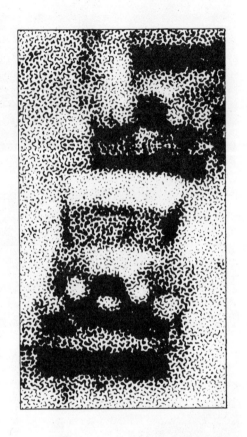

Tony Cashman
The Best Edmonton Stories

Hurtig Publishers
Edmonton

Hurtig Publishers
10560 105 Street
Edmonton, Alberta

ISBN: 0-88830-106-5

Printed and bound in Canada by
T.H. Best Printing Company Limited

Contents

Preface

The first "Edmonton Story" was broadcast in 1951, as a brightener at the end of CJCA's ten o'clock news. In those days, the ten o'clock radio news commanded the same attention that the eleven o'clock television newscast does today, and each station across the country produced its own show. One Sunday night in August, there had been no local news and no "brights" to counter the Korean war reverses which had led off the newscast. However, during the week there had been an incident in the west end, involving nine beavers. The beavers' eagerness in the matter of dam-building had caused flooding in residential gardens, and the offenders had been transported to the Athabasca River. I embroidered this incident to argue that the exiled beavers had a grievance based on history.

Three phone calls followed, one of which was from Edith Hilton, archivist at the provincial library, asking for a copy for the archives. On occasional Sunday nights thereafter I wrote other stories and, as Easter approached in 1952, CJCA's rookie salesman, Garth Olmstead, became involved. By tradition, the rookie salesman was given the Gainers' account, because general manager Alex MacDonald had been known to become a very crusty Scot when the advertising produced by CJCA did not match the quality of the ham and bacon produced by Gainers' packing plant. Garth persuaded Alex that a series of thirteen programmes called "The Edmonton Story" would stampede the public towards Gainers' hams for Easter. Alex became a friend and a real booster of the series, and "The Edmonton Story" was on the air for over nine years.

In 1955 Bob Cantelon, the photographer, entered the scene. Bob was talking to Clarence Richards, and he suggested that Clarence publish a collection of the broadcasts in book form. It was appropriate that Clarence should get involved. He was one of the people who kept Edmonton going. He was an inspirational teacher at Victoria High School. In the 1920s, in order to fill a need for specialized school supplies, he had obtained a bank loan on the strength of some household furniture and had founded the Institute of Applied Art. In the mid-thirties, when Edmonton's football (and other) fortunes were at their nadir, Clarence had provided Edmonton with a football team called the Hi-Grads. Clarence had coached the team and scrounged the equipment. He couldn't scrounge matching sweaters for the players and couldn't afford to buy bootlaces, so the players had to bring their own. But he did give Edmonton a football team. In the late 1940s, Clarence saw that Edmonton needed a publisher, so he broadened the institute's terms of reference to include historical publishing and gave Edmonton Jim MacGregor's *Blankets and Beads*.

Like Alex MacDonald, Clarence became a friend and companion-in-the-cause, though production of *The Edmonton Story* as a book went slowly. The institute's typesetter was a marvellous retired printer named Bill Gimblett, but his union pension only allowed him to work two days a week. Bill would stop often to enjoy a good laugh or to contest the accuracy of something. However, the book eventually took shape, and it appeared in September 1956, just as a 22-year-old Edmontonian named Mel Hurtig was setting up his first bookstore.

Now, as a publisher of national reputation, Mel is making these stories available again. There are some sixty altogether. Forty of them appeared in *The Edmonton Story,* or in *More Edmonton Stories* which Bill Gimblett came out of retirement to set in 1958. These are the stories that seem to have passed the test of time and repetition. Some are told in a different way than they were before, but the story is the same. The first of them — "The Beavers" — is reproduced here exactly as it was read by the late Jack Wilson over CJCA on a Sunday evening in 1951.

TONY CASHMAN

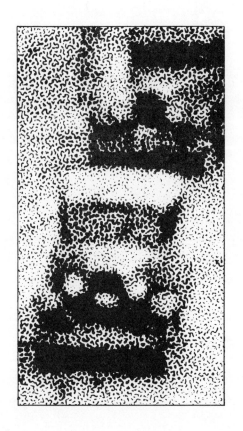

The Beavers

In Edmonton recently, government trappers swooped down on nine beavers and hustled them off to Athabasca. The industrious beavers were munching down city trees to put in their underwater housing programme. People were complaining. The beavers had to go. As they left Edmonton under pressure, the oldest, wisest beaver may have muttered with dark justice, "Well, here we go again. We never get a break in this town. Why don't they ever leave us alone? If it weren't for us, Edmonton wouldn't be here in the first place!"

The wise old beaver was absolutely right. History books may relate that this was once Indian country, but it was really beaver country. The beaver was the lure that brought the North West Company into the Edmonton district in 1795, and a year later brought the North West's huge but lethargic competitor, the Hudson's Bay Company.

The rival traders weren't attracted here by the Indians, or the buffalo, or each other's company. They came loaded for beaver. And the Edmonton district was loaded *with* beaver. As far as Rocky Mountain House, ravines and creeks were straddled by the dams of a thousand beaver towns. Twenty miles due east of modern Edmonton there's a desolate area known as the Beaver Hills. Today the only people who see this district of creeks and lakes are airline passengers. There are no roads or farms in the Beaver Hills. In fact there aren't even beavers any more. But they once thrived in this beaver paradise, and so did the trading companies who hunted them.

Unfortunately for the industrious, flat-tailed animal, his glossy coat was in great demand in fashionable circles of Europe. Local beavers began falling by the thousands into the hands of capitalists, bound for the luxury marts of Europe.

A beaverskin was legal tender along the Saskatchewan. The traders kept their accounts with the Indians in beavers. When the Hudson's Bay Company decided to issue coins in 1854, they called the coins "beavers." There was a big beaver — about the size of a silver dollar. The half-beaver was like a half-dollar, and so on down to the eighth-beaver, built like a dime. There was the likeness of the unfortunate beaver stamped on each coin.

And so Edmonton's economy grew. The Scots of the Hudson's Bay Company organized it. In the 1860s, the discovery of gold on the river broadened it. Agriculture stabilized it. Frank Oliver promoted it. Immigration expanded it. The CPR accelerated it. The CNR buttressed it. Industry balanced it. Oil guaranteed it, and Social Credit cleansed it. But the beaver started it.

If the nine displaced beavers — living in exile near Athabasca — are a trifle huffed at being strong-armed out of Edmonton, they have every right to be.

Go Esks Go!

All together now, to the tune of "Alexander's Ragtime Band," let every loyal Eskimo fan sing:

Come on and cheer, come on and cheer,
Deacon White's great football band;
Come on and cheer, come on and cheer,
They're the gamest in the land.
They can play football like you've never seen before,
Plunge, run or kick up a corking big score,
They're just the fastest gang what am,
Boom bam!
Come on along, come on along,
Let us give the boys a hand.

There's Bailey, kick it hard,
He's the leader of the gang.
So if you want to see the Eskies clean the spots off Calgary,
Come on and cheer, come on and cheer
Deacon White's great football band! Hurrrrayyy!!!

That was their fight song, the song of three hundred Eskimo fans aboard the special train heading for Red Deer on Saturday, November first, 1913. They were going to play Calgary for the provincial championship, and the game was in Red Deer because neither team would go to the home ground of the other.

Calgary teams were Tigers then. The name Eskimos was a product of the scorn the cities heaped upon each other. On an earlier occasion, a southern sportswriter had told his readers that the Esquimaux from the frozen north were coming down to go through the farce of challenging the mighty Tigers. No one forgot an insult in those days. That insult adhered permanently to our football teams.

In 1913 our heroes refused to play the final in Calgary because of some just complaints about the officiating in Hillhurst Park. And the Tigers, on their part, countered with a totally spurious grievance about refereeing in Diamond Park. Our chaps said the head linesman at Hillhurst would set the chains in such a manner that Edmonton had to gain seventeen yards for a first down. The linesman was clearly a blackguard without equal — except for the timekeeper. The university team could tell you about him. The varsity gang had played in Calgary earlier in the season with only two substitutes, and the rascally timekeeper wore the collegians down by letting the clock run overtime. The first quarter alone took twenty-nine minutes to play. The Tigers eventually scored all their points in the elongated fourth quarter and took the game 9 to 5.

The complaint of the Tigers was so weak it's hardly worth relating, but we must put on record the poor calibre of sportsmanship exhibited by Calgary fans. They complained about a game in Edmonton's Diamond Park on Thanksgiving Day which the Eskimos won, fair and square, by a score of 13 to 12. With less than a minute to play, the score was tied 12 to 12 and the Tigers had the ball deep in their own territory, on the 2-yard line in fact. Calgary's captain, Arnold Wark,

13

attempted an end run, hoping to get far enough downfield for a kick into the Edmonton end zone. But our boys were on to this strategy. They chased Arnold along the line of scrimmage and stopped him for no gain. But the referee didn't blow his whistle. He courteously waited for our boys to pick Arnold up and dump him back across the Calgary goal line for a single point. And *then* he blew the whistle and Edmonton won fair and square 13 to 12.

The Tigers and their fans went home vowing never to return. A week before the provincial final, the *Journal* reported: "Coach Deacon White of the Eskimos would rather play in canoes on the Saskatchewan River than play at Hillhurst Park ..." (on the other hand) ... "there's as much chance of getting the Tigers to play in Edmonton as there is of Premier Sifton playing centre scrimmage for the Eskimos."

The situation looked hopeless, but even in this super-charged atmosphere there were cool heads to prevail. If neither team would go to the other, why not have a neutral location — like Red Deer? That made sense. Red Deer it would be — on the fairgrounds. But then came the real sticker. Who would referee? Where was there a man of such blameless character that both sides would accept him? Diogenes, in his celebrated search for an honest man, had a far easier task and he never succeeded. But there were some great men in Alberta in those days. There was one man of such integrity that when the Province of Alberta decided to censor movies, he was appointed our first film censor. He was the choice.

It is unlikely that anyone ever accepted an honour with more reluctance than the Reverend Bob Pearson. On the morning of November first, Bob was stamping his heels around the fairgrounds, levelling the gopher hills, while two special football trains approached Red Deer on collision course. Aboard each train were three hundred fans and two football teams, for there was to be a double-header that day. Preceding the main event, Calgary Mount Royals would meet Edmonton Civics for the provincial junior title.

For the main event the Eskimos had a secret weapon. A rugby football team of 1913 had fourteen players. Nine of them were on the line. With no forward passing and no blocking, it meant that kicking was a vital part of the offence,

14

and it was in the kicking department that the Eskimos had a secret weapon.

At noon the fans poured off the trains and onto the fairgrounds. It cost fifty cents to get in and an extra two bits to sit in the grandstand, but most fans preferred to roam the sidelines, placing bets on the outcome of individual plays. The Mounted Police were on hand in strength and it was said that "they maintained some semblance of order."

Edmonton fans won most of the bets on the junior game as the Civics rode to an 8 to 1 victory over the Mount Royals. Civics were sparked by Frankie Barnes, the architect. Now it may seem strange that a man could have graduated in architecture and practised the profession for three years, and still be less than twenty-one. It does seem strange. So let us say that Frankie was "confused" about his age. Anyway, we beat Calgary didn't we?

Now for the main event. Onto the field trooped the senior teams, the Tigers in their black-and-orange stripes, the Eskimos in their blue-and-white sweaters, and among the blue-and-whites was the Eskimos' secret weapon. It was Percy Hardisty, peerless punter of yesteryear. Percy had come out of retirement for the honour of Edmonton, where his father Senator Richard Hardisty had been chief factor for the Hudson's Bay Company. (He'd also been chief factor in Calgary for two years, but no one is perfect.) Fifteen years had passed since Percy had won games for Queen's University with his booming punts. He was now on the downhill side of thirty-five but still had a few kicks left.

The Tigers roared to an early lead, 4-0 on a field goal and a rouge, and along the sidelines more money was bet on Calgary. Then in the second quarter the Eskimos struck with their secret weapon. Percy Hardisty got away a classic punt which boomed over the head of the startled Dobie. Dobie ran back for the ball, half picked it up, dropped it, and Edmonton recovered on the Tiger 20-yard line. Three plays later Bill Bailey went over for a touchdown and the score was 5 to 4. Minutes later Percy boomed another punt over Dobie's head. Again Dobie fumbled, again Edmonton recovered. Again Bailey hit the scrimmage. Then Campbell went in to score from the 1-yard line and Edmonton led 10 to 4.

By this time Percy Hardisty had retired from the game, and from football. As he got off his second boomer he felt old age catch up with him, all at once, all over. He hobbled to the sidelines, from which he watched the nerve-racking second half. The Eskimos withstood charge after charge and gave up only three points, winning 10 to 7.

There was some confusion afterwards, getting the fans back on the proper trains. The Eskimo supporters were loaded with the money they had taken from the losers, and the losers were pretty annoyed. As the *Bulletin* so rightly said of an earlier contest between the cities (when Calgary had had the presumption to think it could beat out Edmonton for the capital of the province): "Few passions are more desperate or vociferous than baffled greed."

So, all together, let's hear it:

"Come on and cheer, come on and cheer,
Deacon White's great football band ..."

How They Bought Coronation Park and the Exhibition Grounds

They didn't buy them legally, but the stout-hearted city councillors of 1906 had determination equal to their vision and they got around all the barriers — even the legal ones — to supply Edmonton with Coronation Park and the Exhibition Grounds. The class of '06 did not have unlimited vision in all directions. At one meeting it came to the brink of giving female property-owners the vote, but shied away when one of its number denounced that as socialist legislation. But in two swift, quiet weeks of January 1906 it struck quietly to gain us this parkland.

Even more remarkable than a body of elected officials being able to move quickly is the fact that these parks were then miles beyond the city limits. Edmonton had perhaps ten thousand people, and they were accommodated neatly inside 116th Street, 111th Avenue and 92nd Street. Cows found plenty of pasture within these limits and the great real estate boom had not yet begun, but the councillors had vision and they literally went far afield and got us the Exhibition Grounds, Borden Park and Coronation Park — even though the way they got them wasn't exactly legal.

The city charter had them beat right from the start. The charter said they couldn't spend any money for parkland, or for any land, unless the purchase was approved by a vote of the ratepayers. Plebiscites were common in those days, but it took sixty days to set one up, and the boys knew it was impossible to get a sixty-day option on property that was rumoured to be deemed desirable by the city. So they took the only way there was: Mayor Charlie May and Aldermen Picard, Boyle, Bellamy, Manson, Griesbach, Latta, Smith and McLeod bought the land in their own names and held it until a plebiscite could make it legal.

About the fifteenth of January they met in secret — a practice that brings editorial wrath — and appointed themselves agents for the city. They bought the Kirkness property, 140 acres way out east (which now holds the Exhibition Grounds and Borden Park) for $24,500. They bought 100 acres way out west for $18,000. This was part of the Westmount Subdivision, which the Great West Land Development Corporation was about to put on the market. Fifty-three years later some feverish activity transformed this land into Coronation Park just in time for the Queen to plant a tree.

On January 27, 1906, a most wintry of Saturday afternoons, the boys who foresaw the need for Coronation Park held a secret meeting to sign all the agreements. They chose a top-secret location: the dispatcher's office at the CNR station. When the agreements were delivered to the Land Titles Office the following Wednesday, the coup was made public. The boys announced with pride the fine thing they had done, and stood back for the applause — and for the citizens to take them off the hook by voting the money in a plebiscite.

Blushing with honest pride, they awaited the cheers of the multitude. But, poor fellows, they waited in vain. Both locations were denounced as rotten by reason of their remoteness, and the east end location was made doubly rotten by reason of its being a swamp. Moreover the sneaky way they had gone about it suggested to many that the boys had been party to something as unclean as the swamp.

The grumbling of the multitude was so ominous that the councillors didn't dare call for a plebiscite right away. They put it off month after month. It wasn't until December that they gained courage to put it on the ballot, and though it carried, the majority was something less than thumping. That's how we have these acres for fun and games — today and for the future — and it is appropriate indeed that in the centre of Coronation Park we have built a planetarium. It's a fitting memorial for the city councillors who had stars in their eyes.

The Wonderful Street-Railway Charter

Edmonton's street railway was not the first in North America by any means; but from the fuss that was raised over it, you'd never guess it wasn't. The year 1908 was barely underway when the great city of Edmonton obtained from the Alberta legislature a most impressive charter concerning the street railway. Talk about Magna Carta, the so-called Great Charter which the English barons got from King John in 1215! It was nothing placed alongside the charter which Edmonton got from the legislature in 1908. While the English barons — and English historians — called the 1215 document the "Great Charter," King John didn't think much of it. And the English people thought even less of it, because it didn't do a chap much good unless he was a baron.

But Edmonton's Great Charter of 1908 was going to benefit everybody. By its terms, the great city of Edmonton was going to blanket northern Alberta with streetcars. That's right, there would be streetcars for all. Edmonton streetcar lines were given the right of way along any trail within eighty miles of Edmonton. And if the car line to Athabasca, for example, was profitable, Edmonton had the option of extending the line another eighty miles farther.

Well, you can see that the baronial gentlemen who drew up

the Great Charter of 1215 never envisioned anything as astounding as this. The Alberta legislature of 1908, which opened its session on January 16, dealt with only forty-three acts of legislation, and they fill a very thin volume. But one of the acts was the Great Charter. They didn't exactly call it Magna Carta. No, they called it "An Act Respecting the Edmonton Radial Tramway."

In addition to the car line to Athabasca, the charter set streetcars rolling — on paper — to a point or points within the village of Stony Plain, thence westerly to a point at or near Lake Wabamun, and thence to a point or points at or near Lac Ste. Anne. The Edmonton Radial Tramway was to shoot out other lines: one to St. Albert and Morinville, one to Namayo, one to Fort Saskatchewan, Pakan and Saddle Lake, one to Daysland, and another to Lacombe and Gull Lake. However, Edmonton was going to have a contest on its hands before it could get the franchise to operate streetcars in the city of Lacombe itself. Oh yes, indeed! Two other electric railway companies were after that lucrative trade: the Lacombe, Bullocksville and Alix Electric Railway, and the Lacombe and Blindman Valley Electric Railway Company. Edmonton was not to reap huge profits from the Lacombe streetcar riders without a fight.

But the important thing, of course, was the network of feeder lines giving rapid transit to and from Edmonton. In the rosy January dawn of 1908, it was clear to anyone with half a brain that Edmonton was soon going to have a million people. When Edmonton had a million people, and was thereby pronounced full, some place must be found for the tens of thousands still clamouring for admittance. And if a man lived in Morinville, he would need rapid transportation to his job in Edmonton. When towns like Morinville and Stony Plain were full, why, the radial tramway could build out in any direction it chose, and set up its own towns, just like all the big-time railroads were doing.

There was nothing to stop construction of any line. The Great Charter of 1908 gave Edmonton a "big stick" to wield. Clause 4, Section 2 gave us power to "construct, erect and maintain all necessary buildings, machinery, appliances and conveniences for purposes of such tramways and works,

19

including the erection of poles, upon any and all roads, road allowances, streets, highways and lands upon which the corporation deems it expedient."

So put down that shotgun, Farmer Brown, and call off your dogs. The north forty is required for the Edmonton Radial Tramway. We may need it for a car barn. We may require it for a stone quarry. Or we might want it for a coal mine. Don't ask us why a streetcar system needs a coal mine or a stone quarry, Farmer Brown. But it's in our charter, Section 2, Clause 7.

Well, the cartoonist of the Edmonton *Saturday News* was a little amused by this exuberance. On February 1, 1908, he drew a front-page cartoon showing a bird's-eye view of the City of Edmonton, plus "that part of Canada which is NOT within the City limits." His caption went on: "The heavy black line shows the proposed new City Electric Railway, some 200,000 miles in length, of which about ¼ mile of track has already been laid." The caption continues: "The black splotch near the centre is not an accident — it used to be known as the Great Slave Lake, but has now been boarded in, and is used as a skating rink for children." The cartoon shows a few transfer points on the Edmonton Radial Tramway. One says, "Change here for Pacific Ocean — 10 minutes walk." Another says, "Change for Hudson's Bay." And another, "Change here for Halifax — 3 feet away."

The citizens of Edmonton enjoyed the cartoonist's joke. Because, after all, isn't there a lot of truth in nonsense? But there were other doubting Thomases besides the cartoonist of the *Saturday News*. There was apparently one in the legislature. Some timid, small-souled individual in the assembly had a ridiculous clause inserted in the Edmonton Radial Tramway Act. Perhaps this dull cynic was a jealous resident of Calgary. Anyway, it was stated in the Great Charter that any portion of the vast project which had not been completed in five years would be declared null and void. "After the lapse of five years, all powers granted by the Act shall absolutely cease with regard to all tramway lines not actually constructed." It was a ridiculous idea, to be sure, that the project would not be completed in five years, so Edmonton let the five-year clause go into the Radial Tramway Act.

But, somehow or other, that killjoy in the legislature had

guessed right. By the end of 1908, the great city of Edmonton had four mighty streetcars rattling around the town, in a most metropolitan manner indeed. But the streetcars never got out of town. Later on, a private company ran a streetcar line to St. Albert for a brief time. But the Edmonton Radial Tramway just never radiated. The bright vision seen in the rosy dawn of 1908 faded in the light of common day.

Behind Every Successful Man

It was Gus May who usurped the feminine privilege of changing one's mind, and he thereby cost Edmonton the chance to make history in Women's Liberation. On the night of March 6, 1906, the slimmest majority of city council — Gus included — decided in favour of having women vote in civic elections. But then Gus changed his mind. And the motion, and the chance to make history, were lost.

Edmonton came to the brink as Gus and Co. discussed amendments to the city charter. Alberta's first legislature was to meet in about a week and would be amending charters on request. Alderman Thomas Bellamy, for whom the hill is named, was the all-out revolutionary. Tom wanted to open the polls to the ladies on the same basis as men, to any lady twenty-one or better who owned five hundred dollars' worth of property. But the city solicitor didn't think that would be possible. You might admit widows and spinsters, he explained, but not married women. And why not married women? Well, because a married woman couldn't own property. Anything she owned belonged automatically to her husband. Quite so, nodded the councillors. Right on there, Mr. Solicitor. Just wait till we tell our wives! However, they did agree that single women should have a vote and that the legislature be asked to put it in the charter. But they agreed by the slimmest majority, by just one vote, and that brought Alderman Boyle to his feet.

John R. Boyle later went to the provincial cabinet, became minister of education, and used to correct schoolkids on the way they pronounced Egypt. "It's not Ee-jipt, it's Egg-wipt," he would tell the kids. On the night of March 6, John told his fellow councillors they were asking for too much. They were asking the government to pass socialist legislation. The amendment was sure to provoke large discussion in the house and if it wasn't taken out might sidetrack all the other amendments. Gus May was so moved by the argument that he switched sides on a re-vote, and the *Bulletin* was able to report with relief: "Edmonton only escaped woman suffrage, and the possibility of petticoat government, by Alderman May deciding to reconsider what he had done."

Ten years later the Alberta legislature contained only one man brave enough to vote against the Equal Suffrage Act. No doubt there were other honourable members who thought women couldn't cope with the mind-boggling decision of choosing the best candidate, but it was no longer possible to say so. The ladies had made it impossible by becoming full partners in the development of their communities.

In Edmonton they joined whole-heartedly in the booster spirit that built the city in the yeasty years from the declaration of the province to the declaration of the First World War. Booster spirit is heady stuff, potent as the product of the distillery, and it can leave headaches and hangovers too. But it built Edmonton, and the ladies contributed, not only by providing social services but by providing social *life*.

Now this was very important. The illusion that Edmonton was soon to be a city of a million people was constantly confirmed by the appearance of the ladies. How did Parisian women dress at ten o'clock in the evening? That's how Edmonton women dressed at three o'clock in the afternoon. It was an age when styles flowed like the optimism, an age of flowing-feathered hats and flowing furs and flowing skirts. The ladies hauled their flowing finery over the mud streets, unconscious of the footing. They saw the city of a million which their husbands saw. They were young; parties were not just the spice of life but the breath of life. They gave Edmonton a sparkle which delighted Emily Murphy, that ardent crusader for women's causes who came to live here in 1907. In one of her books, she wrote: "There is much tea and tennis, golf, automobiling, dancing, dining and wild riding across the hills, for when people are healthy and prosperous

22

they are instinctively hospitable, and always in a big-hearted, open-minded way."

The mills of this social circle ground exceeding fine, and the rules were set up so that one acceptance produced two obligations and guaranteed an ever-widening circle. Every lady had her set. Each lady in the set had her afternoon for receiving, and on top of regular receiving days there were teas.

Now let's examine the rules of the game, as explained by one of the participants, the late Mrs. E.C. Pardee. Suppose Mrs. A has a tea and she invites Mrs. B. This means Mrs. B owes Mrs. A an invitation to her next tea and also owes Mrs. A a call on Mrs. A's next afternoon for receiving. After that, Mrs. A will then owe Mrs. B another invitation to tea, as well as a call on Mrs. B's next afternoon for receiving. After which ... but you get the idea.

Teas were more complex than afternoons for receiving. The tea might have a theme or be in aid of a good cause. A tea required costumes, all of which were recorded faithfully in the newspapers: "Mrs. Balmer-Watt was Carmen, Mrs. Pardee was Lorna Doone." Carmen and Lorna Doone were very popular. This social whirl kept the ladies hopping, and it wasn't even six o'clock yet. Evening posed an endless chain of dinner parties.

While the ladies were creating the social life needed by the ambitious young city, they were also providing social services, such as the IODE ambulance. The Edmonton chapter of the Imperial Order was the first west of Ontario. It was chartered on November 17, 1905, and the ladies chose the name "Westward Ho!" to indicate the direction the course of empire was taking. The ten founding members then went to work to provide a recognized social need — an ambulance. It was kept at the Fourth Street fire hall, from which point the fire laddies would go racing out to take patients to hospital. A person had two choices — the General, or the Public Hospital in the Boyle Street area. The debts of the Public Hospital were the responsibility of a ladies' aid, and they were paid off by teas, bazaars and bake sales.

Now the ambulance was a generous thought, but there was a problem — its horsepower. The horses were so glad to escape from the fire hall that they always raced to conflagrations, and they didn't change their gait when pulling the ambulance. The

23

thundering rides added unnecessary suffering to suffering humanity, so it was back to the bake sales for the "Westward Ho!" ladies until they had enough to buy a team of trained ambulance horses — handsome blacks with silver harnesses — which made patients easy riders.

The YWCA began with a bake sale. There had been talk of forming one for some time before a house of the proper size became available. It was on 103rd Avenue near First Street. To close the deal and open the "Y", the ladies organized an emergency home-baking sale on the lawn of Mrs. Richard Hardisty.

The Hardisty lawn, at the corner of 99th Avenue and 105th Street, must have had inordinately tough grass. It had to withstand many a fete, including the momentous occasion in 1909 when one hundred delegates of the International Council of Women came to Edmonton on a world tour. The gardens buzzed with interest as the globetrotters told their stories and heard about the current project of the local council: bringing about legislation to stop husbands from selling farms and deserting their wives with the proceeds.

The climax of the afternoon was a sightseeing tour, and the hostesses — full of booster spirit like their husbands — had decided that the visitors would see the sights from the street-car. Edmonton was extremely proud of its street railway, the most northerly on the continent. Once an hour a car clattered down 97th Avenue and behind Fort Edmonton, where the Legislative Building was to be, cruised Rossdale Flat, went over the Low Level Bridge, up Scona Hill and along Whyte Avenue. One hundred strong, the globetrotters piled on the streetcar and rattled away to see the sights which their hostesses found so exciting.

All went well on the outward trip and all went well on the return — until the streetcar reached the foot of the 97th Avenue hill. And then came civic embarrassment, for the power plant was not as dynamic as the citizens. There just wasn't enough juice in the trolley wires to take the car up the hill with all those world travellers on board. So half of them had to get off and wait while the car went up the hill with a half-load and then backed down to retrieve the others.

Before the visitors left they were sure to have been shown the new Imperial Bank, with its three-storey sandstone pillars.

And they'd have been told about the alcove. The Imperial had a corner for women customers only. The Edmonton *Saturday News* said it was so that a lady making money in the real estate game could do her financing without her husband knowing. The Imperial Bank did not hold the city solicitor's view that a woman's property was automatically her husband's, and by 1911 even the city was changing its view. A writer from Oklahoma passed through that year and informed his readers that a married man without property could vote — if his wife owned real estate and he had her permission in writing.

Nineteen eleven was the year the ladies engineered a glittering social function which was a true expression of the booster spirit of the age. It was their contribution to the visit of the Duke of Connaught, the king's viceroy in Canada. A luncheon was required for the occasion, and the ladies decided it would be in the handsomest room in town, which happened to be the legislative chamber of the new capitol building. By this time the building had taken shape and its dome had risen on the skyline. But it was still very much under construction, except for the chamber which was complete with red carpet, brass rails, and panelled walls rising to a distant ceiling. Its size and grandeur affected citizens of that day just as a first visit to the Edmonton Coliseum affected citizens many years later. It was an expression of all that the boosters hoped for the city. So, of course the ladies decided that the luncheon would be there.

Many people, all men, rose to sputter comments like "absurd," "impossible," "preposterous," "simply isn't done" … "no precedent for it in British parliamentary history." But they protested without hope. The lieutenant-governor, Mr. Bulyea, the old dear, caved in just as the ladies knew he would, and on the appointed day the Duke of Connaught and his entourage picked their way past scaffolding and wheelbarrows to reach the red chamber — while famed parliamentarians like Pitt and Gladstone revolved in their illustrious graves.

Through it all, the duke wore his customary look of delighted surprise, but he must have been genuinely puzzled by the bits of coloured string on the cutlery. The string was to identify the owners. In the Edmonton of that day, you couldn't hire anyone to put on a banquet. The ladies had to provide everything themselves, even to the utensils. So in the morning they were in the red chamber marking knives and plates. And at noon they were back, dressed in the height of local fashion, a blend of style and youth and vigour and sophistication and ingenuous optimism, which quite charmed the visitors. And when the procession moved on, the ladies stayed to clean up.

By 1912 a new element was discernible in the growing city, whose population had jumped ten times since Gus May had voted against woman's suffrage. Girls, who had come to district farms with the immigration from eastern Europe, were growing up and coming into the city. They needed help with the language and urban living. Their need led to the foundation in Edmonton of an organization which became national — the Catholic Women's League.

In 1914 male chauvinism suffered a severe reverse hereabouts. Nellie McClung arrived from Manitoba. With Mrs. McClung and Emily Murphy in tandem, the combined thrust of Canada's wittiest, wiliest, most articulate and persistent women reformers was turned full on Alberta. There was no way Alberta could get out of leading the country in admitting ladies to the polls. As the drive came into the home stretch, the reformers had the support of the Equal Franchise League. But, even in support, the league fought a rearguard action for male chauvinism: membership was limited to men only. The end came in April 1916. In the red-carpeted chamber, where the ladies had lunched with the Duke of Connaught, the Legislative Assembly was presented the Equal Suffrage Act.

In that assembly only one man was brave enough to stand and be spokesman for the lost cause. He was Boudreau, Lucien Boudreau, who represented St. Albert and was known as "Little Napoleon." Boudreau grew eloquent in praise of women, but argued that the delightful creatures shouldn't be bothered with voting.

He was a rousing speaker but he couldn't raise a supporting voice in the assembly, not even the voice of John R. Boyle, member for Sturgeon. Ten years earlier, as an alderman of the City of Edmonton, John R. Boyle had loosed his full oratorical powers on Gus May to convince Gus that woman's suffrage was dangerous socialist legislation which would put the legislature in an uproar. But now Boyle said nothing. If he was suffering, it was because it was politic to suffer in silence.

Times had changed. Women had changed them.

The Elephants

In the dim dawn of the world, elephants roamed through Edmonton. That was after the last ocean disappeared and before the last glacier came creeping down from the north. But elephants have roamed through Edmonton more recently than that. There were elephants roaming through Edmonton on Sunday, August 1, 1926. To be precise, they were running at large through Edmonton's west end.

It all began early in the afternoon when the Sells-Floto Circus was unloading its equipment from a special train at the CPR station. The equipment was being loaded on gaudy circus wagons, and the elephants were going to haul the wagons through town to the Boyle Street playground. A large crowd watched the unloading, and the huge docile elephants, with great interest. Now, among the crowd there was a small yapping dog, a dog weighing about five pounds. The dog's yapping got under the thick skin of an elephant named Mary — Mary being about four thousand pounds of elephant. Mary grew more and more nervous. Finally, just as the handlers were about to hitch her to a wagon, she panicked. She began to run, and in a moment the stampede was on. Mary and thirteen other elephants began a wild break for freedom. The crowd stampeded too, and a little girl got a broken arm.

Well, the elephant trainers were almost equal to the situation and they rounded up eight panic-striken pachyderms in a matter of minutes. But six got away. From the CPR station they were last seen disappearing into the west end. Six wildly-trumpeting elephants running loose in Edmonton's west end on a quiet Sunday afternoon in summer! And for the rest of that Sunday there were to be some strange reactions as people recognized the incredible fact that there were elephants in the west end.

What would your reaction be right now if your wife were to say, "Oh, come to the window, dear, and look at the elephant in the garden." This happened at the General Hospital on that strange Sunday half a century ago. You may remember that, at that time, the General Hospital had a garden running all the way down to Jasper Avenue, and the whole block was surrounded by a fence. Sister Superior was startled that quiet Sunday to see a little nun come flying up the hospital corridor. "Oh, come quickly!" the little nun shouted, "there's an elephant in the garden!" The Superior did run to the window, thinking sadly that poor sister had been working too hard for the greater glory of God, and perhaps it was God's holy will that sister should have a vacation. However, there was nothing wrong with sister. There, in the garden, was indeed an elephant. He was an elephant named Snider, an elephant not noted for his sunny disposition. Snider was rooting up potatoes with his tusks and he was being assisted by two other elephants. Well, elephants, of course, are vegetarians; there was no danger of their eating any citizens of Edmonton. But they could trample on them and knock down their fences. As the nuns watched, Snider and his pals were frightened by the yells of their pursuing trainers and they disappeared through the 112th Street fence, making three holes in it as they left.

The most unusual reaction to the elephants was registered by a little lady working in her garden on 116th Street. The perspiring pursuers saw three pachyderms gallop into her yard. When the trainers arrived on the scene, the little lady was indignantly waving her apron at the elephants and shouting, "Shooo! Shooo! Get out of my garden, you dirty beasts!" On 114th Street, north of Jasper, a ten-year-old boy named Bobs Turner was late getting in to tea that Sunday afternoon. Bobs received the usual parental advice on the necessity of ten-year-old boys coming in to tea on time. When asked to explain his tardiness, Bobs explained that he'd been watching an elephant in the garden. An elephant in the garden? The parents smiled at this flight of childish fancy and poured the tea, blissfully unaware that their garden was going to need a major repair job. Up on 121st Street a girl named Alice Williams was walking home. Alice heard a noise behind her, turned around, and saw an elephant approaching at high speed. Perhaps the elephant didn't want to trample her; perhaps he wished only to inquire the way back to Africa. But Alice didn't wait to find out. She ducked into the grounds of Llanarthney School at 121st Street and 102nd Avenue, and the elephant thundered past.

By this time the news was starting to get around. There was a hue and cry of trainers up and down the streets, and all policemen were called out to join the big game hunt. The first runaway to be recaptured was our old friend Snider, he of the big tusks. And credit for Snider's capture goes to the circus clown, a gentleman named Poodles Hannaford. Poodles came dashing into a garden on 112th Street and found Snider eating some flowers with the dainty concentration of a hummingbird. Snider was about to light out again when Poodles had a flash of inspiration. He shouted, "Tail up, Snider, tail up!" That's the command at which a circus elephant raises his tail so that the elephant behind can wrap his trunk around it and they can all go marching around the ring in a circle. Snider raised his tail. Poodles Hannaford raced around behind and grabbed it, and Snider marched solemnly back to captivity, under the impression that he was leading a parade of elephants.

By nine o'clock that Sunday night all the stampeders had been rounded up except Mary, the instigator of the stampede. Mary was still pounding through gardens and fences with a large crowd in pursuit. About nine o'clock they thought they had Mary. They got her into a tennis court, and elephant-man Curley Stewart tried to bolt the gate on her. But at the critical moment Mary charged at the gate, tossed Curley bodily through the fence, and continued on her travels. A little later she was cornered near the cemetery. A local policeman tried to lasso Mary — and did. But as he came in close, Mary tossed him over the fence into the cemetery. Not wishing to take up permanent residence in a cemetery, the policeman withdrew.

Through all this excitement, night watchman George McKay was sitting placidly in his office at Cushing Brothers' factory, at the west end of the cemetery. About eleven o'clock George heard a noise outside. He opened the door and there was Mary. McKay timed his departure through the back door to coincide exactly with Mary's entrance through the front. After kicking the Cushing office around, Mary burst through a wall and headed for some bush just south of 107th Avenue and 116th Street. She decided to make a last stand in that clump of bush. Through the night she trumpeted her contempt for men who try to catch elephants. Mary had a growing audience as the crowds of curious people gathered on the fringes of the bush. But after a night of excitement, Mary surrendered peacefully at five o'clock Monday morning. The circus men brought Trilby, the great boss elephant, to the fringe of the woods. Trilby was one hundred years old and four times as big as Mary. Trilby raised her voice and Mary came trotting out of the bush, ran up to Trilby, and the magnificent old matriarch put her trunk protectively around her. For Mary was, after all, only a little elephant, and as glad as everyone else that Edmonton's great elephant hunt was over.

When the Sky Was Green

Cartmell was the man who said the sky was green. And he was right. He didn't make a fuss about it. He was a calm chap who never made a fuss about anything, even when a store blew up on Rossdale Flat with Cartmell inside it. It was his fellow painters who made the fuss when he persisted in painting winter scenes with a green sky. The others said the sky was blue, but Cartmell wouldn't have any of that in his winter landscapes. In the light he chose for painting, the winter sky was apple green down at the western horizon, and you could keep the green in sight right up to the dome of the heavens.

It took a while for the opposition to see the light — as Cartmell saw it. But he was, after all, an unlikely chap to be lecturing other people on the colours of the sky. By trade he was an interior decorator, and he hadn't even come to Edmonton until he was fifty-two years old. A.B. Cartmell was born in Lancashire in 1871 and in his teens he got into house painting. But decorating houses, especially to late-Victorian taste, did not give him much artistic satisfaction. He tried to be a concert violinist, but when an injury to a finger made that impossible he turned to the twin sister of music.

In 1889 young Cartmell went down to Cornwall to study art for three years at a conservatory run by the distinguished seascape painter, Sir Julius Olson. Sir Julius had his conservatory right on Land's End, just the place to paint the sea in all its lights and moods. There were 130 students in the place. Some of Cartmell's contemporaries went on to prominence, mostly those who could afford to starve while awaiting recognition.

But a man with a wife and family can't afford the luxury of starving, so Cartmell hung wallpaper for a living and painted for pleasure. After thirty years of this he decided he might make a better living, and do some better painting, in Canada. In 1923 he came to Canada, and more specifically, to Edmonton. He chose Edmonton because of snow. He loved to paint snow, and figured that Edmonton would have plenty of the right kind.

He divided snow into three categories. There was soft snow, the kind that used to fall in England and annoy him by disappearing so quickly. There was melting snow, and then there was frozen snow. Frozen snow was the good stuff. It gave Cartmell time to study it and paint it in its true colours — its true colours being anything but white, the colour most commonly assigned to it. Edmonton did not disappoint his expectations in regard to the supply of frozen snow.

In his first years he found high-quality snow so entrancing that he'd paint outside when the mercury was well below zero — holding the brushes in heavy mitts, and keeping his paints from freezing by mixing them with turpentine. He said you had to be outside to consolidate your idea for a picture. As he put it, "You've got to argue with nature."

The controversy about green sky started with his first exhibition. Although most viewers were not sure that Edmonton snow scenes were really produced in glorious technicolour, they were pleased by the colours that Cartmell saw in the snow, colours that in nature became discernible only after intense scrutiny. Red snow they would accept, but green sky was too much.

From 1923 Cartmell began his long, patient campaign to sell green sky. He would arrange to meet people at dusk on a winter evening, and just after sunset the apple-green band would roll out along the horizon and subtones of green would climb up half the sky. It lasted only a few minutes, but he always used to say that any nature scene should look as though it had been painted in one minute.

And he continued to paint snow scenes with a green sky — scenes of Number One Northern frozen snow — and people started to order them. They always ordered them just a little faster than he could get them painted, even when he painted snow from memory during the boring months of summer. Princess Alice, wife of Governor General the Earl of Athlone, heard about his work, and when she visited here during the war, she asked to see some snow scenes. She bought two.

In 1950, when Cartmell was 78 years old, he was in a store near his home when an explosion wrecked it. He was badly hurt and had to spend eight months in hospital. No one thought he would ever paint again, but he worked into his mid-eighties. Edmonton still had a lot to learn.

The 1912 Census

Let us go back again to that fascinating age, the age of the stout-hearted men — the men who would fight for the right they adored — and review one of the historic rows of 1912. The basic ingredients of this row seem harmless enough, but so spirited was 1912 that nothing could be guaranteed in advance to be free of controversy.

It all started in February. That month, the provincial legislature decided to extend the franchise to tenants in Alberta's cities. The legislature decreed that a man who paid rent for his house was as responsible a citizen, and as entitled to vote, as the man who owned his house. Now that seemed harmless enough.

The same month, the great city of Edmonton was made mightier yet by amalgamation with the south-side city of Strathcona, and in a spirit of civic pride the new Edmonton decided to take a census of its additional greatness. The census would also serve as the basis for the next voters' list. Now that seemed harmless enough, but, as we said, this was 1912.

In May the city council appointed Bob Hamilton census commissioner. Bob was a big, jovial, flour-and-feed man. Bob divided the city into twenty-seven districts, hired census takers, sent them out, and in June announced to everyone's civic delight that we had a population of 53,611. Think of it! Bob was congratulated for a good job, and everything was peaceful and quiet for two months. Then, in September, city assessor Tom Walker began making up the voters' list from the census cards. That started the row.

Tom was an incorruptible realist. He had as much civic booster about him as the next man, but he found entirely too much booster spirit in the census. He found that in five small cottages on 97th Street there were alleged to be 172 Chinese gentlemen. All were said to be "naturalized British subjects, entitled to vote." Tom also found the names of 11 Japanese gentlemen, all naturalized British subjects, all residents of the Alberta Hotel. Investigation showed no Japanese gentlemen living there. The list showed still another 115 citizens residing in the Alberta. The patriotic census taker had copied out the hotel guest book for a period of several weeks and entered all the travelling salesmen, vaudeville comedians, and visiting firemen of all trades, as bona fide residents of Edmonton. The Presbyterian General Assembly had met in Edmonton during the time of the census, and the visiting ministers were also listed as bona fide residents of Edmonton the Magnificent.

In one district the total of residents was given as 536. But when Tom and his staff added up the census cards there were only 184 cards. And while the city had been divided into twenty-seven districts for the census, Tom reported that some enterprising booster had rung in a twenty-eighth district. North Edmonton was still a separate village, but someone had added 905 residents of North Edmonton into the population of the city. Nine hundred and five North Edmontonians, all entitled to vote in Edmonton. When Tom did a little more checking on the cards he found only 855, not 905. At the tail end of the list, the enumerator had written: "Fifty residents who refused to give their names." And that's the stuff of which Edmonton's population for 1912 was made up to 53,611. Tom Walker indicated that he would proceed with great caution in making up his list of qualified voters. And then the fun began.

It was shouted loudly — everything was shouted loudly in the age of the stout-hearted men — that "certain interests" were trying to grab control of city affairs by packing the voters' list with phoney names. The *Bulletin* suggested, in the business of the 172 Chinese, that one Chinese gentleman might show up and vote 172 times. On the other hand, Fighting Joe Clarke shouted loudly that Tom was in league with "certain other interests" who were out to defraud the honest tenant of his newly-won right to vote.

Tom growled back that he would continue as he was going, and he intimated that the job would have been easier if Fighting Joe had not been giving free advice to census takers. Yes, when the provincial government decreed that tenants could vote, the City of Edmonton had asked Mr. Justice N.D. Beck for a supreme court ruling on exactly what was meant by the word "tenant." Judge Beck ruled in effect that a tenant was the head of a rented house, the person responsible for paying the rent. Only one person in a house could be classed as a tenant. A son or daughter living at home could not be a tenant, nor could a domestic servant or a boarder. Sons, daughters, servants and boarders were to be listed on the census cards as "occupants," with no voting power. That was Judge Beck's learned interpretation of the law. It was doubtless correct, but it wasn't good enough for Joe Clarke, champion of the underdog. He told the census takers: "Put 'em all down as tenants. Blank blank it, those people are as good citizens as anybody."

In an official progress report to the city council, Tom Walker growled: "I'm going as fast as I can with the voters' list. The work is complicated because every visitor, domestic servant, hotel porter, bellboy and potboy is shown on the cards as a tenant." Bob Hamilton, the jovial man who directed the census, issued a non-jovial statement denying all Tom Walker's charges. Bob said he had carried out instructions to the letter, although he did concede he had taken the broad view of the instructions, rather than the narrow view taken by Walker — and the Supreme Court. In regard to Mr. Walker's remark about potboys, whatever they were, Bob was ready to swear that not one citizen of Edmonton had given his occupation as potboy.

Well, there was already a three-alarm hassle going on over the names when more fuel was added to the fire. H.A. Mackie, representing the labour unions, came up with a list of four hundred names, all bona fide tenants who had been missed by the census takers — probably at the instigation of "certain interests" who were trying to cheat the honest workingman of his vote. Mr. Mackie, with the support of Billy McAdams, fiery publisher of the *Edmonton Capital,* marched on Mr. Walker and demanded that he add these four hundred names immediately. Mr. Walker said he would do nothing of the kind; he would investigate each case individually, and those that qualified would get on the list. "Not good enough," said Mackie and McAdams. They went to the Supreme Court and tried to get an order from Chief Justice Harvey, directing Mr. Walker to add all four hundred. Judge Harvey declined, and in declining charged Mackie and McAdams ten dollars for court costs.

Mackie and McAdams then enlisted Joe Clarke to battle for the four hundred. Joe took up this fight with his customary energy. He said Tom Walker was a liar and a dog; and when mild-mannered Jack Bown, the city solicitor, backed up Mr. Walker, Fighting Joe said the citizens ought to tar and feather Mr. Bown. At the very least, Bown and Walker should resign.

When they declined Joe's invitation, he got a special meeting of the council called to discuss his resolution that they be fired. Seven aldermen signed the request for the special meeting, and it was called for the Monday afternoon of October 22, 1912. Walker and Bown were there for the showdown. So were McAdams and Mackie. But most of the aldermen were not. Most of the aldermen had decided over the weekend that it was the better part of valour to be elsewhere at this crucial moment — so there weren't enough aldermen for a quorum. As the meeting prepared to adjourn, Mr. Mackie stood up and said that the aldermen who had stayed away were a bunch of blank, blank blatherskites. He asked the meeting if it didn't agree with him. And he pronounced his motion of censure to be carried.

Well, this was the end of that memorable row of 1912. The stout-hearted men had so many things to fight about in 1912 that they could devote no more time to this particular row. Mr. Walker pressed on with his voters' list, and some people got on it and some did not. The voters' list was but a pale shadow of the census, but the stout-hearted men did not revise the census downward. Not even Tom Walker suggested that. And to this day, the population of Edmonton for the year 1912 is shown in the official records of the city as 53,611.

The Good Old Summertime

Summer comes to Edmonton in much the same manner that the dawn comes up on the road to Mandalay. One day the trees are like sticks and the hedges like grates, and then, the next day it seems, the leaves are out and it's summer. Age cannot wither nor custom stale the charm of the good old summertime, although there exists a suspicion that summertime was even better in golden days that are past. Yes, there is a suspicion that with all the money that's been spent developing Borden Park in recent years, the spenders have failed to match the jolly atmosphere of the old Borden Park Funland.

It wasn't very big, as funlands go, but it had all the essentials: a roller coaster, a merry-go-round, and a tunnel of love. Tunnels of love were never officially named such — lest someone should rise to protest. They were named "The Old Mill" or something like that, and then everybody called them "the tunnel of love" anyway. The one at Borden Park was named "The Old Mill." People climbed into little boats and floated around through a curving wooden shed, in which skeletons and ghosts would light up from time to time to scare the very dickens out of the nervous. And lest someone still be inclined to rise and protest about the tunnel of love, the operators worked on the theory that three is a crowd; in fact they figured that six in a boat was about right — for decorum and for the balance sheet. The boats were intriguing things. They were magnetized and were pulled gently around the watercourse by a series of magnets; right around and out into the bright sunshine of Borden Park once more, out into the summer sunshine, where the carousel was still turning and the roller coaster was still rocketing.

The "green rattler," they called the train of cars that ran on the roller coaster, and the "green rattler" could rattle at a breath-taking pace indeed. That was because the roller coaster was a permanent structure and was not dismantled and put together again every week like the rides that come to the Exhibition nowadays. The Exhibition now has rides that can hang you upside down and spin you dizzy, but they can't give you half the sudden acceleration of the old "green rattler."

36

And for all that hanging upside down and being spun dizzy, acceleration still offers more exhilaration.

The roller coaster, the Old Mill and the carousel operated in Exhibition Week, of course, but also on Saturdays and Sundays and holidays of the good old summertime — and by appointment to school picnics. They were a private enterprise, the creation of a Toronto showman who built them and operated them on a deal with the city. They appeared in 1913, just after the Exhibition Grounds were moved out to Borden Park. The roller coaster was built along the south fence, and even through the winters its gaunt framework stood above the whole district as a reminder that summer could not be far behind.

But by the 1930s the Borden Park Funland began to fall apart, and this process was possibly accelerated when the Toronto gentleman lost interest, and the city took over the running of it. Part of the Old Mill burned down and the rest was not worth saving. By 1935 the main timber supports of the roller coaster began to show the effects of too many exhilarating rides and too much freezing and thawing in the swampy ground of Borden Park. Prudence dictated that the roller coaster come down, and Merrill Muttart, who was just starting up in the lumber business, was given the contract to finish it off.

Now, of course, it's possible that the old Funland will reappear again, because it's a fact that the good things of the good old summertime do reappear. In support of this statement we would give you the kids, splashing and blowing in the Mill Creek swimming pool on any fine summer afternoon. Fifty years ago kids used to swim in Mill Creek, and their pool was superior in many ways to the one that has now been provided for them by the city. Fifty years ago the kids had to build their own pool and they had to build it anew every summer, after the spring freshets had poured down the ravine and carried away last year's dam.

You can still see where the old swimming hole was — the road that dips down through the ravine at 76th Avenue dips right through it. When the creek had settled down to its normal summer run, the kids would fashion a dam of rocks and logs, about five feet high and thirty feet wide. And while the dam would be something less than watertight, it would back enough water to make a pool a hundred and fifty yards long, thirty feet wide, and in places six feet deep. Porous though the dam was, the logs were tight enough together to prevent the fish getting through, and all summer long the pool was full of suckers — suckers being fish both handsome and delicious if one is eleven years old. That was high life, floating downstream with the current, with the high green bank on the west just a few feet away, and the whistle of the Edmonton, Yukon and Pacific Railroad engine shunting down the narrow canyon above you, and the sun moving just as lazily across the high vault of heaven ... until the sound of rushing water grew louder in your ears, and your head was bobbing against the timbers of the dam, and it was time to swim upstream and float back again.

Edmonton kids have gone swimming in concrete pools since early in the 1920s — thousands upon thousands of kids — and we doubt very much that even one kid of this legion has realized that Edmonton's first three pools were financed from the wreckage of a far greater scheme. Edmonton, in its early days of optimism, was agitated by many a great scheme, and most of them vanished without trace, being founded on nothing more than the optimism which made them seem plausible. But the glorious scheme, known as The Rocky Rapids Power Development, bequeathed to the children and young people of Edmonton a legacy which they enjoy to this day.

The Rocky Rapids are a turbulent stretch of the North Saskatchewan River, about seventy miles upstream near the town of Drayton Valley. The river valley narrows between high rock cliffs, and there the Edmonton Power Company proposed to build a hydro-electric dam and sell the electricity to the City of Edmonton. All the company wanted was an agreement to buy so many kilowatt-hours for so many years. It sounds mild enough, but it sparked a row that ripped the city council apart, spilled out in public meetings and a plebiscite, and, all in all, brightened very considerably the drab war month of November 1915. Night after night, supporters and opponents of the plan stood on the public platform and hurled figures at each other. Even those inseparable lady crusaders,

Nellie McClung and Emily Murphy, were split by the Rocky Rapids issue and campaigned from opposing platforms.

Mayor Henry was against the scheme; Ernie Bowness, the city's efficiency expert, was in favour of it. Then there was G.W. Farrell. He was in favour of it. In fact, Mr. Farrell, the suave Montreal promoter, was probably the originator of the Rocky Rapids power scheme. He formed the Edmonton Power Company to develop the rapids, and while the name "Edmonton" Power Company was chosen with exquisite tact, when you bit through the outer crust of local boys whom Mr. Farrell had picked as directors, there really wasn't much flavour of Edmonton about it. There was the unmistakable slick flavour of Montreal and New York, a flavour that did not appeal to the "stout-hearted men" and spurred on their opposition.

The fight broke into the open at a bruising session of the city council on November 9, 1915. By a split vote the council decided to make the agreement to buy Rocky Rapids power and called for a plebiscite of the ratepayers on November 22. The next week there were public meetings every night — Monday night at Norwood School, Tuesday night at Ross Hall, Wednesday night at the Orange Hall, Thursday night at King Edward Park School, Friday night at the Separate School. Then, on Saturday night, the power company hired the First Presbyterian Church for a mass rally, and the opposition countered by hiring McDougall Church.

The basic problem was simple enough: Edmonton had its own city-owned power plant on the flats, making electricity from coal. Edmonton made the profits from this plant, but the plant would soon require a lot of expanding to keep up with the city. Now, should the city keep on putting its own money into this plant, or should it let the financiers put their money into a hydro-electric dam at Rocky Rapids and buy power from them, and let them keep the profits? Which was the better deal? It might not have been so confusing if the opposing factions had not sought to make their cases crystal clear by figures. In the whole welter of figures that emerged, there was only one demonstrable figure: the city power plant was selling electricity for 2.67 cents per kilowatt-hour. The "fors" and "ag'ins" would start at 2.67 cents per kilowatt-hour, and then in support of their arguments would add in a string of x factors that stretched from the Dominion Cigar Store to the Corona Hotel. Night after night the principals in the Rocky Rapids power dispute stood on the public platform and bombarded each other with figures — Ernie Bowness for the company, Mayor Henry for the opposition. Even the newspapers were confused, apparently. After one meeting the headline in the *Journal* announced: BOWNESS SHOWS WEAKNESS OF MAYOR'S ARGUMENTS. The *Bulletin,* on the other hand, screamed, "Mayor Nails Bowness to the Mast."

There wasn't much time for the befuddled citizens to check the opposing calculations, with only two weeks between the council meeting and the day of the plebiscite. The power company was busy circulating pictures of the dam it was going to build at Rocky Rapids. It would be 108 feet high, it would cost $5.5 million and it would make nice clean hydro-electric power, not sooty stuff made from coal. Mr. Farrell bid for public confidence by announcing that the company would immediately put up a $50,000 guarantee. And, by golly, they did put up the $50,000, and the plebiscite was held on November 22, and 7,988 people were for the Rocky Rapids agreement and 5,226 were against it.

And the promoters of the Edmonton Power Company went away to New York and Montreal and London, and tried to raise $5.5 million to build their dam. Alas, they were never able to raise it. The years went by, and the heat died out of the controversy, and the Edmonton Power Company was dissolved, with the City of Edmonton still holding its only asset — the $50,000 guarantee.

Then, as the late finance commissioner, John Hodgson, expressed it, "We collared that money and built our first three swimming pools with it — in Borden Park, Queen Elizabeth Park and 119th Street." The visionaries who saw the dam rising above Rocky Rapids aimed too high perhaps, but they still accomplished something pretty worth while. Ask the kids of Edmonton on any hot day in the good old summertime.

Bob Edwards on Whyte Avenue

Behind the venerable Hub Cigar Store on Whyte Avenue there was once a wishing well. At the turn of the century it supplied the requirements of the business community and of the settlers and Indians who came to Strathcona to trade. It also supplied two rollicking gentlemen who lived in a very modest suite of rooms above the cigar store. One was Jim Halliday the tailor. The other was Bob Edwards. It was Bob who christened the "wishing well" and when asked what made it a wishing well, he would reply, "Because whenever I draw a jug of water up, I wish I had a jug of whisky to go with it."

This was obviously *the* Bob Edwards, who, for eight months of 1900 lived above the Hub with his carousing pal Halliday, and edited a paper called the *Alberta Sun*. Bob poked irreverent fun at the warring towns of Strathcona and Edmonton. He described the residents of rival Edmonton as "cliff dwellers." He said Edmonton was "a snide place that gives everybody the blues." He wrote that "the homes of Edmonton contain nothing but the enlarged pictures of deceased Ontario relatives."

He poked fun at Strathcona as well. When the town fathers bought Mount Pleasant for a cemetery, Bob wrote that they had bought ten acres — five for each doctor in the town. When the town council sought to express the greatness of Strathcona in an elaborate shield, Bob had fun with that too. It was a wondrous conglomeration of heraldry, proof that the limitations of committees extend to the design of shields. Bob wagged his head puckishly over this figment of collective imagination and commented, "The central figure looks like Halliday ascending to heaven on silver wings."

The doings of Halliday filled the pages of the *Alberta Sun,* presenting an image of Halliday as Strathcona's foremost wit, philosopher, economic consultant and civic boast. There was a current of counter-opinion in the community to the effect that Halliday was a town character and no world-beater as a tailor, but Bob found this view unworthy of space in the *Sun.* To keep Halliday in the forefront, Bob once staged his suicide. He stuffed one of his friend's suits with straw and hung it in the window of their room, where passers-by couldn't miss it. All concluded that Halliday had bade farewell to a world that refused to understand. Bob was hiding beside the open window, recording the comments for the *Sun*.

There was never a shortage of news, even when there didn't appear to be any. One day when the paper was going to press, Bob looked out to the southwest and saw that the sky was very smoky. So he set up a banner headline: RABBIT HILLS ERUPTING!

Towards the end of Bob's only summer on Whyte Avenue, the wishing well began to lose its crystal freshness. It lost so much sparkle that Bob and Jim wouldn't mix it with their whisky. Then the merchants complained. Finally the horses reached the point where they could be driven to the well but couldn't be made to drink. So the townspeople decided to fish down the well and see what was wrong.

Just at this moment Bob and Jim happened to be recuperating from another party. They were standing at the back window above the cigar store, surveying the action with vague, uncertain gaze. Their faces fell open with blank amazement when they saw the townspeople haul a lady out of the well. She was, poor soul, quite dead. Bob's landlord, Arthur Davies, swore that Bob took the pledge and drank his whisky straight from that day forward.

The Rite Spots

Memory may cheat. Memory may add artificial colouring to a far-off summer's day, or slyly upgrade the calibre of Sunday afternoon baseball at Renfrew Park, or add details to an adventure of youth. But memory does not cheat or deceive in one regard — in regard to the Rite Spots.

The Rite Spots were hamburger stands, but such hamburger stands! They served only hamburgers and coffee, and doughnuts, and date squares, and cupcakes, and pies — cream pies, no apple. But such hamburgers, and such coffee, and such doughnuts, and such date squares, and such cupcakes, and

42

such cream pies! Memory can not add one false detail to the fare at the Rite Spots. There was something about it. Just what it was we can't say, because the only people who knew wouldn't say. They were Mr. and Mrs. Clarence Morris, the presiding geniuses of the Rite Spots — of which there were five.

Let us first consider the coffee — that was Clarence Morris's secret. But before we consider it, let us close our eyes for a moment and recapture in memory the fragrance and the smoothness of that coffee. Clarence had his own blend and grind, and it was blended and ground to his prescription by an Edmonton coffee importer. When that was done to his satisfaction, Clarence then had a precise formula for brewing it. Part of the formula was cleaning out the urn after each brew and starting over again with fresh, cold water. It was a fussy routine, a routine from which Clarence would brook not a hairbreadth deviation. But, as we said, and as you'll agree — such coffee! Then, when it was brewed, came the cream, Morris's special brand of cream made exclusively for him by Huff's Dairy. Talk about cream! The Rite Spot coffee cream was richer than whipping cream, and a cup of Rite Spot coffee required only a little bit of it. A little gave a cup that rich creamy smoothness, and didn't overpower the coffee. Talk about the cup that cheers — that was it!

And those hamburgers — those big, juicy, delicate hamburgers — they too were constructed on the Morris plan. He insisted that they be made of brisket of beef, the brisket being the trade name for the shoulder of a steer. There's a little more fat in the brisket, just enough fat, just the very right amount of fat, Clarence figured, to keep the meat juicy, to keep it from drying out. He couldn't always get enough brisket in Edmonton, and when he couldn't he would send to Calgary for more. And he kept one man busy at Rite Spot Number One, cutting it up and grinding it to the Morris prescription. As the full name of the Rite Spot read, "The Rite Spot for Hamburger."

Mr. and Mrs. Morris were truly soul mates. Mrs. Morris held the secret formulas for the doughnuts, the cupcakes, the date squares and the pies. Ah-h-h-h-h, those pies. The Rite Spots never served a piece of apple pie. Mrs. Morris didn't care for apple pies. She liked cream pies and had her secret formulas for all of them — for those banana cream pies, and those coconut cream pies, and those pineapple cream pies, and those chocolate cream pies, and those butterscotch cream pies, and those strawberry cream pies. Ah, just the thought of a piece of that strawberry cream pie, with the whipped cream tracery on top, is enough to make an old Rite Spot graduate positively weak with hunger. And you got a whole quarter of a pie for just a dime. Nowadays, restaurants get eight or nine slices out of a pie, but Mrs. Morris's old Rite Spot pies were cut only four ways. And the date squares? Heck, they were date cubes! Those were depression times, and many a struggling man kept going through a tough day on a two-bit Rite Spot lunch. A big juicy hamburger, a huge piece of pie, a cup of heaven-sent coffee — all for two bits.

Clarence Morris, the hamburger-stand perfectionist, started in Edmonton rather late in life. He had run a restaurant in Turner Valley from the early days of the oil boom. Later he ran a lunch counter at the bus depot in Calgary. Then, in 1933, he and Mrs. Morris landed in Edmonton and opened Rite Spot Number One at Jasper and 105th Street, on the northwest corner. A year later, Roy Josey came into the business and opened Rite Spot Number Two near the CPR building. Then there was Rite Spot Number Three at Jasper and 115th Street, Number Four in Garneau, and Number Five in the Recreation Bowling Academy on 101st Street.

White-haired Clarence Morris literally worked himself to death — may he rest in creamy bliss. Ever the perfectionist, he was at work at six in the morning and stayed until midnight or later, and the last act of the day was one that he considered as important as any other. That was scalding out the coffee urns and washing down the walls for that white shine that Rite Spot alumni remember.

The Rite Spots were casualties of war. The government set strict limits on percentages of butterfat in cream, on the amount of cream that could be used in baking, and on the amount of sugar that could be used. These restrictions torpedoed Mrs. Morris's prized formulas for pies. She sold out her share of the business and retired to Calgary.

And now the Rite Spots are just a series of mouth-watering

memories, memories of those fragrant cups of coffee ... those hamburgers ... those banana cream pies ... those coconut cream pies and those pineapple cream pies ... and those chocolate cream pies ... and those butterscotch pies ... and those strawberry cream pies ... and those banana cream pies ... and those coconut cream pies ... and those pineapple cream pies ... and those chocolate cream pies ... and those ...

The Pipes, the Pipes are Calling ...

Until some time in the 1940s, a towering old gentleman named Colin Fraser used to come down from the north and register at the Leland Hotel. Then he would go over to Gault's Wholesale to call on his friend Bert Johnson and ask Bert if he could get Bill Miller to come up to the room that night and play the pipes. Bill would be pleased to oblige, if he and his bagpipes were not booked for some other Caledonian occasion. He would arrive about eight o'clock and begin to play.

Now it's a fact that the bagpipes are an ear-splitting instrument, even in the great open spaces, and it's a further fact that you can't play the bagpipes without stamping around. So, about 8:03, when the other guests of the hotel had traced the source of the clamour, they would set up a clamour of their own. The night clerk would request that Colin Fraser go listen to the bagpipes somewhere else, but the old man would stand to his full height, his eyes would fill with fire, and he would say, "You make us stop, and never a northern man will again cross the threshold of your hotel — ever!" And the night clerk would give up and Bill Miller would stamp around the room blazing away on the pipes; and old Colin would rock on the bed and call out the tune he would like to hear next. Deep in his memories, old Colin was a happy, happy man. His memories were of another Colin Fraser, his father.

In the deep subconscious of Edmonton there are memories of this first Colin Fraser and of the tunes he played with his bagpipes over a century ago. In the Edmonton of the Hudson's Bay Company, New Year's was not complete without Colin

Fraser to pipe it in. Long Colin Fraser, the Highland man, would bring his pipes fifty miles, or a hundred miles, or a hundred and fifty miles to pipe in the New Year at Fort Edmonton. The fort was full of Highland men — and island men from the Western Isles. That's where the company liked to hire its boys for the fur trade. They were big boys, immune to winter and rough weather, and they weren't given to backing up when a fight was brewing. The company hired so many of these boys that Gaelic was the leading language of Edmonton, and when the Reverend George McDougall opened the first school here in 1870, his first task was initiating his Gaelic-speaking students into the mysteries of English.

If Fort Edmonton had such a strong Gaelic flavour, New Year's Eve at the fort had an equally-strong Gaelic flavour; because the eve was Hogmanay. Hogmanay was even more precious to Scots in business in wild northwestern Canada, than to Scots doing business at home. Hogmanay without a piper was like apple pie without the cheese; and that's why Colin Fraser would bring his pipes fifty miles, or a hundred miles, or a hundred and fifty miles, to pipe in the New Year at old Fort Edmonton.

Colin Fraser was a professional piper. In 1828 he had made a coast-to-coast tour with his pipes — well, anyway, from the coast of Hudson Bay to the Pacific coast. When Sir George Simpson, the dynamic little governor of the Hudson's Bay Company, had been planning a tour of company holdings in North America, he had asked for a piper to give his tour more class. Sir George was great for class in the wilderness; a few miles before reaching a trading post he would change to a silk topper and tailcoat. He figured a tall Highland piper, with bagpipes blazing, should precede him in every dramatic entrance.

London headquarters liked to humour Sir George. So, early in 1827, the company had instructed its agent at Stromness, in the Orkneys, to hire a piper at thirty pounds per annum. The agent turned up young Colin Fraser in the village of Ullapool, and the youth was duly booked for a Canadian tour. While the company did not deny the old precept about "paying the piper," it nevertheless approached the matter with caution. On April 4, 1827, the agent at Stromness was advised: "It will be requisite to keep the piper within due bounds on his reaching you, to prevent him getting out too much in advances." On April 27, the agent was advised further: "You may make out a regular contract for Colin Fraser the piper, and advance him a little money; care must be taken however that he does not get from Mr. Simpson and your good self more than fifteen or twenty pounds at the utmost."

Late in June, 1827, a company ship stopped at Stromness and picked up Colin Fraser. Colin reached York Factory on Hudson Bay in the fall, and in the spring of 1828 he began his Canadian tour with Sir George Simpson's party. Colin was an absolute sensation among the Indians. The Indians had seen Highlanders before, lots of them, but never so tall, fair and god-like an individual as Colin Fraser. Nor had they seen such a musical instrument as his bagpipes. Nor had they heard such sounds come out of a musical instrument. Marching ashore with his measured piper's tread, and dressed in his best kilt, Colin Fraser did seem close to God indeed. An Indian once asked him to intercede with the Great Spirit, but Colin declined politely. He said later, "The petitioner little realized how limited is my influence in that quarter."

While Colin's Highland music was a sensation among the Indians, it didn't fit the working requirements of the French-Canadian boatmen in the Simpson party. Simpson wrote in his journal of the expedition: "The second day out, we asked Colin Fraser to give us a few of his favourite strathspeys on the bagpipes. They went off quite well to the ear of the Highland man, but as yet made a poor accordance with either the pole or paddle." So Colin Fraser, may it be forgiven him, was obliged to add some French songs to his repertoire, and the Simpson canoes would come swinging around the bend into view of a fort, while Colin blew a snappy *"Sur le Pont d'Avignon"* through his pipes.

Colin stayed with Governor Simpson for a number of years after his tour; then in 1835 he went to Jasper to manage the Hudson's Bay post there. In 1846, wandering artist Paul Kane found him at Jasper, and Kane noted that Colin had a Cree wife and no less than nine "interesting" children. Colin had more after that, and there were some fine athletes among them.

It was during his time at Jasper that Colin began travelling to Fort Edmonton to pipe in the New Year. In 1850 he was transferred to Fort Assiniboine on the Athabasca River and in 1853 was made post manager at Edmonton. From 1854 to 1862 he was running things at Slave Lake. Then in 1862 he was moved down to Lac Ste. Anne. And at the start of these years he would snowshoe fifty, or a hundred, or a hundred and fifty miles to pipe them in at Fort Edmonton. His last New Year was 1867 — he died suddenly in April of that year at the age of sixty.

Colin Fraser came to Edmonton no more, but the melodies lingered on and so did the stories of his piping: how he used to spend long winter evenings at Jasper House, playing the pipes and dancing to his own shadow on the wall; how he would spend evenings at Fort Edmonton, pacing the balcony which ran around the third storey of the Big House, pacing around and around, all evening long, setting the wild echoes flying with the skirl of his pipes.

Of course, bagpipes are a taste. Some people will say, "Play on ... play on ..." while others will say, "Hold! Enough!" before the piper has got decently warmed up. That's what the other guests of the Leland Hotel would say when Colin's son came to Edmonton in modern times. But the music of the pipes is wild, stirring stuff, and this was wild, stirring country when old Colin Fraser used to come to pipe in the New Year at Fort Edmonton.

In those days there was nothing at all of the Edmonton that lights up so brilliantly to greet the new years of the present century. There was nothing to see but the dark woods extending to the edge of the frozen river — dark woods illuminated by the snow. But up on the high cliff, where the Legislative Building now stands, Fort Edmonton stood, the one pinpoint of light in the primeval forest. The great central hall of the Big House would be noisy with the celebration of Hogmanay. Then all would go quiet, and into the coppery glow of that barbarically splendid hall would come Colin Fraser, to pipe in the New Year.

Big Island

Old Edmonton's favourite picnic spot lies deserted now. Only wild birds and the occasional canoe paddler stop there any more. The place has been so completely forgotten that its name has meant nothing to two generations of Edmontonians. The name is Big Island.

Big Island is sixteen miles up the river, one of a series in the twisting stream between Edmonton and Devon. There's Midnight Island, Fraser's Island (named for pioneer lumberman D.R. Fraser) and Big Island, named for its size. It covers seventy acres, about twelve city blocks, and in its days of glory it was one of the beauty spots of Alberta. A grove of giant poplar trees grew there. Fed by the rich river mud they grew eighty feet tall and a foot and a half thick. Big Island was in its prime just before WWI, in the golden age of the picnic.

The true picnic-lover of that age would scorn the eat-and-run picnics which families of today enjoy. A hasty car ride to Victoria Park by four or five people is not a picnic. To begin with, a picnic is something that requires at least three hundred people for a quorum. It starts in the morning, and there must be a three-hour boat ride to get to the picnic ground. There must be a barrel of beer in the woods, and the picnic dinner must last for two hours. There must be political speeches, and at least one of the orators must be a sitting member of Parliament, of the Senate, or of the provincial legislature. Then, in the evening, there must be a three-hour boat ride home again — time for a full-fledged dance on board. That is a picnic.

And that's what they were like in the palmy days of Big Island. Many Edmontonians of those days were transplanted from Ontario and the mid-western states, where a picnic without a boat ride just wasn't a picnic. The boat was supplied by John Walter, the man for whom Walterdale is named. John Walter's boat was the *City of Edmonton,* a 132-foot sternwheeler, which he built here at his lumber yard and used on weekdays for his lumbering operations upstream. On Sundays and holidays the *City of Edmonton* was a pleasure boat for the pleasure of up to four hundred Edmontonians at a time.

It only cost a dollar for the round trip. The holiday crowd would board the steamer at her dock below the Low Level Bridge. As last minute arrivals scrambled for a place, she would cast off at ten-thirty in the morning and — making a sturdy six miles an hour against the current — would reach Big Island at one-thirty in the afternoon. There she would tie up and pour her human cargo out into the poplar groves for an afternoon of speeches, races, eating, and idle browsing through the woods. On the other side of the island, in the narrow channel between island and shore, there used to be thousands of logs bobbing in the water. That channel was a storage log-boom for Walter's mill. Logs from upstream were diverted into this channel and dammed up there until they were needed at the mill on Walterdale Flat. There were often five million board feet bobbing in the water, and there was something quietly satisfying about sitting idly on the bank and watching the logs.

That was the charm of the old-time picnic. You could listen to a politician defend or denounce the Conservative party (it didn't really matter much which), or you could steal away and listen to the rippling waters. About eight o'clock in the evening, when the sun was sinking slowly in the west, the *City of Edmonton* would pack its picnic crowd aboard again and cast off for home. Big Island — isle of enchantment — did not disappear around the bend to the music of softly strumming guitars. It disappeared to the music of the Lynch family orchestra, strumming with great vigour in the main lounge of the boat. The orchestra pounded all the way home to Edmonton. Captain Abe Pearce, up in the wheelhouse, took the long way home, criss-crossing the river to keep out of the current, and running his engines as slowly as possible. He could stretch the return trip out until ten-thirty for the benefit of the dancers and the people on the decks who were talking with their heads close together. That was a picnic — the *City of Edmonton* and Big Island, and sixteen miles of river between.

But the boat and the island have fallen on evil days. The *City of Edmonton* had to be abandoned in 1918, though you can still see the outline of the boat's flat bottom in the sand bar below the High Level Bridge. When the boat was abandoned, the island was abandoned too. There's not much to see at Big Island now. The giant poplar trees have long since been logged over and the typical prairie bush has grown up between the stumps. In 1921 our city council bought the island to make a prison farm. They were going to send bad actors literally "up the river." These gentlemen might have done great things for Big Island; after all, look what they did for Australia. However, the plan fell through and the island lay deserted until 1950 when the city had a better idea — to drill for oil there. The island was close to the Leduc-Woodbend field, and the city, as usual, was close to financial despair. We had high hopes of striking it rich. We drilled down, but when we got there the D-3 was bare. So Big Island was abandoned again, perhaps for the last time. And it's all by itself now, an island that has known better days — in fact, some of the best days in the history of our town.

Silver Heights Peony Gardens

In 1921 George Brander was seventy-six years old. But he was from Nova Scotia so you will understand that he was only middle-aged and just the right man to start the Silver Heights Peony Gardens. If you lived in the Edmonton of the twenties or thirties you'll remember the gardens, remember them as the most sumptuous banquet of colour that Edmonton has ever enjoyed. There were eight acres of peonies, and from June to August they were never still — with a quarter of a million blooms swaying and bobbing in the breeze that blew across Silver Heights.

The fact that George Brander had lived seventy-six years without growing a single peony was no deterrent to starting in then. He not only had longevity on his side, he had heredity: his father James Brander had been one of the orchard pioneers of Nova Scotia. A native of Huntly, Scotland, James left in 1826 when he was nineteen, and came to Nova Scotia to farm a clearing in the forest on the wild south shore of Northumberland Strait. James made the clearing himself, and to get seed at planting time he would walk sixty miles to Truro. Once he came back from Truro with a small pack of apple seeds, and although he had no formal education in apple growing he raised a successful orchard from that first packet. This instinctive finesse with growing things was clearly inherited by his son George, who was born in 1844.

For most of his life George was successful at farming, and also at business — with a general store at Northport, Nova Scotia. In 1907, when George was sixty-three, he joined the other young men going west. Mrs. Brander had died, and when their son James the doctor went west to practise at Ponoka, George went too. He kept busy at a number of things, and in 1910, when the country around Provost opened for homesteading, George decided that he, too, would be a homesteader. He filed on a quarter section, spent the required three years clearing and breaking, and then sold it for a profit. Then he moved into South Edmonton, where his son James was in general practice.

The real estate boom was at its rosiest bloom when George moved into Edmonton. Son James bought fifty-four lots in remote Silver Heights — out east of Mill Creek — on the assurance of Mr. Latimer, the real estate agent, that he would double, nay triple, his money in a short time. Silver Heights got its romantic name from its topography. There was a bump on the prairie ten feet higher than the surrounding country, so, in the spirit of the times, this bump was labelled Silver Heights.

Dr. Brander did not triple his money right away on this investment in Silver Heights. He didn't even double it. In fact he didn't get a nickel back. Through 1914, 1915, 1916, 1917, 1918, 1919 and 1920 he didn't sell a single lot. But he paid the taxes on them and kept possession, even though nothing developed out there but weeds and poplar scrub — which every year grew up higher around the survey stakes.

George Brander thought there should be something else growing there. He persuaded his son to try some vegetables, and they grew all right, but vegetables were too dull for the elder Brander. So they bought a couple of peonies from Taylor's greenhouse and planted them in front of the son's house at 10652 on 81st Avenue. They thrived and the old chap was so taken with peonies that he ordered a big load of roots from Holland, and Silver Heights was transformed into something more impressive than the real estate promoters ever dreamed of.

52

There are eight kinds of peony blooms. The most common is the "bomb" type, and the peonies did appear to explode all over Silver Heights. George Brander soon had all fifty-four lots — five acres — in peonies. The gardens were bounded on the south by 93rd Avenue and on the east by 85th Street, and in a short time they jumped 85th Street onto three more acres rented from Claude Losie. It is appropriate that the large apartment project on the east side of today's rushing 85th Street is known as Alldritt Gardens — but the Alldritt Gardens will never look anything like Brander's. You'll never see 350,000 peonies blooming on 17,000 plants.

Now, of course, George Brander didn't need all those peonies, but he liked them. Everybody liked them. And when someone would say, "Mr. Brander, you're making a real contribution to Edmonton," the old chap would straighten up with honest pride. In the days when Edmonton couldn't afford to buy much entertainment, Sunday drives to Silver Heights made rich entertainment.

George had a guest book about which he was very particular. Some Sundays there would be two thousand names added to the book, for the gardens were a sight worth driving to see on any Sunday from June through August. George had two hundred varieties of peony, from early-blooming Siberians to August-blooming Chinese peonies, and so there was always something new to see even if you drove out every Sunday.

The Brander Gardens formed the most attractive showroom Edmonton has ever boasted. In the blooming season people would stake out the bush they wanted to acquire in the fall. Tradition holds that there is only one proper time to transplant a peony: nine o'clock in the morning on the fifteenth of September. But once transplanted, they're a permanent addition to any garden. They live for a hundred years.

As the gardens grew bigger and bigger George found the winters longer and longer. To pass the time until he could get out with the flowers again, he would weave baskets — in an ancient style he had learned from his father — and give them away to friends. But when spring came he would be off like a young colt, riding to the end of the Bonnie Doon streetcar line and walking the other five blocks to his beloved gardens. His last summer was 1933 when he was eighty-eight years old.

His son the doctor kept things going for a few years, and then George Lambert, the doctor's son-in-law, took over and kept Silver Heights looking the way the old man had made it. If it hadn't been for the war, the gardens might have gone on forever. But peonies take a lot of manpower; they take one man per acre, working all the time, to keep them hoed and raked. Peony gardens were rather low on the wartime priority list, and the gardens on Silver Heights gradually went out of existence.

But it must not be supposed that the peonies went out of existence. The plants were dug up, divided into fifty thousand roots and sold through Woolworth's to grace gardens all around Edmonton. And it's a safe bet that many of the peonies you now see blooming in Edmonton came from Silver Heights — where George Brander started a new life at the age of seventy-six.

Wallace Howe

From his plug hat to his bulky shoes, Wallace Howe was a cartoonist's conception of Great Britain personified. He was literally and figuratively a stout fellow — sturdy of build, sturdy of character, sturdy of purpose — and his wonderful sturdiness of purpose was shown in its highest colours when, in his late fifties, he undertook to learn to play the bull fiddle. It was in the interest of Edmonton's cultural growth that Wallace Howe took up the study of this ponderous and singularly unrewarding instrument. He was a man of many parts, besides the thumping, unmusical parts allotted to the bull fiddle in orchestral arrangements, and this project was typical of the public spirit he showed for Edmonton in the many years he lived here.

Wallace Howe was born in Manchester, England, in 1867, and like many an English townsman he came to Alberta in the early years of this century to become a farmer. Like most of these English townsmen, he took only a short time to see the error of his ways. In 1910 he became a townsman again, a citizen of our town, and here he resumed his interrupted career as an auctioneer. His first stand was in the Mortlake Block, just east of the Plaza Hotel. Then he auctioned things at McDougall Court. Then he was going, going, gone again — to a place on 101A Avenue, across from the McLeod Building. It was towards the end of his active business life that Mr. Howe turned his talents to the bull fiddle.

As we said, he was approaching sixty, an age when most men are glad to concede that you can't teach an old dog new tricks, but Wallace Howe decided it was about time for an exception to the rule. He was fond of music — classical and theatrical music. He liked to hear it produced by amateur groups, and he noted that there was a shortage of amateurs to play the string bass in these groups. So Wallace Howe determined to strike a blow for music in Edmonton: he undertook to master the bull fiddle.

A bass player's life is a dreary routine of tump-tah, tump-tah, tump-tah, tump-tah. Indispensable though he is, he labours in obscurity. There are no concertos for the instrument, and in those days young ladies did not take up the bull fiddle as an accomplishment. That changed, of course, and years later the Edmonton Symphony Orchestra employed a smashing redhead in the bass section — progress that Wallace would have appreciated more than most. But in those days young ladies took up the violin. That's why there were lots of violinists for amateur groups but no string bass players. And that's precisely why Wallace Howe decided to tackle the elephantine instrument when he was approaching retirement age.

He didn't tackle the instrument unaided — not even Wallace Howe could attempt that. He enlisted the aid of Percy Humphrey, who used to teach the violin and allied instruments on 97th Street. Mr. Humphrey always said that Mr. Howe was the best pupil he ever had. Wallace was soon playing with the Edmonton Symphony Society, learning his parts with Mr. Humphrey and then going home and working at them with Churchillian determination. It may be that Wallace's career as an auctioneer laid the groundwork for his musical adventures. There's a definite rhythmic pattern to the chant of an auctioneer, a relentless, driving rhythm. Perhaps Wallace was mastering the philosophy of the bull fiddle through all those years.

In 1935 he joined in the founding of the Edmonton Civic Opera Society. The artistic director and driving force of this society was Mrs. Carmichael, a sturdy lady who had come to Edmonton in more moneyed times when name vaudeville performers played the Pantages Theatre and when the Macdonald Hotel was on the circuit of name dance bands. She had come to the Macdonald as Jessie Van Loo, leader of an all-girl dance orchestra. At the conclusion of that engagement she accepted another with Dr. Jimmy Carmichael, the whimsical dentist, and she stayed in Edmonton to contribute her teaching and organizing talent as a civic duty. Mrs. Carmichael's operettas and the Glenora Club's annual winter carnival were the only shows in town. The skating club would work all year to create a one-week ice show at the Gardens, and Mrs. Carmichael would marshal the entire resources of the small city to produce four nights of *The Desert Song* at the Empire Theatre. Wallace Howe contributed his fiddling and organizing abilities to this effort. He was president of the Civic Opera in its second year, and he played in the orchestra. It was only when he reached the biblical age of seventy that Wallace laid down his fiddle, but he stayed on in the executive branch of the Civic Opera.

He was glad to do so because he was a tireless worker for the things of life that are good and beautiful. Now it happened that Wallace Howe believed that a good drink of Scotch or a good bottle of beer belonged among the things that were good and beautiful, and that conviction had led him into an earlier public-spirited venture: the Moderation League. In 1916, the Province of Alberta had placed a complete prohibition on good drinks of Scotch and good bottles of beer, and Wallace Howe and his friends were grieved and annoyed. They thought moderation, not prohibition, would eliminate the evils of drink and would also preserve the good things about it. So they organized the Moderation League of Alberta, to work for a change in the liquor laws. General Griesbach was president of the league and Wallace Howe was vice-president and secretary.

Wallace wrote pamphlets and organized public meetings — and he was a doughty performer on the platform. Heckling reached furious heights at these public meetings, but the old auctioneer liked hecklers because he usually came out on top. He was imperturbable and unshakable. Wallace said that telling a man he couldn't drink a nice bottle of beer in his own home was un-Christian and un-British. The voters backed up the Moderation League. In the special plebiscite of 1924, they set the government up in the liquor business.

With prohibition going, going, gone — and Alberta safely on the way to moderation — Wallace Howe turned to other pursuits, like the bull fiddle and the Burns Club. Yes, although he was the personification of John Bull, and although he had been born in Manchester, his parents were Scottish and he inherited a deep affection for the writings of Robert Burns. He helped to "keep the flame" in the Edmonton local of that worldwide brotherhood. Right up to his death in 1942, at the age of seventy-five, he kept up his interest in the Burns Club, in the Edmonton Civic Opera Society and, yes, in moderation. And for nearly twenty years after he had passed on to thump the fiddle in support of the invisible choir, he still played a part in the productions of the Civic Opera Society. During the curtain calls on opening nights, patrons would note Mrs. Carmichael receiving a bouquet of roses of a particular shade. They were from an old admirer, Wallace Howe. He had provided for them in his will.

The Municipal Airport

"Busy weekend at airport," announced the *Edmonton Bulletin* in 1932. "Two departures on Sunday." Of course these were no ordinary flights by ordinary pilots. Two heavily-laden freight planes had taken off for the north, flown by men with names like Brintnell, McConachie, McMullen, Hayter, Berry, Gilbert and May. With the enthusiastic backing of the small isolated city of seventy-five thousand people, these men were making Edmonton the gateway to the north and the bush-flying capital of the world.

Now you might guess that Edmonton was the bush-flying

capital because there was so much bush on the airport. There were no concrete runways in those days, but there were runways all the same — places where the grass wasn't as high as it was on the rest of the field. The City of Edmonton had invested six hundred dollars in 1927 to bring the airport up to licensing standard and make it the oldest municipal airport in Canada, but money for upkeep was scarce. That was why airport manager Captain Jimmy Bell greeted kindly the proposal of a dairy farmer, who lived on the northeast corner, that he pasture his ten cows on the field.

The farmer had a little girl and the little girl had a dog, and the two combined to keep the cows off the busier stretches of runway — most of the time anyway. When a cow strayed into the danger zone, a pilot planning to land could always break into Bossy's contentment by buzzing her off to higher grass.

The legendary pilots who challenged the north went to their joustings in some pretty flimsy aircraft — as two little old ladies discovered one afternoon. The airport was a Mecca for sightseers on fine days, so when Jimmy Bell and a mechanic noted the ladies peering at a plane at the other end of the airport's lone hangar, they paid little attention. The ladies' precise English parasols and round flowered hats proclaimed them to be little old English ladies out for some soft summer air. They had made the long journey to see an airship face to face — a scientific marvel they had only seen before as a blurred shape, buzzing in the blue distance. As they themselves buzzed around a Cirrus Moth biplane belonging to the Flying Club, they expressed surprise at how small an airship was when met at close quarters, and they began to speculate on what the thing might be made of. One lady decided to find out. She raised her parasol like a lance, pointed its tip at the side of the plane, and thrust. Rrrrippp, went the fabric.

"My word, the thing is made of papah," she said.

"Oh, but it can't be made of papah," said the other little old lady. The first old lady raised her parasol and thrust again. Rrrrippp, went the fabric again.

"No, by jove, I think it's made of cotton."

"Oh, but it can't be made of cotton."

"Well, maybe this part is made better." Up went the parasol. Rrrrippp, went the fabric over the engine — just as

Jimmy Bell and the mechanic arrived at the double to end the investigation of what airships were made of.

Cows were part of the decor at the municipal airport in 1932, and a horse was added by Captain Maurice "Moss" Burbidge, the fierce but friendly fellow who ran the flying club. Moss had a legendary fondness for animals. An English country squire at heart, he always had a couple of dogs with him at the airport. He buried two of his pets there. And once, later, out in Victoria, when he was burying a pet sheep, his hired man asked him if he'd "like to say a few words."

So it was no surprise to the boys when Burbidge arrived at the airport one day and said he'd bought a broken-down horse and needed help to get it there. There are at least two stories of how Burbidge bought the horse. One is that he bought it on Kingsway from an Indian who was driving it to the slaughter house to sell for fox meat. The horse was lame in three legs and not much better in the fourth, and out of compassion Burbidge paid the Indian what he expected to get from the packers.

The other version is that he bought it from a junk dealer on 96th Street. The horse had collapsed from exhaustion, malnutrition and lack of the will to live, and the junk dealer was beating it to try to instil some motivation. Burbidge couldn't stand the sight of an animal being mistreated, and he barked in his fiercest manner, "You can't do that!" To which the junk man replied, "It's my horse. I can do what I want with it." To which Burbidge replied, "No, it is not your horse. I've just bought it." Upon which he threw a ten-dollar bill at the sadistic junk man, and being unable to persuade the poor horse to get up and walk to green pastures, he drove out to the airport and got help from the boys.

At this point the stories converge. It's agreed that the boys ran a sheet of canvas under the horse and carried it to the hangar — the old number one hangar. They put the battered animal down in the grass and it began to eat and recover. Scott Reed, the lapidary, witnessed the fact that it ate lying down. Scott's father had insisted that a horse had to stand to eat, but Scott saw this one eat lying down until it gained the strength to stand again.

The grass around the hangar had to be kept down with a single mower so any grass the horse ate was gratefully acknowledged. And the horse was well behaved around airplanes, as it showed on the night of the big thunderstorm. That night there was a violent electrical commotion, and it seemed to 'Arry — the cockney handyman who served as night watchman — that Captain Burbidge would not want his pet to be out in the storm. So he took the horse from its usual place behind the hangar and brought it inside. When the elements had subsided a bit, 'Arry phoned the boss of the Flying Club to report proudly: "I put your 'orse in the 'ang-gar, Mr. Burbidge."

Burbidge, the animal lover, was immediately filled with more concern for his airplanes than for his horse. A frightened, kicking horse could have kicked all the club's wooden and fabric airplanes to pieces — think what the little old ladies had wrought with their parasols! He came streaking out in his car, fearing the worst. But the horse was standing quite calmly in the corner where 'Arry had tied it. It was standing just as though it belonged there. Which it did, in 1932, when this was the bush-flying capital of the world.

Chief Ensor

Nineteen eleven was the year that Edmonton's dairy inspector was moved to describe the manager of the Edmonton City Dairy as a liar, and the manager of the dairy was moved to return the compliment through the press. Nineteen eleven was the year the city health officer socked the city tax commissioner right in the commissioner's office. Nineteen eleven was the year the city council refused to spend five hundred dollars to send the health officer to a convention in Chicago — until one alderman suggested things would be so much better with the health officer out of town, that it would be money well spent. Nineteen eleven was the year the city council dedicated to firing Commissioner A.V. Bouillon. It was also the year in which R.W. Ensor was chief of police.

Mr. Ensor's brief and turbulent term as police chief was a by-product of the row over Commissioner Bouillon. Chief

Lancey had resigned in February 1911, saying that he could no longer abide Commissioner Bouillon's domineering habits, so Edmonton looked around for a new police chief and the lot fell upon R.W. Ensor, a staff sergeant with the Mounted Police.

On first inspection, the new chief appeared singularly well qualified for the job. In the first place he was Irish. Then, he had served eight years with the Mounties and had distinguished himself by breaking up the cattle-rustling gang at Stettler. He had pursued the rustlers for a year and convicted seven of them. (Edmonton should have been a ripe field for a man like Chief Ensor, because, judging from the newspapers of the time, civic government was full of horse thieves.) Ensor had another qualification — he was a total abstainer. And though he looked like a man who could eat twelve pounds of meat per day, he was a vegetarian. A man of many theories on health, he could be seen stowing away huge salads at the old Shasta Café. Policemen were sometimes referred to as bulls, and Chief Ensor carried his personal resemblance to that testy animal into his relations with the public, the press, and the men under his command. It was not unusual for a public official of 1911 to be cantankerous (the commissioners that year put up signs in the civic offices instructing civil servants to be civil to the public) but Chief Ensor rather overdid the cantankerous bit.

The chief got into no trouble during March, his first month on the job, but by April he was feeling that he knew his way around and he issued a cantankerous order: "Policemen who are off duty through sickness will have their wages docked." The chief, you see, was a health nut and did not believe in sickness; weakling cops who did believe in it would have to pay for the privilege. Ensor's men were ready to dispute the point, and on April 5 Constable Jimmy Hoyle wrote a letter to the chief, suggesting that the weather and the danger made constabulary duty hazardous and made a constable subject to illness. According to Hoyle, the chief called him into the office and said, "It is the height of impertinence for any man to ask me to cancel an order I have confirmed. You are discharged."

Now, if the chief had to fire someone, Jimmy Hoyle was an exceedingly poor choice. Jimmy was the hero of the local force, having only two years before arrested Oscar King, the murderer who had killed two men and buried them beside the Clover Bar Bridge. The *Journal* rose in wrath to point this out, to point out that Jimmy had been sick only one day in all his years with the police force, and to point out further that he had been a model of deportment — while a cop "who only a few nights ago was caught in a poker game on Fraser Avenue," and another, "who has been suspended once for drinking but is going on as big jags as before," were still on the force. The *Journal* named the offenders too. Newspapers crusaded at all levels in 1911.

Edmonton had three papers — the *Capital,* the *Bulletin* and the *Journal* — and about the only subject on which they ever agreed was Chief Ensor. Two days after he had fired Jimmy Hoyle, the papers were calling for the chief's downfall again. He had fired Hughie Steele, the senior man on the force, for "complicity" in the sick-pay letter. The chief refused to discuss with the press the departure of Hughie Steele. Another few days and he announced that Bob English, the popular clerk of the court, was fired. When Bob was dismissed, the *Journal* reported: "The chief of police refuses to discuss it. When approached, he draws into his shell like a turtle and emits sounds which could only be understood by a pedigreed grizzly bear."

The chief was getting remarkably poor press notices, even for 1911, but his reviews went from poor to worse. On the night of April 19 he ejected one C. Winther Caws, a mild-mannered Englishman, from a political rally at the Thistle Rink. Here's how the *Capital* described the incident the next day: "During a speech Mr. Caws rose mildly to his feet and said mildly, 'I'd like to ask a question.' 'Put him out!' said someone, quoting a customary phrase at political meetings. The chief must have thought one of his former officers in the mounted police had coughed behind him. He jumped towards the offending person who had dared ask a question without showing his licence. No one knew who the chief was because he was in ordinary clothes and it was not clear to the crowd why this unknown person should take upon himself to evict any man. But Ensor saw the door. He heard the man ask a question. His mind moves in a cross between a muddled jog and a slow canter. He acted according to his lights. The man must be put through the door. He was marched out of the hubbub, into the calm and quiet of the starlit, moonstruck night without."

On having marched C. Winther Caws into the street, Chief Ensor returned to his seat in the rink and was immediately accosted by a prominent citizen, Mr. A. B. Groff, who demanded to know by what authority he cast people out of political rallies. Without condescending to explain that he was chief of police, Mr. Ensor told Groff to pipe down, or he would join C. Winther Caws in the calm and quiet of the starlit, moonstruck night without. The next morning Mr. Groff discovered who the burly bouncer was, and he stormed into the chief's office to demand an explanation — but he came out again as quickly as he'd entered, propelled by the chief. Mr. Groff then proceeded direct to the city commissioners to tell them what Ensor had done. The commissioners thought it was rather funny, so Mr. Groff then proceeded direct to the newspapers, who didn't think it funny at all. Then Mr. Groff proceeded to the office of his lawyer, Fighting Joe Clarke, champion of the underdog, and Joe thought it was great sport and said they would charge the chief with assault and bring him into court.

C. Winther Caws hired a lawyer too and filed his own charge of assault. "I am not always the inoffensive and mild person the press has so romantically depicted," said C. Winther Caws. "I have rights. I do not propose to be ridden over roughshod by an apparent civilian, who happens to be suffering unduly from an inflated idea of his importance as a public servant."

Oh, well said, Sir! To the prisoner's dock with Ensor! However, an impediment appeared to this objective, in a manner typical of 1911: they couldn't get the chief to the dock, because no magistrate would hear the charges. One magistrate said he was a public servant like Ensor and therefore might be prejudiced. Another said he'd just that day been ordered by his doctor not to hear any cases of any kind. The RCMP magistrate said it was a city affair and he really had no right to intrude. Coises! Would justice never prevail?

Justice was in parlous shape all right, but it prevailed. Joe Clarke went right to the Supreme Court, and that highest tribunal appointed a country magistrate to come to town and hear the charges. After many days of heated discussion in the papers, Chief Ensor came to court and pleaded not guilty to assaulting C. Winther Caws. The magistrate found him not guilty on that one, and then the chief pleaded not guilty to assaulting Mr. Groff. "I merely led Mr. Groff to the door," he said. But the magistrate found him guilty in this case and the chief was fined — one dollar.

The papers, meanwhile, were trying and convicting the chief on a number of other charges, and had decided "Ensor must go!" Early in May, Edmonton's automobile drivers joined the chorus. There were only two hundred such drivers in Edmonton in 1911, but they made a great deal of noise. They were incensed at the chief because he had ordered prosecution for any motorist who did not paint his licence number on his car lamps in figures five inches high. Since the car lamps were only three inches high, how the devil were they to comply?

Even the sunny glow of springtime failed to melt the papers' dedication to the principle that Ensor must go. One fine day in May the *Journal* reported: "The sun shines brightly on the policemen. Heretofore the city has always supplied them with nice white military hats for summer. In other years it was not the custom for the chief to wear such a headgear, but it's understood that Ensor will prevail upon the city to buy him a brand new one. And if the city will not comply it is understood that a Panama hat, with the words CHIEF on the top and sides will be provided. However, if the city feels it cannot stand the expense of luxuries, the chief might be induced to go without a hat — as there is a vacant spot on the top of his head where his title could be inscribed."

Ah, 1911. Edmonton was not so big then, nor so wise, but Edmontonians did have fun. Except perhaps for Chief Ensor.

Frank Clarke's Spectacular Ride

The most spectacular performance ever seen on the Connors Hill ski jump was the work of Frank Clarke. Frank was not a skier. He was better known as a partner, with his brother Ed Clarke Senior, in enterprises ranging from turn-of-the-century gold dredging to latter-day tire shops. Frank was also known as a chap who couldn't say no to a bet. Back in 1913, when tap-dancing was in its first vogue and Alex Entwistle held tap-dancing contests at the Dreamland Theatre on Tuesday nights, a pal had bet Frank he wouldn't enter a contest. Frank had taken the bet and had also taken the second prize of five dollars (based on the applause of the audience) and he was a consistent winner from then on. Frank and his prize money were soon parted, with his pals waiting outside, waiting for him to stand a treat at the nearest saloon. But his success as a tap-dancer encouraged him to take on any and all bets, and that's how he happened to turn in the most spectacular performance ever seen on the Connors Hill ski jump.

However, before we come to that we'd better explain how the ski jump happened to be there in the first place. It was the product of a splinter group within a club known as the Sons of Norway. The Sons of Norway were very active here in the early years of the century. They used to have some fine Scandinavian shenanigans at the Mechanics Hall on 103rd Street and at the old Separate School hall on the same street. The older, more settled sons were content with indoor recreation, but the younger sons didn't think that recreation should end at the smorgasbord. On December 19, 1911, eight of them founded the Edmonton Ski Club.

Haakon Floen, who worked for Hardisty's Transfer, was the first president, and Johnny Haugan was the secretary. Johnny and his older brother Hans were sons of Telemarken, Norway — the town that lent the term "telemark" to skiing. With Gilbert Sorenson — also a ski-club member — they strung lines atop power poles for the City of Edmonton. Then there were Ole Olsen and Evan Bolsing, a couple of carpenters; Halvor Lilleboe, who owned an apartment house; and Otto Sven, the tile setter.

It was clear to all of them that Edmonton had snow equal to any found in Norway, and snow that was at least equally persistent. Also, Edmonton had hills equal to many in Norway. The only thing lacking was skis. But a friend of theirs, a lodge brother named Asle Sippola, had gone farming south of Entwistle and had found a splendid stand of birch in the neighbourhood. Asle planed their skis out of the native Alberta birch and half a century later was still making skis for discriminating sportsmen from that stand of birch.

With the skis in hand, the boys still needed toe-irons and harnesses, so they went to a shoemaker and drew a diagram of a ski harness. He fashioned some according to the sketch, although he made it clear that he thought these Norwegians were like the Norwegian entertainer who "yost goes nuts at Christmas." They then described a toe-iron to a blacksmith on 98th Street. With much effort and much head-shaking, he succeeded in bending and cutting a piece of iron into the right shape. They ordered eight sets, and in January 1912 skiing came to Edmonton.

Their first hill was in the west end below 113th Street, a spot beloved by generations of young Edmontonians who liked to go downhill fast. But the skiers had hardly appeared before they were locked in a controversy with the snowshoe fans. Cyril Waites and the Alpine Club used to clop around the country in snowshoes, and they figured that skis were a foreign fad that couldn't last. Haakon and Hans and Johnny and Gilbert and Ole and Evan and Halvor and Otto decided that some dramatic demonstration was required to quiet the Alpine Club, so they challenged the snowshoe brigade to a race. The Alpine Club accepted and invited the Ski Club to choose the route. The Sons of Norway chose wisely and well. They would race from the High Level Bridge to Whitemud Creek. They knew they would flounder and fall over deep-crusted fields, but on crusted river ice they couldn't lose. They didn't. They won the race with two miles to spare, and skiing was here to stay.

In the summer of 1913 the members of the Ski Club figured that Edmonton was ready for a genuine old-world ski jump. They leased part of Connors Hill, rounded up some spare timbers from the city, and went to work putting up a seventy-foot slide. The construction was no problem, because Ole Olsen and Evan Bolsing were carpenters, and Gilbert Sorenson and the Haugan brothers were used to working atop poles. Skiing caught on so firmly and so fast that in February 1915 the club organized a western tournament that attracted entries from as far away as Duluth and Colorado, and attracted six thousand spectators to Connors Hill. The war gradually ended the boom in skiing, as it ended the boom in everything else; and it also ended the skiing career of Haakon Floen, who went away as a captain with the 49th Battalion and lost a leg in the fighting.

But when Haakon returned, he was still organizing for those who could ski, and the organization grew so rapidly that by the early 1920s the Norwegians had become a minority in the Edmonton Ski Club — just what the founders had hoped. Even when the original Connors Hill jump was condemned and torn down in 1925, the sport continued to flourish. The club organized the first ski trains to Banff and had meets on the hills along the river. One memorable meet was held on the Highlands Golf Course, down a hill so short and steep that the contestants had to finish their runs out on the river. That would have been no problem — if it hadn't been for the eight inches of open water running over the ice. One thoroughly soaked competitor growled, "They oughta call this a ski regatta."

Through the years of ski "regattas," the Ski Club plotted and planned to get back onto Connors Hill with a bigger and better jump than the one that had been condemned. In 1935 they engineered a reality out of their dreams and you can see it to this day — in fact you can drive right under it. And while many a spectacular performance has been made from this jump, there has been none as spectacular as the one Frank Clarke made from the old jump, back in 1913.

One day shortly after the jump opened, Frank and his betting pals were on the hill inspecting it, and one of Frank's pals bet him five dollars he wouldn't go off the jump riding a shovel. A bet was a sacred thing. Frank took it.

They borrowed a shovel, and Frank mounted the ladder and gazed down into the awful depths. He was a little sorry at this stage, but a Clarke knows no retreat. He took his seat on the shovel, making himself as comfortable as possible, and grasped the handle in front of him, planning to steer with it. His friends gave him a push, and he was off. Down, down, down he went — faster all the time. Down to the bottom of the jump, then up, up and out! Out into space, riding graceful as you please on a flying shovel. He skimmed lightly over the icy slope. He skimmed closer ... closer ... closer. We shall draw the veil of charity over what happened next, but Frank was happy about the liquor regulations of those days, which insisted that he *stand* at the bar to treat his friends with his winnings. They could all stand and toast the most spectacular performance ever seen on Connors Hill.

Edmonton Gets on the Railroad

The events of Wednesday, November 8, 1902, have not been duplicated, certainly not in Edmonton, and almost certainly not in the whole long history of the whole wide world. November 8, 1902, had everything. It had a happy ending, nobody got hurt, and it had the wonderful slapstick atmosphere of that era, slapstick which could rise to the highest comedy. The events of November 8, 1902, began at eight-thirty in the morning, on the Canadian Pacific right of way, a few blocks south of the depot in Strathcona. That was the day the Edmonton, Yukon and Pacific Railway was to be connected to the CPR, giving Edmonton a direct railroad link with the outside world. It was a long-awaited day.

First of all, W.J. Pace and a construction gang showed up at the appointed place to put in the connecting switch. Then, at 8:30 A.M. the morning train for the south rolled out of the Strathcona depot; rolled over the appointed place, and rolled out of sight. Then Mr. Pace told his boys to get busy. And then things started to happen. A uniformed policeman of the town of Strathcona stepped forward. He presented Mr. Pace with an order from the town of Strathcona, instructing him not to try to connect the EY & P to the CPR. Mr. Pace was unimpressed. He told the policeman so in picturesque terms and told his boys to get on with the job. But the policeman and the town of

Strathcona and the Canadian Pacific Railway had anticipated Mr. Pace's reaction. The cop pulled out a warrant for his arrest. Mr. Pace ignored the warrant, too. He again told his boys to get busy. But the boys stood in greater awe of constituted authority (especially the uniformed kind) than of Mr. Pace; they didn't want to be arrested. They held a conference, and while they conferred something else arrived on the scene.

It was a switch engine puffing down from the CPR roundhouse. The engine was well manned by boys from the CPR shops. They ran it up to the spot where Mr. Pace was proposing to connect the Edmonton, Yukon and Pacific, and they then proceeded to run it back and forth over the spot — back and forth. It was quite impossible to put a switch on a track with an engine on it. Mr. Pace said, "Okeh, boys. Let's go around to Mill Creek and work on the bridge." So they trooped away, leaving the switch engine and the policeman in command of the situation. Yes, at nine o'clock on November 8, 1902, the day seemed to belong to Strathcona and the CPR.

But by ten o'clock news of the skirmish had reached across river to Edmonton. And by eleven it had spread through Edmonton like wildfire. Edmonton was mad. Hoppingly so. Why, away back in April, the railway committee of the Privy Council had authorized the EY & P to connect up to the CPR. And here was the CPR in cahoots with Strathcona, trying to block the connection by skulduggery, blackguardy and treachery. Edmonton knew why. Yes, it was because the CPR owned half the town of Strathcona. That was the "consideration" for which the CPR had agreed to build its terminal on the south side. Unlike Edmonton, Strathcona enjoyed a direct railroad connection with the outside world; and enjoyed crowing about it, too. As half-owner of the town, the CPR was its greatest booster. Anything the CPR could do to preserve Strathcona's advantage in the matter of railroads, the CPR was glad to do. At least that's the way Edmonton figured it. Afterwards, the Canadian Pacific denied any such motive, but nevertheless, at noon on November 8, 1902, a CPR locomotive was chugging back and forth on the part of the right of way that W.J. Pace and associates were trying to connect with the EY & P.

Lunch tasted pretty sour to many Edmontonians that day. They determined that if mere force was going to decide whether or not the switch went in, Mr. Pace and his associates would not be at a disadvantage with the CPR. Shortly after lunch, several busloads of vigilantes started out for Strathcona. Down McDougall Hill they rode, across the Low Level Bridge where the tracks of the Edmonton, Yukon and Pacific were already laid, up the long Scona Hill, past the CPR roundhouse, and to the spot where the CPR engine was shuffling back and forth on sentry duty.

The patriots from Edmonton were ready for anything. But, like Mr. Scrooge at one point in *A Christmas Carol,* they were not by any means prepared for nothing. And that's all they could do when they reached the scene. While they had come to support Mr. Pace and company in their just cause, Mr. Pace and company were nowhere in sight. There was the engine, the cop, and an interested crowd of south siders — but nothing else. Two o'clock passed ... three o'clock ... four o'clock. At five o'clock, when darkness began to fall on that winter day of November 8, 1902, it appeared almost certain that the day had gone to Strathcona and the CPR.

Then about 5:15 along came Mr. Pace, strolling casually up the line from Mill Creek, and whistling softly to himself. His attitude was so mild, so lamblike, that you would never have guessed it was just a cloak for a clever stratagem: W.J. Pace had something up his sleeve. He looked around mildly, conversed mildly, and then it was 5:25 ... and a runner from the CPR roundhouse came down and told the crew of the sentry engine they would have to chug back to the roundhouse for a few minutes and let the evening train from the south pass through. The guard-train chugged away. As it left, the train from the south came into view. It rumbled past. Then ... W.J. Pace gave a sharp whistle. His boys came streaking out of the bushes (they'd been hiding there for some time); they came streaking out of the bushes and started pulling up the tracks. The crowd of Edmonton patriots prevented any interference. The boys got the tracks up in short order, and before the guard-engine could get back from the roundhouse, they had the switch in place. Edmonton had a direct rail connection with the outside world. November 8, 1902, belonged to Edmonton, belonged to the history of railroading and to the history of the whole wide world — our dark, weary and sinful world, which can certainly use more bright spots like this one.

70

The Thistle Rink

The fans at the Thistle Rink were so tough they had to be kept in cages. The Thistle Rink was on 102nd Street behind the King Edward Hotel. Among its many uses were political meetings and hockey games, so it shook to its foundations with partisanship on many a night, before the night in 1914 when it went up in such a blaze that the curling rocks burned up.

There were wire screens down both sides of the rink, and that was because hockey was less of a spectator sport for the spectators of seventy years ago. The fans would get into the game. In January nowadays, if you see a lady out with a parasol, you'll think the poor girl is heading for a crack-up. But in January 1906, if you saw a lady out with a parasol, you would be sure she was heading for the South Side Covered Rink to get in on a game between the Strathconas and the hated Edmonton Thistles.

There were no cages to hold back the fans at the South Side Covered Rink, which was beside the CPR tracks, a little north of Whyte Avenue. If a hated Thistle got too close to the boards on a dash down the ice, the lady could jump from spectator to participant with one accurate swipe of the parasol. A gentleman with a cane could also get into the game, and even an unarmed man could get a piece of the action with his fists.

Across the river at the Thistle Rink the cages kept the parasols and canes out of action, but the screen couldn't restrain the fans from getting into the game with coal. The coal had a parallel with modern military tactics where you confuse the enemy by throwing up "bogeys" on a radar picture. When the hated enemy was threatening to score, the fans would confuse the attackers by throwing puck-sized pieces of coal on the ice.

The hockey season, ironically, used to start on Christmas Day, when Edmonton would play Strathcona. On New Year's there'd be a return match in the rink of the other team. On Christmas Day the season would open in an atmosphere of peace on earth, good will towards men — with certain obvious exceptions. It would continue on New Year's in an atmosphere of auld lang syne — with certain obvious exceptions.

71

The proprietor of the Cameron House, which was at the south end of the Low Level Bridge, the only bridge on the whole river, found that hockey was great for business. On Christmas Day he would have the Strathcona fans going to Edmonton and returning. On New Year's he would have the Edmonton fans going to Strathcona and returning. A man, whose aggressions were being neutralized by the sentiments of the day, could stop in at the Cameron House and have them recharged at the bar. All the hotels of the Thistle Rink era were good contributors to anything involving sport, because any sporting event brought an increase in patronage. Nowadays, following an event, fans will listen meekly on television or radio while "experts" tell them what happened. But in the Thistle Rink every fan was an expert. He was bound he'd be heard. And the kindly hotel keeper had a forum open for him.

Hockey, soccer, harness racing, boxing, lacrosse and baseball — everything but cricket — meant business for the hotels, so they didn't contribute much to cricket but they did contribute handsomely to the building of Edmonton's first baseball park. This was in 1907, when the Thistle had been going five years and the South Side Covered Rink for three. Some of the boys formed a joint stock company to sell shares and built Diamond Park, down below McDougall Hill. This was to replace the cow pasture up along 102nd Street near the CNR tracks.

This venture lost five hundred dollars less than it might have done, because the team that was brought in to play at Diamond Park had a catcher named Ford who was pretty good, and at the end of the season the company was able to sell Ford to the Pacific Coast League for five hundred. Although the shareholders lost their money, the hotel keepers figured they got theirs back over the counter. During the hockey season there would be some kind of two-game series with some kind of trophy at stake almost every weekend. Teams from Calgary, Regina and North Battleford would be in town to challenge for the Brackman-Ker Trophy or the Secord Shield or some other Edwardian horror. There would always be action when Edmonton played Calgary or Regina for the Secord Shield — as Harold and Guy Deeton, Walter Campbell, and Russell Johnson could testify. They all played for the Thistles.

72

But the most action came when Edmonton played Strathcona for no other prize than the prestige of humiliating a cross-river rival. The action would start as the bus carrying the Edmonton team arrived in Strathcona. Although some people complain of the high-sticking in hockey games today, the Thistles used to have their sticks high and ready the moment they entered hostile territory. Insulting urchins would meet them first, and from there to the rink the citizens of Strathcona would leave off singing "God rest ye merry gentlemen" to come out of their houses and hurl verbal ammunition — and other ammunition provided by the fact that this was the age of the horse. At the rink, the ladies with their parasols would be waiting to get into the game.

But when the Strathconas came to the Thistle Rink a week later they had it easier. At the Thistle the fans were kept in cages.

Two-Gun Cohen

A book has been written about Morris "Two-Gun" Cohen, who rose from London dock hand to Alberta ranch hand, to Edmonton real estate operator, to sergeant in the Canadian army in the First World War, to general in the army of Nationalist China. Right here, we would like to enlarge on one phase of Morris Cohen's career: his contribution to fun and games when Edmonton was young and exuberant, and fun and games were terribly important. One of Two-Gun's many contributions was a gambling den he operated on the seventh floor of the Macdonald Hotel. He lived in the adjoining room, and he operated his gambling den in the Macdonald secure in the knowledge that the last place the police would look for a gambling den would be the Macdonald Hotel. Little wonder that Morris Cohen was equal to the subtle diplomacy of the mysterious East and rose to a position of power and influence in Nationalist China. When the Japanese surrounded Shanghai in 1932, they found the defences of the city being organized by Morris "Two-Gun" Cohen, the former Edmonton real estate man.

Morris landed in Edmonton about 1907. He had worked among Chinese dock hands in his native England, he knew the language and the customs, and he was soon up to his heavy eyebrows in the affairs of the local Chinatown. In 1908, Dr. Sun Yat-sen, the founder of the Republic of China, came through Edmonton on a tour of North America. Morris Cohen was among the people invited to meet Dr. Sun, at a reception in the home of Attorney General Charlie Cross, and Sun Yat-sen was so impressed by Morris that, a dozen years later, he invited him to join the Nationalist staff in China.

Two-Gun was always much in evidence around election time. The arrival of Morris Cohen at Lewis Brothers' Café was an election tradition in the days of real sport. He would pass the word that on a certain night at a certain time he would be at Lewis Brothers' Café to sell the Chinese vote; and at the appointed hour he would be there waiting for the bidders.

It was at Lewis Brothers' that Morris Cohen made his most elaborate contribution to the gaiety of Edmonton. The café was on First Street, across from the present Rialto Theatre. By day, and by evening, it was a select restaurant for discriminating diners, but by night the temperature rose and it became a jolly sort of club for jolly chaps like Morris Cohen. Even the riffraff was high class at Lewis Brothers'. Once, when Chicago got too hot for Lester Gillis (alias Baby Face Nelson), that friend and confidant of John Dillinger sought the peace and quiet of Edmonton for a while; and he could usually be reached at Lewis Brothers'. For this Rabelaisian crowd, Morris Cohen devised that classic practical joke: "Going to see Marie."

Like any practical joke, it required a victim, and the victim required for "Going to see Marie" was a stranger. When the boys spotted a stranger in the café in the later hours, they would put the plan into action. They would ask the stranger if he was lonely; and the stranger would concede that he was. Then they would suggest to the stranger that he go to see Marie. And who was Marie? Well, Marie was a lady who lived in a little house over on 102nd Street just north of Jasper Avenue. And what was Marie like? Well, Marie was a very attractive lady indeed. And was Marie likely to be lonely, too? Oh, very definitely. Well, so far so good, but was there any

74

drawback? Did Marie, by any chance, have a husband? Oh yes! Ho ho! Ha ha! Marie had a husband, but he was a railroad man; he'd be out on the train. Sure. But there was something one had to do. Marie was very fond of chocolates; one had to be sure to take her a box.

When the boys saw the stranger buy a box of Frank Lewis's best chocolates and saunter out into the night, they knew the game was on. They would race out quietly and go over to Second Street. One of the boys would nip into the little house — which was vacant, of course, and which made the game possible — while the others hid in a junk yard across the street to watch the fun. The victim would arrive and knock timidly on the door. Behind the door, one of the boys would slip blank cartridges into a pistol. The victim would knock again. The door would fly open. There would be a bellow of rage and a voice would shout in effect: "So you, sir, are the cad who's been hanging around my wife, while I, a poor but honest man, have been out working on the railroad. You, sir, are unfit to hold a place in human society." With that, the blank cartridges would be banging off, the victim would streak into the night, and the boys hiding in the junk yard would collapse with laughter. One victim ran all the way to the CPR station, found a train just leaving, and rode all the way to Wetaskiwin.

Alex Riddell, later Edmonton's deputy police chief, first heard about "Going to see Marie" when he was a young constable on the beat. Alex was beating the sidewalk along 102nd Avenue when a wild-eyed man raced into his arms shouting, "Save me! Save me!" When Alex investigated the little house he found the boys from Lewis Brothers' sitting on the sidewalk, shouting with laughter and eating the chocolates.

When you consider "Going to see Marie," nothing else that Morris "Two-Gun" Cohen achieved seems too surprising.

The Happy Time

That was the happy time, the time before Edmonton took on the sobering responsibility of being a city or being a provincial capital — 1904 in the first case and 1905 in the second.

The horse trough at 95th and Jasper was a symbol of the happy time. Your old world capitals might have had their glorious public fountains but they didn't have anything like our horse trough. It held a fascination for railroad builders and lumberjacks and other strong men who sought their livelihood in the bush. When they came to town for a spree they would amuse themselves and the populace by jumping into it fully dressed, splashing and thrashing, and blowing like whales.

Your old world capitals might have had their reigning operatic queens, but Edmonton, in the happy time, had Jessie Cameron. Jessie studied music in Paris and made her name known in New York, but that came later. When she was the toast of Edmonton, Jessie was the chubby blonde daughter of John Cameron, who had a coal mine by the Mounted Police barracks and for whom Cameron Street is named. In those days the river steamers used to come up to Edmonton from Prince Albert and the Battlefords. The steamers would lie at Fraser's mill on Riverdale Flat, and the captains would invite Jessie to come down on summer evenings and sing on the deck. People would come to the brow of the hill to hear the sweet voice of a child singing "the old songs," and the town was so quiet that her songs filled the valley. The capitals of the old world, for all their operatic queens, had nothing to compare with Jessie; for all their magnificent choirs, they had nothing like the choruses of railroad builders and lumberjacks who splashed by day in the 95th Street horse trough. On Saturday nights they liked to take the Fifth Street ferry out to midstream and bombard the echoing bluffs with "Sweet Adeline."

Your old world capitals might have had their statues of generals on horseback, but here in Edmonton we had that genuine stuffed horse that used to stand on the sidewalk in front of the Great West Saddlery. It was a monument to the taxidermist's art, probably Frank Wolfe's. The only trouble was the dogs. On a drowsy summer day a dog would come ambling along the wooden sidewalk, and he would see the horse. He would come up cautiously and investigate further with his nose."Aha," he would think to himself, "my remarkable sense of canine smell, which helps compensate me for my poor sight, tells me this is indeed a horse. Dogs like to bite horses; I am a dog, therefore I shall bite this horse." And the dog would begin attacking the stuffed horse with all possible gusto and with all appropriate howls and barks. Then a boot would come flying out from the Great West Saddlery and the dog would go flying up the dusty street, and a minute later the clerk would come out of the saddlery to retrieve the boot and put it back in stock. No, your old world capitals might have had their statues of kings on horseback, but they had nothing the equal of our Great West Saddlery horse.

The sidewalks along Jasper were wooden, of course, but they were once the occasion for a mighty slick advertising stunt. One morning, giant footprints appeared on the sidewalks — painted there, that is. Inside each footprint was a sign saying: "Follow the giant footprints to Edmonton's popular store." Now there weren't many stores. There was the Bay, and Johnstone Walker's, and Joe Morris's, and Larue and Picard's, and Gariepy and Lessard's, and the store with the most intriguing name: Brown, Sage and Curry. But no one ever found out which of them was supposed to be Edmonton's popular store — because every merchant got out early with his own yellow paint-brush and painted giant yellow footprints turning into *his* store. There were giant yellow footprints all along Jasper, turning into popular stores.

Edmonton's municipal administration was consistent with the demands of this simple time. All services were provided from one building, the original Number One Fire Hall, which Kenny McLeod erected for the town in 1893. The town, not the village. The village moved up to town status that year, and the fire hall, just north of Jasper on 98th Street, served as police station, town office and town meeting hall. It also served as bunkhouse for some town employees who were given a free bed in return for being on hand to turn out with the volunteer fire brigade. Among the lads who enjoyed this arrangement was W.H. Clark, who founded the Clark Lumber Company. When the fire bell clanged in the tower above, lads like Clark or Art Ormsby or Billy Barnhouse would reach for their clothes and slide down the brass pole while citizens with horses raced to the hall. The prize for the winner was five dollars. The first team to the hall got to pull the pump wagon to the scene of the conflagration.

Even at the peak season for public works, the number of municipal employees did not exceed twenty-five, and the staff did not include a janitor. But the police held a continuous warrant for a vagrant named Pete, and when the town fathers felt the hall looked a mite grubby the police would pick up Pete and put him to work with a mop.

The town fathers met upstairs and so did the citizens at large. There was room enough for all — for the men anyway. There was one rousing meeting in 1899 when Mackenzie and Mann, the railroad builders, outlined their plan to extend the Edmonton, Yukon and Pacific Railway. One phase of the plan was to extend it to Edmonton. Yes, they were going to bring it over from Strathcona by way of the Low Level Bridge, and in return for certain valuable concessions from the great town of Edmonton they would build a terminal within a few blocks of downtown Edmonton. The boys all applauded and went home figuring Edmonton's place in the sun was guaranteed. And Mackenzie and Mann fulfilled their end of the agreement to the letter. They fulfilled the letter all right, but the spirit was lacking. They built a terminal within a few blocks of downtown Edmonton but it was down on the flats — and a pitiful matchbox of a terminal — not the grand station the boys had pictured on top of the hill.

Now the town fathers who could get janitor service for nothing, and fire protection for nothing, were obviously very resourceful men. But the full extent of their resourcefulness is revealed not in a balance sheet, but in a story the late Bob English used to tell. The revealing incident occurred shortly after Bob became city clerk. It seems there had been a meeting of the city council. And it seems that the police had raided a bootlegger and seized several bottles of evidence. After the council meeting, some of the boys fell to discussing the case of the bootlegger and the great amount of evidence the police had seized. And, well, the boys agreed that the police had seized *so much* evidence that it would surely not all be needed to obtain

78

a conviction. So they poured a round. And there was still so much evidence that it seemed there could be no harm in pouring another round. And another round. And another round. And another. And another. And another.

In the morning Bob English had to inform the boys that the case was coming to trial that day and all the evidence was gone. Were the town fathers unequal to the occasion? Not on your life. They rushed out to another bootlegger, bought enough to refill the bottles, and the first bootlegger was convicted — as he jolly well ought to have been.

That was the happy time.

Boom Times — 1908-1914

On a golden day in 1911 a prominent Edmonton lawyer was talking to a friend on Jasper Avenue. "Yes," said the lawyer, "I'm subdividing my farm. It's halfway between Edmonton and St. Albert. I haven't decided yet whether to make it a suburb of Edmonton or St. Albert."

That was the spirit, the spirit of the great real estate boom, when Edmonton was going to be a metropolis and every town and village was going to be a city. St. Albert was going to be a city. Of course it was. What could stop it? And St. Albert was not to be alone. Onoway was going to be a city. Wolf Creek was going to be a city. Tofield, Rocky Mountain House, Grouard, Fort McMurray. All going to be cities. The newspapers of that golden age are full to the brim with optimistic advertisements about cities like Tofield and Onoway. But they were not cities yet. And that was the great thing, because it gave shrewd investors the opportunity to get in on the ground floor, to buy now, and to have five or six centrally-located lots ready to sell at a handsome profit when the city materialized.

In the golden age there were real estate offices all along Jasper Avenue, up First Street, up 97th Street, and along Whyte Avenue. A conductor and his motorman had a real estate office in their streetcar. They had a map of the subdivision they were plugging nailed up in the motorman's compartment, and they did a right good business. They were "runners" for the gentlemen who were promoting the subdivision, drumming up trade on commission. When a company was pushing a subdivision of its own creation, it would have about ten runners in action.

New subdivisions all came about in the same way. The operators would get hold of a farm, usually a quarter section, and have it surveyed into streets and lots. You can get about thirty city blocks into a quarter section and you can get ten lots to a block, so that made a total of about three hundred lots available for shrewd investors. In the boom time Edmonton grew farm by farm to its present dimensions. If the farm was ten feet higher than the surrounding countryside, the promoter might call it "Something-View," like Fairview up east of the airport. If it was ten feet below the waterline in spring, it might be called "Something-Dale," like Allendale. Having christened his farm and having had it surveyed, the promoter would then print his maps and send his runners out on the streets.

The runners, like all the real estate crowd, had a phenomenal knack with a map. Their control of a map was an art now lost forever. They could unroll it without tearing it, hold it steady in a high wind, point out a choice lot with a deft wave of a thumb, and never break stride. They acquired their art through constant practice. The length of Jasper Avenue, on a good business day, you could see maps opening and closing with the precision of window blinds. The runners would often make immediate sales on the street, but most of their work consisted of getting the customer into the net and luring him to the office, where the promoters would gaff him.

Runners were not to be confused with curbstone brokers who also worked in the open. The curbstone brokers were the pet peeves of orthodox real estate men. Curbstone brokers were the sort of gentlemen who commonly seek a livelihood by following racehorses from city to city and whispering sure-fire tips to betters. Most of them operated around First and Jasper, or around the railroad stations. They were skilled at picking out a stranger who had just arrived in Edmonton. They would engage the stranger in conversation, get the conversation around to real estate, and then usually sell the stranger a lot. Their operating expenses were practically nil. They would take an option on a lot, for maybe a dollar, then transfer the option to the stranger for a hundred dollars. It was perfectly legal, but orthodox operators felt that curbstone brokering lacked tone and caused them unfair competition.

Even so, the orthodox brokers did well. Billy McNamara, mayor of the city in 1914, used to say it was a wasted lunch hour when he couldn't make fifty dollars over the lunch table. When the boys had a good day with the lots, a favourite form of celebration would be a night in Cronn's Café. Cronn's had circular booths, and the fun lay in drinking champagne and ringing the booth solid around with empty champagne bottles.

The charming thing about the great boom was the way you could build up a fortune for ten percent down. The boys celebrating their good fortune in Cronn's might be celebrating a good day with Glenlyon lots. Glenlyon is still deep in farm territory north of Calder, but in 1911 investors were urged to buy fast. Said the ads, "Glenlyon will double, yes, treble your money in a reasonably short time. Do not fail to take advantage of this unprecedented opportunity."

Now, let's see how we make a fortune, on paper, by buying lots in Glenlyon. Suppose a lot is worth $300. All right, we buy it for $45 down and $30 a month. We figure we'll treble our money as the ads promised. That means we're going to get $900 for it when we sell. So we figure we're worth $900 for an investment of only $45 cash. It doesn't take long to build up a fortune at this rate. Meanwhile, the promoter who sold us our lot in Glenlyon takes our $45 and puts it down on a $450 lot, which he figures he'll be able to sell for $1200. So he adds another $1200 to his estimated fortune. Our $45 goes round and round, making everyone wealthier. As long as someone with a new set of $45 keeps coming into the game, optimism runs high and the boom grows bigger and grander. It was great fun while it lasted.

Streetcar lines were a prize attraction for buyers in new subdivisions. The real estate boys thought they were a prize worth fighting for. W.J. Magrath, who opened the Highlands in 1911, paid $20,000 to have the white-sign streetcars extended out there. That was one way to do it, but the best way for a real estate man to get a streetcar line was to be on the city council. The original plan for the west end called for the streetcars to run out along the St. Albert Trail. But the tracks were diverted straight north along 124th Street, the better to serve the subdivision of Inglewood which some of the councillors were promoting.

There was another row about the 107th Avenue car line to the west end. Early in 1912 the city council passed estimates for running the streetcar line out along Vermillion Avenue — that's 106th. Then, a couple of months later, the committee of aldermen in charge of such things announced suddenly that the car line would go along Nelson Avenue instead — that's 107th. The change caused comment on the street and in the press. At the next meeting of the city council a spoilsport alderman stated that certain aldermen on the committee, not mentioning any names, had tipped off their friends in advance about the change; and that the friends, along with certain aldermen on the committee, not mentioning any names, had taken advantage of the information to corner the choicest real estate on 107th Avenue. There was an embarrassed silence in the council chamber. The mayor broke the silence. He asked the spoilsport if he could prove it. "No, I can't prove it," he said, "but I know —— well it's true." So everyone breathed a sigh of relief and got back to business as usual.

One of the lasting achievements of the boom time was Edmonton's civic centre — the area of Sir Winston Churchill Square and the City Hall. The area had been left undeveloped because of the competition among 97th Street, Jasper Avenue and 101st Street. The empty area in between seemed ideal for a civic centre, a sort of village green scaled to a great metropolis.

In July 1912 the city council stopped the sale of city-owned land in the three blocks north of the market square. (Those three blocks have since become two, due to the rearrangement of streets). It turned out that the city owned only two lots in all those blocks, so the gentlemen who owned the rest were soon banded together trying to sell them to the city. And, though you'd scarcely believe it, some owners were also members of the city council.

Lots in the proposed centre were being bought at high prices, to be sold at even higher prices to the city council. When the prices were added up, they came to a total of

$2,712,193.34. That was a great deal of money. It was all to be cash, too. None of your fifteen percent down and ten percent per month. All cash. Many pairs of hands were rubbed in eager anticipation.

Plans were drawn up, public meetings were held, and the council declared formally on March 18, 1913: "The municipal council of the City of Edmonton deem it advisable to establish a civic centre, being a park or open space for the purpose of building thereon various buildings of a public or semi-public nature, and laying out the said lands in an ornamental manner."

To acquire the land, council deemed it necessary to create a debt by borrowing $2,712,193.34, and this proposition went to the burgesses as a money by-law on March 28, 1913. But alas for the promoters; the rate payers would not buy this one — not at the price.

And the joke of it is that Edmonton got the land for a civic centre anyway. When the boom collapsed the owners let the property go. The city took most of it for taxes and in the process saved $2,712,193.34 plus interest, and forty years later built the City Hall and Sir Winston Churchill Square.

The Hudson's Bay Land Sale

It was the Sunday evening of May 11, 1912, and even to the most unobservant of men it was abundantly clear that something was afoot. Something unusual was going on in the streets of downtown Edmonton. Men carrying chairs and boxes and tables and campstools were hurrying along with a look of eager determination. They were clearly not fleeing from fire, flood or invasion; they had not, all of them, all of a sudden, gone mad. They were in a hurry because the big secret of the Edmonton real estate boom had leaked out. They were in a hurry to get in line and get in on the biggest land sale of the boom — the sale of lots in the Hudson's Bay Reserve. The big secret had been guarded well by the Hudson's Bay Company, but you can't stop people putting two and two together; and by the process of putting two and two together, the secret had been deduced. Before we go into the secret, perhaps we'd better explain the background of the Hudson's Bay land sale.

Back in 1870 the Hudson's Bay Company had sold out Rupert's Land (which included the present prairie provinces and Northwest Territories) to the growing Dominion of Canada. The company had struck a hard bargain: $59 million in cash and the rights to a lot of choice land. Around every trading post, for example, it had the right to reserve one thousand acres, and around old Fort Edmonton the company had reserved a thousand acres, running from the river back to 118th Avenue and from 101st Street west to 121st Street. That was the Hudson's Bay Reserve. The designation still appears on land titles. As early as 1883 the company had begun selling lots in the reserve — $25 for an average lot and $35 for a corner. You could buy the corner of Jasper Avenue and 104th Street, for example, for $35. The pioneer merchants, Larue and Picard, once got this corner in trade for an alpaca coat.

It wasn't until the first real estate splurge of 1906 that there was much demand for lots north of Jasper Avenue. By the second splurge in 1909 there was demand for lots anywhere. But the Hudson's Bay Company decided to sit tight on the northern half of their reserve. They clung tight to the area from 108th Avenue north to 118th, and from 101st Street clear across to 121st. They clung tight while real estate promoters pushed the great city of Edmonton around and beyond them. While the promoters were beating up the value of distant subdivisions like Dovercourt and Sherbrooke, they were, of course, making the lots in the centrally-located Hudson's Bay Reserve even more valuable. "The Company of Adventurers of England Trading into Hudson's Bay" sat back, rubbed their hands in anticipation, and waited till the iron was hot.

On April 24, 1912, the first intimation appeared in the papers. It was drawn up like a legal notice and said the company would offer for sale a number of business and residential lots centrally located in the City of Edmonton. The sale would start on May 13. That was a Tuesday. But more exciting still, there would be a public lottery on the Monday before the sale. In the lottery, shrewd investors would draw numbers out of a barrel to decide the order in which they would be allowed to buy lots. There would be only fifteen hundred tickets, and each ticket holder would be allowed to buy four lots. The drawing would start at two o'clock Monday afternoon, but to make sure that everyone had a fair chance, the exact location of the lottery would remain a secret until six o'clock Monday morning. The location would then be published in the morning *Bulletin,* and the advertisement would not be taken to the *Bulletin* until just before press time.

As we said, the company guarded the secret well. Shrewd investors were uncontrollably curious about the secret location. They trailed officers of the Hudson's Bay land department, hoping the officers would give the location away. They tried bribery. But they finally figured it out by the process of putting two and two together. On Saturday afternoon a dray was observed to pull up in front of a little unused church on 103rd Street. The draymen were observed to take out a huge safe and wheel it into the church. Then they wheeled a couple of steel barrels into the church. Aha! No more than a dozen passers-by witnessed this operation, but they were a dozen passers-by with but a single deduction: why else would a safe and two steel barrels be wheeled into an unused church, if not for the Hudson's Bay land sale?

By eight o'clock Sunday evening there was a middling crowd of people patrolling up and down in front of the old church, people who were eyeing one another to see whether they were all in on the secret. Fenton Aitken was patrolling with a friend. Suddenly he turned to the friend and said, "Let's just lean up against the doors and see what happens." That started it. In a flash there was a line-up of thirty people. Inside the hour they were lined up down to 102nd Avenue. And through the night the rumour flew, and the line grew. It grew right around the block and back to the church again. And, as we said, the most unobservant of men could not have been unaware, on that night of May 11, that all the gentlemen rushing along with boxes and campstools and chairs were up to something important.

It was a good-natured crowd. People who feel they've put something over are generally good-natured. When the official announcement of the location appeared in the *Bulletin* at six o'clock that morning, there were 1,285 men in line. By that time, some were cooking breakfast over open bonfires. One party had played cards all night by light from car headlamps.

By nine o'clock there were 1,500 in the line. They all signed a petition and sent it to the Hudson's Bay land commissioner, stating in effect that since the gang was all here, let us get on with the draw. The land commissioner was disturbed at his morning shave in the Corona Hotel, and he was not at all happy to discover that the secret had not been kept. He rejected the petition bluntly. The draw would start at two o'clock. It had been advertised for that time, and there would be people coming in from the country who would be left out if it started earlier.

About ten o'clock a trainload of fifty shrewd investors arrived from Vegreville. But they were too late. The line was too long. The 1,500 tickets were gone long before they got near the church. A couple of operators tried to crash the line at the 400-mark. They clung to a fence and would not be dislodged. However, when they couldn't be dislodged, they got such a pummelling that they were pleased to accept a police escort to neutral territory. Others tried to buy places. One prominent man offered $3,000 for three places near the head, and was turned down. Arthur Davies, the former mayor of Strathcona, was eighty-seventh in line. He sold out for $1,000. And way around near the end, place no. 1442 was sold for $55.

One's place in the line, of course, had no bearing on the draw. Mr. Aitken, first in the line, drew ticket no. 910, which meant that 909 other investors would choose lots before he could. The man who drew ticket no. 1 had been 742 in the line-up. The man who drew no. 2 sold for an undisclosed amount of cash to McDougall and Secord. McDougall and Secord then proceeded to buy the choice corner lots on Kingsway at 101st Street. Paddy Dunne drew ticket no. 10. He bought four lots and made more money out of them than most shrewd investors. That is to say, Mr. Dunne didn't lose any money. The most money of all was probably made by a visitor from Winnipeg, a chap named Ed Alexander. Ed's Edmonton friends had hustled him out of his bed in the Corona Hotel and got him into the all-night line-up. Ed drew ticket no. 5 and sold it the same day for $5,000.

For days afterward, the barbershops and drugstores of Jasper Avenue were full of signs advertising less desirable tickets for sale. It was many weeks before the excitement died down. The Hudson's Bay Company moved to keep it alive by building a handsome paved avenue diagonally across the Reserve. That was Portage Avenue, the present Kingsway. The city laid two handsome lines of streetcar tracks along Portage Avenue, and on either side of the handsome street the building lots traded furiously. But, like most building lots in Edmonton, hardly any of them were being built on. After a year, the company grew a little concerned about this and it built a cluster of houses around 109th Street and 111th Avenue — a very nice cluster, too. But still nothing happened. Eventually it became clear that nothing was going to happen. The lots would not be built on ... the car tracks on Portage Avenue would not be run on ... the boom was going to bust ... and the Hudson's Bay Reserve was going down with the rest. The excitement of the Hudson's Bay land sale had been the peak of the boom, but the sad fact is, it broke the boom.

The boom had kept going on a little money circulating rapidly, with a little new money being added all the time. But then the Hudson's Bay Company had come along and suddenly taken two million dollars out of circulation. With Bay Reserve lots on the market, promoters of distant subdivisions could not sell their lots. The boom structure began to tremble. It quaked violently, then crashed down flat. The crash came in 1914. People could not pay the instalments on their lots. They could not even pay the taxes, and even when they could pay, they figured it wasn't worth the trouble.

In 1916 a number of lot holders in the Bay Reserve banded together and went to court to try to have their instalments stopped. They argued that they had already paid enough for their land, more than it was worth, and asked the court to declare their accounts paid in full. Their lawyer, Gerald Penton, K.C., likened the Edmonton real estate boom to the famous South Sea Bubble. He said, "The people were suffering from a mental aberration." The court was sympathetic, but there was nothing it could do. There was nothing anybody could do. And even though the Hudson's Bay sale had broken the boom, it had still provided its finest hour.

Dad Sharples, the Host with the Most

The Strathcona Hotel could tell many a story, if hotels were vested with the power of speech, and the most interesting tales that the old hostelry might spin would be about its first proprietors. Dad Sharples and his wife ran it from 1891 to 1895, and they ran it in a way that Punch and Judy might have done.

Dad Sharples was short and fair, with a moustache and twinkling blue eyes. Mrs. Sharples was short and plump with twinkling blue eyes like those of a china doll. They were a lively pair and never more lively than when they'd been at their favourite refreshment. Dad didn't mind a little drink, and the more he had the less he minded. Mrs. Sharples didn't mind a little drink either, and the more she had, why, the less she minded. This often gave hotel guests some unexpected entertainment.

One evening at dinner, for example, the guests in the dining room were startled to see the door from the kitchen fly open. They were even more startled to see their host, Dad Sharples, come flying out of the door followed closely by a cauldron of boiling raspberries. And then their hostess appeared and hurled invective after her departing husband. A few minutes later, Dad came back warily into the dining room and apologized to the guests for the disturbance and for the language of his better half, which, he conceded, was " 'orrible." Dad had left all his "h's" in his native Liverpool, where he'd spent a hectic youth challenging the tough guys of the waterfront to goes at fisticuffs, goes in which Dad was almost uniformly unsuccessful.

From Liverpool he had gone to sea as a steward, and in 1888 his ship, the *Polynesian,* had put into Montreal. Here Dad decided to end his sailing career. He deserted, or, as he put it so charmingly, "I left the ship at midnight." He immediately entered the service of the Canadian Pacific Railway as a dining-car steward on the Rocky Mountain run, but he lost his job through too much zeal. The laundry service was slow, so Dad used to wash out the serviettes himself and hang them on the bell-rope to dry. But there came a trip when Sir William Whyte (the high priest of the CPR for whom our Whyte

Avenue is named) was making an inspection tour of the West. In Dad's diner he found a long line of serviettes hanging from the bell-rope — most contrary to regulations. That ended Dad's career as a dining-car steward, so he spent the summer of 1891 in Moose Jaw, enjoying his second favourite hobby, which was painting.

But in the fall he was invited to rejoin the Canadian Pacific as manager of the railroad's new hotel in South Edmonton. It was to be called the Edmonton House, because the railroad was backing the south-side town as the real Edmonton, figuring that the old trading-post town on the north side would wither away.

Dad and Mrs. Sharples spent eleven days in Winnipeg, outfitting the new hotel right down to the liquor. Then they set up in business on Whyte Avenue. Well, they didn't exactly start business on Whyte Avenue because in the beginning the hotel faced east onto 103rd Street, which was then known as Railway Street in honour of the railroad that was making the new south-side Edmonton more dynamic than the tired old place on the north bank.

The street was much lower then than it is now. There was a broad stairway leading up to the main entrance — so broad that three men on horseback could ride up abreast. And three men actually did one night. They were Charley Bremner (for whom Bremner is named), Captain Boag (for whom Boag Lake is named), and Billy Fielders. They came from around Clover Bar; the hotel was a sort of halfway house where good fellows from Clover Bar could meet kindred spirits from Edmonton. Boag, Bremner and Fielders rode their steeds right into the bar and found the party so good that they stayed for three days.

Dad didn't bat an eye when the trio rode in. He always tended the bar personally and he not only served, he provided the entertainment: he played the piano and sang. His favourite song was an epic of the English music halls: "Daddy Wouldn't Buy Me a Bow-Wow." Dad had an interesting variation on this song. With every drink he took, he'd make a chalk mark on the piano and add another "wow" to the song. So, as a sociable evening went on and on, the song would become "Daddy wouldn't buy me a bow-wow-wow-wow-wow-wow-wow-wow."

A frequent attender of these singsongs was a bow-wow named Punch, a fox terrier that someone had given to Mrs. Sharples. Punch had the run of the hotel. And he appeared in the following incident that Dad described in his diary: "One day we had a Mr. White from Ottawa, comptroller of the Mounted Police, as a guest of the house. I took him up to show him his room. I was giving him some pointers on how we had clean sheets for the beds for all our guests. I overstepped the mark by pulling down the counterpane and sheets to show him the snowy white linen. Great Scot, what do you suppose I exhibited to his gaze? Nothing less than the fox terrier coiled up in his bed."

When Mr. White came through a year later on his next inspection, he managed to set fire to the bedclothes while smoking in bed. But Dad told him there'd be no charge. "Never mind," he said, "that makes up for the dog in your bed the last time you were here."

Land Office Business

"Edmonton is usually a quiet place, a very quiet place. There are people who say it's positively dull." Yes, there are people even today who make this charge about Edmonton. But we're quoting from the *Edmonton Bulletin* of June 20, 1892, and the man who made the admission was Frank Oliver, one of Edmonton's great patriots. Mr. Oliver continued: "On Saturday last, it was, if possible, more quiet than usual — until about three o'clock in the afternoon. After that hour and until late midnight, it was undoubtedly the most alive, lively, excited, exciting and generally interesting place in all Canada. There was the biggest kind of circus on. There was more fun than could be furnished by a barrel of monkeys."

Well, something pretty drastic must have happened to cause this sensation, and it had. Strathcona had invaded Edmonton and tried to steal the land titles office. Yes, at three o'clock on that Saturday afternoon in 1892, the Dominion land agent had tried to move the office quietly from Edmonton to the south side. The land agent was Timber Tom Anderson, a Strathcona patriot — but he hadn't moved quietly enough. He had arrived at his office on Jasper Avenue with a team and wagon, and the teamsters had gone inside. There had been nothing sinister in this. A small crowd had watched with idle curiosity. A somewhat larger crowd had seen books and ledgers being moved out. Then curiosity had become anger. Strathcona was trying to steal Edmonton's land office in broad daylight. A large crowd milled angrily around the embattled teamsters while the news spread through town like wildfire, bringing a huge crowd on the run. Anger became action. To keep the land office records from moving south, the crowds unhitched the horses from the wagon. Then they unhitched the wheels from the wagon, too!

Presumably muttering something like, "Coises, foiled again," Mr. Anderson hurried to the Mounted Police barracks and came back with two constables. While the Mounties could see the situation, they could see equally well that there was little they could do about it, even though Mr. Anderson had an order from the Dominion Inspector of Land Agencies, Mr. J. McDonald Gordon of Ottawa, authorizing the transfer to Strathcona. Mr. Gordon had given him the order the day before, and then, reasoning perhaps that discretion was the better part of politics, Mr. Gordon had gone off to inspect some distant land agency and left Mr. Anderson to execute the transfer. However, the determined citizens of Edmonton forced a "stay of execution."

As the crowds milled excitedly, a new peril presented itself in the shape of reinforcements from the south side — four wagons, any one of which was quite capable of moving the land office across the river. But the wagons were forced to go back empty. Excitement reached fever pitch at eight o'clock that night when Mayor Matt McCauley presided at a town meeting in front of the land office. By unanimous voice-vote, the town passed resolutions full of determination and displeasure, and wired them to Ottawa. After the meeting some citizens formed a "Citizens' Guard" around their threatened building, while others passed the time hanging the land agent in effigy. Yes, as the *Bulletin* said, "There was the biggest kind of circus..."

The Sabbath was calm, but excitement flared again on

Monday. Word spread through Edmonton that the Mounties were coming from Fort Saskatchewan to deprive Edmonton of its heritage. To meet this peril, Edmonton quickly re-formed the Home Guard, which had been organized seven years earlier during the Riel uprising. By noon, five hundred armed men were gathered by the town hall. Mayor McCauley told them that they were organized to keep the peace, but most figured it was to keep the land office. So they waited for the new peril. And how did they feel as they waited? Well, Winston Churchill expressed it fifty years later when he described where and how Britain would resist Hitler, if Hitler tried to barge in uninvited.

Like Britain in 1940, Edmonton waited for an invasion that never came. The Mounties didn't enter the town; they stayed outside, across Latta Ravine at Jasper and 91st Street, while Inspector Griesbach came in to see what all the threatened shooting was about. The southsiders didn't come back for the land office. Neither did Mr. Gordon, who had authorized the transfer. The whole affair seemed to be blowing over. Then it flared again.

A party of young bloods from Strathcona tried to kidnap the beloved fire bell of the Edmonton volunteer fire brigade. The bell stood on the lawn in front of the wooden fire hall on Jasper East. The raiders came in, in the spirit of Oxford students who set out to pinch a policeman's helmet. And there was a marked similarity in the appearance of their objective, except that it weighed eight hundred pounds. It was so heavy that the raiders were just loading it on the wagon when they were discovered. The Edmonton fire brigade never turned out to a fire as it turned out to protect its bell. The battle lasted twenty minutes, a fierce thing, a regular Donnybrook. At the end of the twenty minutes the raiding party retired to Strathcona — with honour, but without the bell. To this day the bell is still north of the river. Only it's now stored in the city's Cromdale warehouse near the Exhibition Grounds, a much safer distance from any raiding party which might come from south of the river.

Bob Chambers, Motorman for Glenora

In Bob Chambers's day the Edmonton subdivision of Glenora was a semi-rural community that dozed peacefully among the woods and ravines. Its standards were safeguarded by the Carruthers Caveat, which required that no house built in Glenora could cost less than $3,500. There was no rush of traffic to disturb the peace. No cars rushing up Groat Ravine. No trucks tearing down 102nd Avenue. About the only thing that moved on 102nd Avenue was the neighbourhood streetcar, Glenora's chief link with the outside world.

The neighbourhood trolley was a stub car that never got uptown. From 1912 to 1932 it padded back and forth between 124th Street and 142nd Street, running on uncertain schedule on a single uncertain track. No more was needed. There was no Jasper Place, no Capital Hill, no Crestwood, no Parkview, no Laurier Heights. There was only Glenora, and not much of that.

A number of motormen drove the neighbourhood trolley. There was rollicking Bill McLellan, who, one winter night in 1919, bounced the car right into the third ravine. But the motorman who gave the trolley its true flavour was Bob Chambers, the literary Scot. Bob mounted the motorman's stool in 1916, and when the Glenora car rattled into history in 1932 Bob moved to the south side and made a portable Burns Club of the McKernan Lake car.

"Bob had his ways," as the Scots put it so nicely. We say a man is "eccentric" or is "a character," but the Scots say "a man has his ways," which implies that a man is entitled to his ways, and is a man for a' that. Bob certainly had *his* ways.

He was impatient and sometimes downright nasty with adults who disagreed with him on Robbie Burns, his favourite poet. On the other hand, he was the soul of patience with the neighbourhood boys — who made a snowball target of his streetcar, figuring possibly that a boy's a boy for a' that. (And he had two of his own, who were put through university on his motorman's salary.) Bob always watched over the kids of Glenora on Saturdays, when he would see the little ones walking up the avenue to 124th Street to spend their penny allowances at the Princess Confectionery. He couldn't bear to have them walk home again, so he would call them aboard the car, stop along the line wherever they lived — he knew where everybody lived — deliver them to their homes, have a chat with their mothers, and then remount the car and rattle off to the bush at 142nd Street.

On his way towards town, Bob knew what time each businessman and university student should be boarding the car, and if the passenger wasn't in sight Bob would stop and wait for him. On the other hand, he had a mania for leaving 124th Street right on schedule. He waited for no man at that end. The blue-and-white streetcar could be halfway up from Jasper Avenue, full of homeward-bound Glenora people, and the motorman on the blue-and-white could be blowing his whistle frantically. But if it was time to go, Bob would go.

It was one of his ways. However, just three blocks down the line he might stop the car for a full five to seven minutes for a visit at the MacRae's garage. Some garages still maintained the gracious tradition of the blacksmith shops they had replaced. MacRae's was one of them, and if Bob looked in and saw that MacRae had a pot of coffee on the stove, it was his way to stop for a coffee break. Passengers who lived near would get off and walk home. And the passengers Bob had stranded at 124th Street would catch up.

Casual as he was about stopping for coffee, Bob was punctilious about stopping for trains. In those years, when a motorman came to a railroad crossing, he had to get down from the car, step out in front and look both ways to make sure no trains were coming. On every run down 102nd Avenue, Bob would cross the vanished grade of the Edmonton, Yukon and Pacific, for the grade hugged the east bank of Groat Ravine. Every time Bob came to it, he would get down with great ceremony and make sure the trolley was in no danger from the infrequent and improbable collections of boxcars that used to run on the Edmonton, Yukon and Pacific. On the other hand, the rules of the EY & P required that the trains stop at 102nd Avenue while the fireman got off and looked for traffic. It was a grand sight to see Bob and the fireman bowing to each other and waving the other through.

Bob's territory was a wonderful spot for a philosopher like

himself. Thoreau would have enjoyed strolling in the rustic tranquillity of Glenora. So would Wordsworth or any nature poet. Bob's misfortune was that he drove the only thing that moved in Glenora, so it provided sport for the young, as well as transport for the mature.

In providing sport for the young, Bob's hardest time came in winter between four and six in the afternoon when school was out. Many a time, as Bob stepped down from the car to check the railroad for trains, he would be awaited by a crowd of adventurous boys. They would be hiding behind a hedge with an arsenal of snowballs. Their target was the coal stove in the motorman's compartment, those stoves with the delightful sooty smell that threw their heat a full three to four feet.

Bob would get down from the car. The door would be open, the target in view. Then would come the volley of snowballs, crashing into the cab to explode against the stove with wonderful clouds of steam. The boys would run ... Bob would shake his head patiently ... push the door shut ... drive on a block or so, then stop the car and patiently sweep the snow out again. It was a harmless prank, and a boy's a boy for a' that.

On other winter days Bob would run into a boy-made snowbank alongside Government House. The bigger boys would spend a couple of hours rolling large snowballs on the wide boulevard in front of Government House, now part of the Provincial Museum. When Bob rattled west, the adventurous youngsters would roll the snowballs out into the road and in between the tracks of the single-track car line. A dozen three-foot monsters standing in a row, they waited Bob's return — while the boys watched from behind the Government House hedge. A block away Bob would see the snowballs and pour on the current, trying to convert Car Number Fifteen into a snowplough. On he would come with fearful speed, as young hearts behind the hedge beat high with adventure. Group Captain Donovan Ferris, who had some later high adventures with the air force, and in the north as a bush pilot, had his first real taste of adventure watching Bob Chambers head for a line of snowballs. Here he comes ... Splump, and the first snowball vanished ... Splub, and the second one vanished ... Splush, and the third one vanished ... Spll-ll-ush, and the fourth one went ... Spllllubbbbbb, and the car came to a halt. And Bob would get out with his broom and patiently sweep the snow off the track — and then rattle on his way up to 124th Street. It was a harmless prank, and a boy's a boy for a' that. Bob is gone now and the streetcar is gone, and the 102nd Avenue on which they ran is gone too, gone with the rush of progress.

Donald Ross, Our First Hotelman

When it opened in 1912 it was called Donald Ross School. That was logical because Rossdale was named for Donald, and it was appropriate because Donald was an early champion of public education. When the school was closed sixty-three years later, it was made headquarters for the Commonwealth Games, and that was appropriate, too, because the landlord of Edmonton's first hotel was a great believer in fun and games.

Donald was a comfortable, heavy-set man with mild eyes looking over a mild moustache, a mild voice that could turn a comic phrase or turn away wrath, a ruddy complexion gained from his Scottish youth, and an even ruddier nose gained from good fellowship. Unlike most of our fur-trading Scots who came to Edmonton the direct way — some of them all the way by water transport — Donald took a long, looping route. He landed in New York seeking his fortune, and failing to find it there, worked his way across to San Francisco, then north along the Pacific coast, then up through British Columbia's Cariboo gold country, and then back through the Yellowhead Pass to Edmonton.

He arrived in 1872, so soon after the settlement had been opened for claims that he was able to claim seventy acres of Rossdale by virtue of being the first man there. He started a market garden, and mined coal from the hillside under McDougall Hill; and in 1876 he turned the second floor of his house into a dormitory called the Edmonton Hotel.

Our first hotel was just below the U-turn at the foot of McDougall Hill, and it was a hotel with bath — one bath with one roller towel. On one occasion, a guest complained about the towel, and in the voice that turned away wrath Donald assured him, "Strange, twenty men have dried their hands on that towel this morning and you're the first to complain." Once, when there was no room at the inn, Donald allowed a late arrival to sleep on the pool table. In the morning the guest objected to paying the full rate of fifty cents for such a hard bed. "Well, if you don't like that I can charge you the pool room rates, sixty cents an hour." Then there was a discriminating group, who sniffed at the accommodation and announced it just wouldn't do. "I guess you'll have to go to the next hotel," said Donald sadly. "Where's that?" "Winnipeg!"

On the day of the school vote — December 20, 1884 — Donald threw the weight of his guests into the fight to set up a tax-supported public school system. There was strong opposition to the proposal, mostly from the Hudson's Bay Company, which owned most of the property and would be the heaviest contributor. The company imported employees who had property in Edmonton, from points as distant as Athabasca to vote against it. But Donald persuaded his guests to get involved on the side of public education. The day was viciously cold, so he lent them his monstrous coonskin coat for the trip to the polls. Of course they were all eligible to vote: didn't they swear they were? Matt McCauley, the returning officer, said afterwards that every time he saw the coat coming he knew he could count another "yea" vote, and at the end of the day the "yea's" had prevailed by fifty-four to forty-three.

Donald became a member of the first school board. In 1894 the board put up Edmonton's first high school, an imposing structure made of bricks, which peered over the bank and looked down on the hotel. Unfortunately it was built on top of Donald's old gopher-hole coal mine, and when the mine shaft collapsed the school did too, and it had to be torn down. Donald wouldn't have planned it that way, but then he couldn't help seeing the humour of it either.

When other hostelries ended his monopoly of the inn trade Donald went into competition. He drove a horse-bus across the river to meet trains at the south-side station, and he would walk the platform soliciting the custom of incoming passengers. "Edmonton Hotel, gentlemen, it's a temperance hotel." With this, he would close a large hand over his large bright nose while his eyes twinkled merrily.

97

It was indeed a temperance establishment for a long time, due to the stubbornness of the territorial authorities in Regina. They finally relented and agreed to a bar licence, on condition that Donald provide forty rooms. He only had slightly more than thirty in the old homestead and its two annexes, so he went to work with a carpenter and partitioned the original dormitory into eight separate rooms.

As building materials for the growing Edmonton were hauled across the river from the CPR terminal in Strathcona, the bar of the Edmonton Hotel became a favourite stopping place of the teamsters. "They like to rest their horses before driving them up McDougall Hill," said Donald.

Donald's duties as host left him plenty of time for his market garden. With the aid of a brick hothouse he was a man for all seasons and drove around town on a wagon, selling his wares and quenching his thirst now and again from a bottle under the seat. His skill with growing things led to an easy working friendship with the most famous guest of the Edmonton Hotel, the great plant culturist Luther Burbank.

Burbank came here several times, the first in 1894, looking as always for wild plants which might be tamed in his great gardens at Santa Rosa, California, and which might transmit their wild quality of toughness to their pampered, cultivated cousins. Burbank was enchanted by the tiger lily, that red lily which flares in the woods of northwestern Alberta, and which, had it not been for the wild rose, would have become our provincial flower. Burbank decided he must experiment with the wild tiger lily.

To his friend Donald Ross he entrusted the job of supplying him with bulbs of the tiger lily. Mr. Ross, in turn, delegated his responsibility to the Ross children, and on summer afternoons they would dig up tiger-lily bulbs in the woods of present-day Rossdale. They had to dig deep into the cool earth, four or five inches, to get the bulb from which the tiger lily sprang. In the summer holidays of 1895, Donald Ross Junior spent two weeks digging them from the farm of Ezekiel Keith at Clover Bar. He dug one thousand in those two weeks, and off they went to Mr. Luther Burbank, Santa Rosa, California, by first class mail. The bulbs of the tiger lily always rode first class. Burbank found it easier to get them into

California that way, the sovereign state of California being even then very nervous about beetles and bugs.

From these wild bulbs, Burbank developed the paler, larger tiger lily that has a place today in many an Edmonton garden, a memorial to Luther Burbank and his buddy Donald Ross.

The Journey of the Ad Club

There is a belief that whooping it up with civic pride was invented in Calgary and that Calgary has a patent on it. But let no man deceive you, least of all any man from Calgary. Staid old Edmonton once whooped it up with more civic gusto than ten Calgarys. It happened in the last year of our first boom, when optimism was high and Edmonton was close to having a million people, of whom sixty thousand were actually in residence.

There was true booster spirit heating the air in those days. Doubters breathed it in and were converted. Some were so completely saved from their doubts about Edmonton that they went out to evangelize the whole world. This fervour reached its height in June 1914, when 196 Edmonton boosters chartered a twelve-car train and whooped it up for Edmonton through Winnipeg, Minneapolis, Milwaukee, Chicago, Battle Creek, Detroit and Toronto. This was the famous excursion of the Ad Club — Ad for Advertising.

Their expedition was foreshadowed by three boosters who had carried the name of Edmonton down New York's Broadway two years earlier, on August 20, 1912. The booster trio were S.S. Franklin, B.H. Taylor and Russell White, and they braved much to make their assault on Broadway. On June 25 they left Edmonton in a Stoddard-Dayton motor car, a sixty-horsepower contraption with a high tonneau in back. They followed the route later taken by the Ad Club as far as Toronto, but instead of halting there they carried on through Kingston, Troy and Albany to New York.

It took them eight weeks. The car had brakes to begin with, but these fell off somewhere in Minnesota and our heroes learned to stop by gearing down through high and second into low. However, they eventually wore out the lower gears and had only high to run on. To stop, they would run part way up a hill and coast back to the bottom.

To everyone along the way they spread the miraculous news about Edmonton, particularly to the farmers who pulled them out of the mud and gave them free meals. And on August 20 they were able to carry the news to New York, the town where most of the capitalists lived, the chaps who would really appreciate knowing about Edmonton. Franklin, Russell and White mounted a big red EDMONTON banner on their car and spent the day chugging up and down Broadway. That was really whooping it up for Edmonton. Calgary had never had the benefit of a one-car motorcade on the Great White Way.

And don't forget that Edmonton had to compete for attention — with Wetaskiwin, for example, which had a city publicity commissioner, a chap named M.M. Gillis, who used to pound out letters to millionaires advising them to invest some of their millions in Wetaskiwin. For a few heady days in 1912 it seemed that Mr. Gillis's campaign had bagged a real millionaire when it was announced that a capitalist named H. Ewan McDavin was going to build a $50 million automobile plant in Wetaskiwin. He actually unloaded some building material which everyone came to see, and Wetaskiwin was cracking at the seams with booster spirit. Until word came down the line from Tofield that a millionaire named Ewan Halton was building a $50 million auto plant at Tofield. And until the police announced that H. Ewan McDavin and Ewan Halton were the same man, that he was also known as Halton S. Ewan, H.S. Ewan Davin, Ewan Dawson and Ewan S. McDowan, and that they had warrants for him under all his names.

This was a setback, of course, but only a setback. The booster spirit soon gathered a fresh head of steam as all the boosters for all the centres in Alberta cheered each other on. They were rivals, but they were allies as well. There were enough millionaires for everybody as long as everybody boosted hard enough.

The boosters liked to charter trains and tour the new lines that the railroads were opening up, cheering on the townspeople of the new communities. There was once a junket by the Edmonton Board of Trade on which a man was fined $35,000 for failing to boost Edmonton properly. The victim was "Judge" Tipton, the old, south side, real estate man for whom Tipton Park is named. Judge was on a special booster train touring eastern Alberta, and at the towns en route he was handing out pencils advertising his real estate firm. The pencils bore the name and address of the firm and said the firm was in Strathcona.

Strathcona that very year of 1912 had amalgamated with Edmonton to make a metropolis mightier than all others. The boys called it treason for Judge to be spreading propaganda for Strathcona on a Greater Edmonton booster train. They convened a kangaroo court right on the train. Using an *International Harvester Almanac* as a "criminal code," the boys decided that Judge was guilty beyond doubt and that the fine would be $35,000, the first instalment of which was to be paid immediately in the form of drinks for everybody; and the balance to be paid in a hundred years.

That was the spirit of the booster years, the years when every man with an idea was given a respectful hearing. Even the chap who was going to pave the Saskatchewan River and run streetcars on it to Winnipeg was given a hearing. And the noisiest expression of the spirit that moved people in the boom years came in June 1914, when Edmonton boosters chartered the train, from which to spout the praises of Edmonton all the way to Toronto.

The Edmonton Industrial Association organized the excursion so that Edmonton would not be shouted down at the convention of the Associated Advertising Clubs of America. The convention was being held in Toronto, and ad clubs from ninety cities would be there to advertise the charms of their cities — at the tops of their voices. Edmonton had to be heard. The local boys figured that a dozen railroad carloads would do the job, and they left the CNR station on Saturday, June 13, serenaded by the Edmonton Newsboys' Band, their train a-splash with banners bearing mottoes like "Six thousand in 1906 — sixty thousand in 1914."

The boosters included seventy women, among them Mrs. J. Percy Page, who was later first lady of the province. The boosters borrowed a special club car from the Northern Pacific Railway — one with a bar, a pool table, a poker room and a barbershop. And they published their own paper on board: *The Edmonton Spirit.*

The third day out they crossed into the United States and chugged through Minnesota, handing out pamphlets on Edmonton to the capitalists who gathered at every station to see the train. They also tossed out "booster pennies." These were the old pennies, the ones bigger than a quarter; and around each one, like the ring around Saturn, was an aluminum disc advertising Edmonton. Thousands of booster pennies went out of the train windows.

In Milwaukee the Board of Trade took the boosters on a tour of the breweries. In Chicago the Chamber of Commerce showed surprisingly little jealousy about Edmonton's future greatness and organized a motorcade of fifty limousines to take our boosters on a tour of the city. At Battle Creek, Michigan, the great Dr. Kellogg, inventor of Corn Flakes, came out personally to show "our people" around the Corn Flakes factory. Detroit gave the booster train proper deference, and then on June 23 the train hit Toronto for the advertising convention.

The editor of the Toronto *Globe* described Edmonton as "the wonder city of Canada, the growth of which has astounded the world." The boosters talked to all kinds of capitalists. On the third day our mayor, Billy McNamara, announced that the trip had already been worth $5 million to Edmonton and that an English syndicate had taken an option on eighty acres of industrial land — for which Billy was the agent.

A headline in the *Journal* announced: EDMONTONIANS ARE CONSPICUOUS AT TORONTO! And the *Journal* reporter said that our boosters were "telling the world about Edmonton." It was too bad that we were limited to eight minutes in the oratorical contest which came on the fourth day, because our spokesman, W.A. Milne, couldn't possibly say in eight minutes everything the world wanted to know about Edmonton; especially when his actual speaking time was reduced by the applause (from the Edmontonians), which greeted every claim.

Our man might have won first prize for our town if he'd embroidered the truth a bit, but he stuck to facts such as "Edmonton's growth has astounded the world," and "every school child is in the movement that has made Edmonton the fastest growing metropolis in North America." As a result, the orator from El Paso, Texas, won first prize, but the judge said our man had outshouted the representative of Los Angeles, and that was something to be proud of.

The convention broke up on June 24, 1914, and our gang dispersed for home, confident that they had told the world, and that the growth of Edmonton would continue to astound the world. But four days later Archduke Franz Ferdinand was shot to death at Sarajevo, and the world went to war and forgot about Edmonton for thirty-three years — until oil was discovered at Leduc.

The boosters who whooped it up in 1914 were disappointed. But they weren't wrong. They didn't expect too much. They just expected it too soon.

The Glorious First of July

There was a hot time in Edmonton on the night of July 1, 1893. It was the night of Dominion Day, and to re-create the events of that night we have the account of a man who was there. The man's name was G.D. Clark and he was better known as a photographer than as a raconteur of Homeric tales. Before the turn of the century he was a partner of Frank Mathers, Edmonton's original photographer. He managed to be on hand with his camera at many an historic moment in Edmonton's past. In his later years Mr. Clark used to be seen around Edmonton selling prints of his original pictures.

Mr. Clark didn't have a camera to record the blazing events of Dominion Day, 1893, but he was there. And in 1931 he wrote an account of the events, had the account printed on a single sheet of paper, and sold copies around town. He sold one copy to Dr. F.S. Macpherson, to whom we're indebted for the copy we're using here. We're going to leave it just as Mr. Clark wrote it. Rewriting it could improve its grammar and give a more understanding view of the Indian people, but would destroy its authenticity. It's a priceless bit of Edmonton history.

THE GLORIOUS FIRST OF JULY, 1893 — BY G.D. CLARK

Edmonton's first display of fireworks came about in this manner in the days when sport was real sport. The Sports Committee decided on fireworks. Not having sufficient funds, they started a drive, ending with good success. The merchants, private parties and farmers throughout the district donating about 950 dollars. The fireworks, being ordered, arrived in due time. On the evening of July first, they were conveyed to the race track on the Hudson's Bay Reserve. The grandstand being situated about where the Empire Theatre now stands on 103rd Street, though facing north, and the circular track being north of the grandstand. On the southwest quarter of the track, the Indians took up their camping quarters, being shaded with poplar trees at the time made an ideal camping ground for some thirty or forty teepees, forming quite a picturesque scene. The grandstand being filled to capacity at dusk, the dancing booth going on in full swing, the Indians quite content by their camp fires with all the gorgeous apparel, all patiently waiting for sufficient darkness to witness the fireworks. All in readiness, Mr. Ibbotson and T. Lauder undertook to set the fireworks going.

Unfortunately, Bill Ibbotson knew as much about setting off fireworks as I know about punching holes in a modern barbed-wire entanglement, equipped with a pair of eiderdown boxing gloves. Mr. Ibbotson being at that time a courteous merchant, although when he undertook to deal with the fireworks, he got into a real argument, not a verbal one either. It was proved right then and there beyond a doubt, that the fireworks knew more about Bill Ibbotson than Bill Ibbotson knew about the fireworks. Tommy Lauder took first hand to fire some of the sky rockets, but the result was not pleasing to Bill Ibbotson, so he took on the job. The fireworks being in two large cases, one the size of two upright piano boxes, the other about 10 feet long by four feet square on the ends, both being open at the time. Mr. Ibbotson, with the help of others took all the fireworks out of the 10-foot box and piled them up in the small box — all tangled up like a crow's nest. Taking the 10-foot box, and placing it alongside the pile of fireworks on its end, he mounted the box and shouted to Tommy Lauder: "Hand them up and I'll set them going." "All right," says Tommy. Rooting around in the pile of fireworks, Tommy dug out a sky-rocket about as big around as his HEAD, and handed it up to Bill Ibbotson, who, in turn, struck a match on his breeches, and then touched the fuse end of the rocket.

Before that rocket got on its way, it let out such a blast of sparks it set the whole pile of fireworks into action. It was wiz-wiz-wiz ... biff-biff-bang ... siz-siz-siz... The infernos of hell (let loose at both ends and the middle) could not have been worse. Flying skyrockets by the hundreds shot into the packed grandstand, and in less time than it would take you to bat your eye at a pretty, passing girl, that grandstand was cleared. Some of the crowd on top of the grandstand jumped right off the top and did not care if they landed fair and square on top of somebody's head — which I honestly believe some of them did. Others went down between the seats, into the ground. The yells, screams, and shouts of everybody. It was not a matter of when, where or how you were going, it was GO, and go HARD. Everyone on that grandstand that got no fireworks put up their backs, got the wind up their backs aplenty. That grandstand was cleared proper. Tommy Lauder — always being a brave little firefighter — leaped into the pile of fireworks grabbing a full armful. He lit out over the baldheaded prairie. The going was good, but when that armful of fireworks started going off, he dropped them and got out of that, awhooping. I don't know what direction of the compass he took to make good his escape — or whether he went up or down. I do know that those short legs of his automatically shifted into high gear and I believe they were in higher gear at that time than they ever were before.

The fireworks were going good — having a strong desire to show the Indians what they could do. It was wiz-wiz, biff-biff-bang right into their happy hunting grounds. Scaring all the horse sense out of their cayuses, so much so that they snapped their rawhide halter shanks like cobwebs. The skyrockets striking the teepees amidships and punching holes in them to such a size that a full-grown mule could stick his head in without bending his ears, and look all around inside. Some of the skyrockets were right onto their job, taking nice heavenly curves and coming straight down the smoke flaps of the teepees, bursting inside and blowing all the pemmican and bannock out of their cooking utensils. The war whoop that went up from all the Indian chiefs stampeded every Indian tribe for parts best known to themselves. Most of them leaving all their earthly belongings, some of the mothers even left their papooses behind, believing that their white brothers and sisters openly waged war upon them without any declaration thereof. So firm were they in this belief that it took the Mounted Police several weeks to round them up and bring them back to Edmonton to claim their deserted belongings.

As for the writer, he had a full measure of excitement with thrills galore. While witnessing the glorious performance, a skyrocket (about the circumference of a good-sized tomato can with a five-foot shank) cut loose in the center of attraction making one beeline for me. Being doubled up with laughter at the time, and unable to move, that scorcher of a rocket passed directly between my legs. I took one leap in the air and when I got back on terra firma my pants were well above my knee caps. But still laughing and looking around to see what was coming next, I did not have to look long ... a four-foot spin-wheel hopped out of the flying fireworks and took after me in dead earnest. It was my move again, and I did move. I didn't run, I did not have time to. I simply streaked it out of that. There was nothing on God's earth that could keep up to me — let alone overtake me — on this occasion.

On this eventful evening, kind providence was with us all. It was a miracle that no one was hurt. So ended the first display of fireworks in Edmonton. It was the best display of fireworks pulled off in this town or any other white man's town. Should any other city or town in the whole universe

have a better display of fireworks to tell or write about —
Edmontonians will take their hats off to you. But remember
— Not Before.

Well, there it is, The Glorious First of July, 1893, written by
G.D. Clark, a man who was there.

The Sunday Ball Game

My grandfather never missed the ball game and always wore
his black suit to it because it took place on a Sunday. Jim
Younie, the mathematics teacher, would come at one o'clock
and choose a seat in the sun, having calculated that by three
o'clock when the game started, the sun would have travelled
thirty degrees to the west and put him in the shade of the
grandstand roof. The large lady with the voice to match would
also come early, in order to get a place directly behind the plate,
from which judgement seat she could get on the back of the
young umpire, John "Lefty" Ducey.

In the mid-thirties the ball game was played at Renfrew
Park on Sunday afternoons. Historic Diamond Park — sacred
to the memory of Beans Reardon, Babe Herman and Raw-
Meat Rogers — was on the brink of demolition. The glory of
Boyle Street had dimmed. The centre of attention was
Renfrew, which printer Henry Roche had converted from a
soccer pitch to the finest ball park in the West. There were ball
games at Renfrew during the week. They started at 6:15 P.M.
because there were no lights. But *the* ball game was played on
Sunday afternoon.

In the days preceding Sunday, people going past the fire
hall would ask Phil Horn how he thought the game would go.
People with business at the CPR station would ask George
Green how he thought the game would go. Fans would stop
Buck Eaton on the street and ask him how his pitching arm
would be on Sunday.

The ball game started at three and had to end by six. Times
were set by city by-law so that fans would not be diverted from

107

their religious obligations. Even within the permitted hours, one could listen to "Bible Bill" Aberhart giving the bankers hell on CFCN, but it was far better sport to hear the large lady with the matching voice give it to Lefty Ducey. And the greatest sport of all came on the Sunday that Ducey turned on his tormentor and barked, "Ahhhhh, shuddup!"

The lady was not the only critic among the fans. Bill Matthews, the insurance man, liked to gather his cronies in the right-field bleachers and watch for displays of incompetence. Any lapse was greeted with cries of "What a league! What a league!" Bill and his pals had a mission. They had to ensure that the unbelievably high calibre of baseball was maintained. This brings up a vital point about baseball, the strangest contradiction in all the realms of sport. While athletes in other lines have improved in forty years, baseball has gone the other way. Athletes today sprint faster, vault higher, dive deeper, lift greater weights, throw the football with more accuracy, and toss the caber farther, but baseball has witnessed a steady decline. Ask any old-time fan and he'll tell you. The fact that Henry Aaron can hit more home runs than the immortal Ruth only confirms the sad decline of standards. The ball itself is no good anymore. It is made of cowhide rather than horsehide, and even Henry Aaron can knock it out of shape with one puny swing.

The fans were great too, in the good old days, because the ball game was not entirely a spectator sport. Like Bill Matthews and the large lady, Pepper the butcher always had a contribution to make. When a batter lofted a pop foul that disappeared from view and then thonked the grandstand roof, Pepper the butcher would yell, "Up in Nellie's room!" And when a shortstop had to subdue a bounding ball and threw to first base too late to catch the hitter, Pepper would yell, "Twenty minutes late!"

Mickey Conti was another great fan, though Mickey seldom saw any of the game. He was the concessionaire and he ran his own game under the stand, matching customers double-or-nothing for hot dogs and pop. If Conti broke even on tosses, he'd made money because he was wagering wholesale cost against retail; and though it wasn't much, there wasn't much money in the ball park on a month of Sundays.

108

Admission was by good will offering, called hopefully a "silver" collection, to ward off coppers and nickels. Dollar bills were a forlorn hope, though there was one group of select fans who pumped folding money into the park. These were the merchants who sponsored the teams.

Frank Wolfe of Edmonton Motors often had a team in the league of the year. Chris Diamond of the Shasta Café had many teams known as the Shastas, and he was such a fan of his own teams that he once imported a phenomenal young pitcher from Rocky Mountain House. The pitcher's wages were to be two dollars a game and all the steaks he could eat, but the young man's capacity for steaks was even more phenomenal than his work on the mound, and with beef at thirty cents a pound the café found that it couldn't afford him. Harry Cohen of the Army and Navy had teams called the Cardinals, and he bolstered one of them by offering slugging outfielder, Pete McCready, employment in the stockroom. Once, when Harry found Pete asleep on the job, Pete awoke with a perfect rationale for his nap. "You wouldn't want me to be tired out for the game, would you, Mr. Cohen?" The game wasn't for two days but Pete did have a point.

The fans came down on Sundays to see Pete hit for extra bases at dramatic moments. They also came to see him do his non-baseball specialities, such as climbing the screen. If Pete were to end an inning with a sensational catch in the outfield, he might come dashing in across the diamond, brush past Lefty Ducey as he bent to dust the plate, charge the backstop, grab two fistfuls of wire screening, and go up the screen like the monkey at the Borden Park Zoo.

George Green used to make charges from right field which also delighted his fans. An unbelievable decision by the umpire would act as a cavalry bugle setting George in motion; and right field was the ideal spot from which to begin the charge, because the offending umpire had lots of time to see him coming and George had encouraging fans beside him all the way. Some mistook George Green's displays of disbelief for anger. On his long run from the outfield his disbelief was mute, but when he confronted the offender it became histrionic, and terpsichorean as well. George would fling his cap to the ground and dance on it, calling on the fans, calling on the heavens, calling on the umpire, to deny the evidence of his own eyes, to deny that the runner had been called safe when he was out a mile. And though George could move heaven and earth, he never moved an umpire. An umpire is unfit to dwell in either place.

The fans participated in two ways: by cheering the heroes and demoralizing the opposition. I belonged to a juvenile rooting section which sought to demoralize Randall, as a contribution to the cause of the Shastas and Cardinals. Elmer Randall pitched for Wetaskiwin and flung the ball so hard that the heroes had trouble hitting it — when they could see it. However, we thought we could get to Randall.

He was obviously a farm youth and would therefore lack the sophistication that came from frequent association with streetcars, with the doughnut machine in the Metropolitan Store, the American Dairy Lunch and the elevator in the Tegler Building. We decided that reminders of agricultural pursuits would distract Randall from his purpose of throwing the ball past the heroes. So he faced a barrage of: "Hey, Randall, it's time to feed the pigs!" "Hey, Randall, the cows are getting out; go shut the gate!" "Hey, Randall, it's time to collect the eggs!" "Hey, Randall, where's your Ironman pants?" (GWG Ironman pants were worn for agricultural pursuits.) Randall weathered the barrage and kept setting the city teams down with three and four hits, but he never threw a no-hitter. Perhaps we achieved that; it would be nice to think so.

Now it is just possible, for all things are possible, that the ballplayers of the thirties were not the supermen they seemed — that Elmer Randall and Buck Eaton and Dave Fenton and Herman Loblick and Clayton Dolighan and Mickey Duggan and Chief Jimmy Rattlesnake were mortal after all, and that the shows they provided on Sunday afternoons were amateur baseball.

It may be that fans and players made the games important by common consent because Edmonton was a small and isolated city of eighty thousand. Edmonton today is eight hours from London by plane. Then it was eight hours from Calgary by train, and Calgary was days from anywhere. Even the American network radio stations didn't come in till after dark,

110

and daylight endured till ten. When the baseball season ended in late summer all would be quiet. Deacon White had given up the one-man struggle to keep inter-city football going, and there would be no hockey until December when the weather was cold enough to form natural ice in the Gardens. So it's just possible that the fans invested the Sunday ball game with all the drama which is now spread over many sports and many events. It's just possible.

Evergreen and Gold

Marion Alexander chose the colours of the University of Alberta. Marion came here with her husband, Dr. Will Alexander, who was one of four professors recruited to put the university in business in the fall of 1908.

There was great enthusiasm for the new university, but the enthusiasm was not by any means unanimous and the opposition popped up in surprising quarters. Emily Murphy was bitterly opposed to it. The plans called for a medical school some day, with a hospital in connection, and Mrs. Murphy was an ardent worker for the Edmonton Public Hospital and figured the University Hospital would be undesirable competition. Frank Oliver was against it too. The Honourable Frank told Dr. Alexander it was a lot of damfool nonsense, which could well have waited. And the *Calgary Herald* was opposed to all "merely provincial" universities. The *Herald* figured that provincial universities would be so academically puny that a degree from one of them would mean little. There ought to be one western university for the four western provinces. It ought to be centrally located and ought to be on a transcontinental railroad. A subtle way, indeed, of proclaiming that the one, the true, the logical, and the inevitable place for the western university was Calgary. However, the university was not going to be in Calgary; it was going to be in Strathcona. Uncle Sandy had seen to that.

It is quite inaccurate to suppose that Mr. St. Laurent was the first political figure in Canada to be known as "uncle." The

111

Honourable Alexander Rutherford, first premier of Alberta, was known as Uncle Sandy. Uncle Sandy was a resident of Strathcona and a staunch champion of all her just civic ambitions, which included the provincial university. So, without telling anyone about it, least of all anyone from Calgary, Uncle Sandy bought an entire river lot in old Strathcona for a campus. It is only regrettable now that Uncle Sandy did not buy Windsor Park at the same time, as it could have been had for little extra cost. (About 1900, Windsor Park was traded for a shotgun.) Having decided on the location, Uncle Sandy then decided on the first president.

The university men in Alberta were divided into two camps in those years. There were McGill men and Toronto men. There were, to be sure, some Queen's men and Dalhousie men and even Oxford men, but not enough to form a camp. The Toronto men thought that a Toronto man should be president of our new university, but Uncle Sandy was a McGill man, and Uncle Sandy was certainly not going to entrust the institution to anyone less than a McGill man. The most eminently qualified of all McGill men was clearly Dr. H.M. Tory. A few years earlier, Dr. Tory had come west to establish McGill College of British Columbia, a sort of academic outpost of McGill where British Columbian students could take two years' instruction in Arts and then go to Montreal for the final instruction that would make them genuine McGill men. Dr. Tory was the McGill man for the new job in Alberta. Mr. Rutherford sought him and signed him, and Dr. Tory went on the provincial payroll on January 1, 1908.

He lured four academics away from older institutions to staff the professorial chairs. Dr. Alexander was enticed from the University of Western Ontario for twenty-five hundred dollars, more than double his previous salary, and he arrived in the fall to begin the task of turning out Alberta men. It was to be three long years before they succeeded in turning out any. The university was on the top floor of Queen Alexandra School the first year, and the proud city of Strathcona boosted the enrolment to forty by promoting all grade eleven students to university. In the makeshift years the future campus was a favourite strolling ground for Dr. Alexander and his wife Marion and their friends. It was then a sort of common pasture

112

for Strathcona, and Will would take a golf club with him and whack the ball over meadow and dale, while he conversed, or pondered within him, whether Aristotle was on solid ground in his "theory of the mean."

In the fall of 1912 the university moved to the campus, and into the first building on the campus, Athabasca Hall. Athabasca Hall was a building that had everything; it had the students, the dormitories, the dining room, and the offices of the professors. Dr. Alexander and Dr. W.A.R. Kerr shared an office which had been designed for a bathroom. It had a tiled floor which tilted towards the centre, so the desks of the professors tilted too.

A couple of years later Dr. Tory decided that the building that had everything obviously had *too much* of everything, and he demanded an Arts Building, for instruction only. The government was not enthusiastic — with the boom flattening out — but Dr. Tory was so persistent that Mr. R.T. Jeffers, the provincial architect, was instructed to design a very economical Arts Building. His design was a distinct disappointment to the university people. Most of them thought it would look like a jail, although a few optimistic people thought it might look no worse than a factory. But work was started on Mr. Jeffers's design, and they had the foundations laid when Dr. Tory could endure the prospect no longer. He ordered work stopped, ordered a new design with two wings and a convocation hall, and he had much of the foundation knocked out. Today there is still visible evidence of the change in plans — you can see cracks in the wall-joinings where the wings have settled.

The contractors built away with a will during the summer of 1915, and it appeared definite that they would be finished in time for the fall classes. But then came a hitch — the money was finished before the building; there was no money for the roof. Dr. Tory tried to borrow some from the provincial government, but by this time the boom had not only gone flat, there was also a war on. The government had no money for Dr. Tory. He then tried the friendly bankers, but they gave him the same reasons. So he went to the head office of the contractors, George Fuller and Company of New York, and Mr. Fuller proved to be a real "friend of the university." Said he, "Don't worry about it, Dr. Tory. We'll put the roof on and you can pay

113

us when you're able." So they put the roof over the Arts Building and Convocation Hall, and it opened on time in the fall of 1915.

When the students returned that fall, the whole campus was again in the full colours which Marion Alexander had chosen for the university. In fact, the whole countryside and the river valley were displaying the colours. Marion had chosen them on the first walk which she and Will had taken to the future campus. They had come to the top of the hill and looked down into the valley and across to Edmonton. The poplars were at their golden peak and glowing in the sunlight, a dramatic contrast with the evergreens. Marion had decided, literally at a glance, that evergreen and gold were going to be the colours of the university. She went to Johnstone Walker's and spent an hour rummaging at the ribbon counter, one of the longest and most prestigious counters in the stores of that era. Eventually she turned up two ribbons which recorded exactly what she had seen on the campus. The university Senate quickly made them official.

The Jolly Undertaker

Sam McCoppen was a man Charles Dickens might have created; even the name Sam McCoppen has the ring of Dickens about it. Sam was the jolly undertaker, from 1915 to 1934.

McCoppen lived for eighty-eight years, right up to 1954, and they were years bulging with activity. Undertaking was just one of his activities. You could write a long series of books about him, like the series about Tom Swift and his string of fabulous inventions. For example, you could write a book called *Sam McCoppen and his Summer Resort.* When McCoppen came to Edmonton from the east in 1905, he sought to develop weedy Edmonton Beach as a summer resort. He might have succeeded if the lake hadn't deserted the beach. Then there could be *Sam McCoppen and his Varsity Tuck Shop.* In this volume you'd include the kids he helped through university

114

with timely loans; you could also work in the provision of his will, which left a scholarship fund for students. You could write another book describing his part in establishing the Kiwanis Children's Home. Then there could be *Sam McCoppen and his Tugboat;* in the 1890s Sam used to run a tugboat out of Port Colborne, Ontario, and later out of Sault Ste. Marie. Then, perhaps, there'd be *Sam McCoppen and his Ship of State;* Sam was an alderman of the City of Edmonton from 1918 to 1921, and in 1922 he campaigned for the mayoralty. The next book could be called *Sam McCoppen and his Apartment House;* he owned quite a few of them from time to time in the days when apartment houses were an Edmonton rarity. And there would have to be a book called *Sam McCoppen and his Hotel at Islay.* This story ends with a big fire — which was also the end of the hotel — but it leads to the story of *Sam McCoppen, the Jolly Undertaker.*

When his hotel burned down in 1915, Sam was left in a poor position financially. With the collapse of the business boom, many gentlemen were in the same position. Observing that the undertaking profession was not subject to the uncertainties that had blighted his other enterprises, Sam decided to be an undertaker. He came back to Edmonton, and although he was now fifty years old, he set out to learn this new trade. He went to work for Connelly and McKinley, then located on 100th Street just off the old market square, and by 1917 he felt he was ready to go into business for himself.

McCoppen was a stout man with a ruddy face and a ready laugh. He smoked a pipe which was seldom allowed to go out. He wore a seaman's cap and a yachtsman's blue blazer, and like many a man who has commanded a tugboat or even some more humble form of water transportation, McCoppen retained the nickname of "Captain." Sam McCoppen was an improbable sort of man to be an undertaker; but then, he was an improbable sort of man in any case. In hot weather Edmonton's Jolly Undertaker had a stunt he used to enjoy hugely. He used to send flutter-fans out to patients at the Royal Alexandra Hospital, fans inscribed: "Compliments of Sam McCoppen, your favourite undertaker." The phone number at Sam's funeral parlour was 6-6-6-6. Sam used to pronounce it "Sick-sick-sick-sick," and rub his hands together

115

as if to say that such a state of affairs was a promise of good business for McCoppen.

One of the most subtle jokes he worked was at a meeting of a fraternal organization, one of those get-acquainted affairs. Every man present was called on to stand up and state his name and business. The Jolly Undertaker could see a splendid opportunity. He sidled across the room and got in next to a couple of doctors, Dr. Fred Sites and Dr. Bill Farquharson. Dr. Fred Sites, when his turn came, stood up and stated that he was a member of the medical profession. Dr. Farquharson stood up and also stated that he was a member of the medical profession. Then Sam McCoppen stood up and said, "I follow the medical profession."

The Jolly Undertaker would also advertise on election nights — through the *Edmonton Journal*'s slide projector. Before radio took over election results, the *Journal* used to flash the latest returns on a screen downtown. The screen was set up on McDougall Church, with the projector in a second-storey window of the *Journal*. It used to be a great sport to advertise on such nights. Several times during the night, Sam's advertisement would appear on the screen. There'd be a picture of the Jolly Undertaker wagging a knowing finger and saying, "I'll get you yet..."

Well, they finally got Sam McCoppen. But it took them eighty-eight years.

Vernon Barford and the Finer Things

Vernon Barford's last public performance was marked by the Victorian charm, the confident mastery of the situation, and the jaunty precision that he gave to every performance. And Vernon Barford believed strongly in "performance."

That was one of the artistic convictions he brought with him from England in 1900, and which he impressed on the musical life of Edmonton for more than sixty years. He maintained that people should give a first-rate performance of something within their capabilities, rather than flounder on something beyond them. That was one conviction of his, a conviction upheld by his choirs, choruses and operatic companies.

He also imparted to his singers, and to the musical life of Edmonton, his conviction on song — a song being something that one listens to as one sings it; and when the song becomes intense, no shouting please! Don't spread the emotion too thin in time of crisis. Condense it for most telling effect. It's the sort of conviction you would expect from an Oxford graduate of the 1890s, which Vernon Barford was. You might also expect an Oxford graduate of the 1890s to try some wild romantic notion like going out to Canada and becoming a pioneer farmer in Saskatchewan, and he did that too.

People who can picture from memory Vernon Barford directing the chorus at All Saints' Cathedral or accepting top prize for his junior choir at the musical festival, or adjudicating at the festival, or giving one of his articulate talks to the Women's Musical Club, might have some difficulty picturing him on the prairie outside Qu'Appelle, Saskatchewan, magnificent in the corduroy knickerbockers which English gentlemen wore in the country, and urging a team of oxen to break the prairie and thereby create a ploughed field. But he was there all right. He came out in 1895 and stuck it gamely for a full year before deliverance appeared in the form of a job as organist and choirmaster at the Anglican church in Qu'Appelle.

But after four years of that, he decided that the twentieth century did not belong to Qu'Appelle but might belong to Edmonton. So he struck out for Edmonton and landed here in a January thaw in 1900, and became musician number one. His peers always made him number one. It started the week he arrived. A chap named Reg Wilkins had been playing the piano for dances in this frontier town of three thousand, but when Reg heard Vernon play he insisted that Vernon take over.

In April 1904 Vernon Barford directed Edmonton's first operatic production, *The Chimes of Normandie,* at Robertson's Hall. Be it amateur or professional, perils and pitfalls lie in the path of any musical production, perils artistic and financial. The Edmonton Operatic Society planned to get around the artistic perils with Vernon Barford, and for the financial ones

117

they elected J.J. Anderson of the Union Bank to be president of the society.

Seemingly armed against any eventuality, *The Chimes of Normandie* went into rehearsal in November 1903. The society had chosen *The Chimes* because an Edmonton tenor named Dickie Day had sung tenor lead in a production at Nelson. But after six weeks it became apparent that Mr. Day was really a baritone. He dropped down a role, and a northern freighter named Tom Kelly was appointed tenor. The role of the miser was sung by Howard Stutchbury. The two feminine leads were the choir directors from the First Presbyterian and the First Baptist churches. Rounding out the company was a chorus of forty-five and an orchestra of twelve. The bandbox stage of Robertson's Hall was firmly and fully packed when the whole company crowded on, but at least it didn't take long to paint the scenery for that small stage.

As the big night approached, the production almost foundered on a miscellaneous pitfall. The costumes had been rented from Chicago, and when they arrived in Edmonton a grimly efficient customs official decreed that the society must pay full duty on them, even though they were only rented. While Edmonton's cultural progress hung in the balance, a frantic wire was dispatched to Ottawa, to Edmonton's M.P., Frank Oliver. Frank Oliver pulled the appropriate strings and the costumes came in duty-free.

Came the big night — and another fall. At the end of the second act the tenor fainted. Tom Kelly, northern freighter, was impervious to the elements but the first-night excitement got him. A husky tenor is a bulky enough stage property even when he isn't wearing a suit of armour. But Mr. Kelly rallied quickly, as a knight in shining armour should, and he sang his part through to the end. Tom Kelly and *The Chimes of Normandie* were a success.

In 1908 the same crowd teamed up to produce the first regional musical festival in North America. In 1907 Governor General Earl Grey had proposed a nationwide festival of music and drama, to be held in Ottawa and to be open only to entries from provincial capitals. At that time Edmonton had been a provincial capital for two years, and Earl Grey's lieutenant in Alberta, G.H.V. Bulyea, thought Edmonton must have something to offer. His Honour knew but one musician, Howard Stutchbury, so he discussed it with him. Fortunately, Mr. Stutchbury knew a good many musicians, chaps like Vernon Barford, W.J. Hendra and Jackson Hanby. They got together and talked it over. They rejected the idea of sending groups from Edmonton to compete in Ottawa. This would no doubt be a boon to the cultural life of Ottawa, but would do nothing for Edmonton. "Why not," they said, "have our own musical festival right here?"

There was the usual flaw in this plan — none of them had any money. So they again called on Mr. J.J. Anderson, the bank manager, and put him on the board. With a little help from the Union Bank and the enthusiasm of one hundred musicians, Edmonton staged the first regional musical festival in North America on May 5, 1908. One hundred musicians competed in eleven different classes. The festival used two halls on 103rd Street right across from each other: All Saints' Cathedral and the Separate School hall.

It has been a long time since that first festival, when the *Bulletin* wrote: "This has been the greatest musical event that Western Canada has yet known, drawing talent from various points in the province, between Edmonton and Cardston." (One extremely talented gentleman came from Olds. He competed as a tenor, a baritone, and a bass, singing the same song each time.)

The festival concluded with a grand concert in the Thistle Rink, the historic hall on 102nd Street behind the King Edward Hotel. Vernon Barford conducted a chorus of two hundred and an orchestra of forty, while two thousand people crowded in to listen. It was an impressive occasion in early Edmonton. The chorus and orchestra were all in evening dress, while just outside, anyone venturing off the sidewalk could be plunged inches-deep in mud.

Vernon Barford was involved in the musical festival for more than half a century, including those thin years of struggle when two of the harbingers of spring were the firemen playing catch in front of the 104th Street fire hall and H.G. Turner going in and out of stores along Jasper Avenue, raising a dollar here and a dollar there to help stage the festival. Although Vernon was a pace-setter he never seemed to be in a hurry. He never ran. Nor did he walk. He strolled — with a cane for effect — and his dress and manner always suggested that he had a yacht tied up around the corner.

His last public performance was given in the 1960s, in the last of his nearly ninety years when he was living at the Westbury, then the Savoy Plaza. He had become quite unsteady on his feet by this time, unsteady and slow, but as jaunty and confident as ever. He would go out for a stroll two or three times a day, though by this time the cane was a necessity. One evening in the rush hour he found himself caught on the wrong side of Jasper Avenue. The traffic was thick and fast, and although there were traffic lights at 111th Street, Jasper Avenue was too wide to get across in the allotted twelve seconds.

But he was equal to the occasion. He started out with the green light, making the best time he could. When the light changed, he held up his cane to hold back the traffic. He proceeded unsteady but undaunted across the full ninety-nine feet. He mounted the curb on the south side at last, mounted the curb as though it were a podium. Then he turned, raised his cane like a baton, flashed the familiar smile and bowed to the audience.

The High Level Bridge

THE STUPENDOUSNESS OF THE HIGH LEVEL BRIDGE IS AMAZING. That was the proud headline in the *Edmonton Journal* back in 1913 — the year the bridge opened. The headline was a banner atop proud views of the High Level Bridge, a bridge the like of which you could see nowhere else in the world, a bridge almost half a mile long and 157 feet high. The stupendousness of it all was indeed a matter for civic pride. In fact, so stupendous was the bridge that it had not one opening, but four.

The first opening was on June 2, 1913, when the first Canadian Pacific Railway train pounded across the upper deck. The second opening was on August 11, 1913, when the first streetcar of the Edmonton Radial Railway rumbled across. There were reporters on the first streetcar and one story was headlined: GIVES PASSENGERS CHILL AS THEY GAZE INTO THE ABYSMAL DEPTHS BELOW. Superintendent Woodruff noted that many passengers found the view of the abysmal depths so chilling that they averted their gaze from it. However, he added that in averting their gaze they did not make the operation any safer thereby. The start of streetcar service on the high bridge was accelerated by some weeks in order to provide faster service to the Exhibition, which was to open the following Monday and which was comparable in stupendousness to the High Level Bridge.

Opening number three came on August 31, 1913 — a fine Sunday. The contractors had finished the pedestrian walks on the Friday, and after a day for settling, the pedestrian walks were thrown open on the Sunday. A steady stream of Sunday strollers turned out to try the high level walk. A society editor predicted that the bridge would become the favourite promenade of Sunday pedestrians. And another reporter said it would be a grand place for morning "constitutionals," as it afforded a "glorious blow of the freshest of air, plus the exhilaration that is felt when at a great height." So that was opening number three, and the fourth and final opening was set for Saturday, September 13, when the contractors would finish paving the traffic deck with wooden blocks.

The contractors paved away at a steady sixty feet per day and on September 11 the job was done, and the owners of buggies, wagons and motor cars prepared for an interesting weekend. However, the fourth opening was postponed by the CPR. The postponement came over the financial arrangements. The CPR's share of the cost was to be $1,544,000 and the CPR had put up its money. The City of Edmonton had agreed to put in $286,000 and this had been paid. The federal government had agreed to contribute $125,000 and this had been paid. The provincial government had agreed to complete the financial arrangements with $175,000. But this had not been paid, so the CPR padlocked the traffic deck until such time as it was.

The government pointed out that the legislature was to open on the following Monday and that in a few weeks it would have the money appropriated by the house. But the argument fell on deaf ears; the CPR would not take an IOU from the Government of Alberta. The friendly bankers would not lend the government $175,000 till payday, so the traffic deck stayed padlocked.

Three weeks went past while the legislature wrangled about many things but didn't get around to voting the money to unlock the bridge. After three weeks, on October 6, 1913, the *Capital* ran a handsome picture of Edmonton's new pride and joy, noting acidly that the thing would be open for motor traffic when the province paid its share. There wasn't much hue and cry from the public over the padlocks, because there wasn't much motor traffic, and the wagon drivers had been using the Low Level Bridge and the McDougall Hill lift for many years. So there was no move to storm the barricades.

There was an early freeze that fall and McKernan's Lake blossomed with hundreds of skaters, and the streetcar service over the High Level Bridge was stepped up to one every five minutes to handle the crowds bound for the lake. So who cared if you couldn't drive a car over the bridge, as long as the streetcars went every five minutes? The election campaign came on with Billy McNamara running to oust Mayor William Short, and McKernan's Lake figured in the campaign. A real estate agent tried to sell the lake to the city for $78,400 to be developed as a resort, but it turned out that McKernan's Lake was owned by candidate Billy McNamara, and the boys on the city council suggested that Billy make the city a present of it! Billy didn't, but he won the election anyway and it was comparatively quiet. "Only one serious fight at the polls," said the *Journal*. So who cared about the traffic deck?

In fact, when the legislature finally voted the money and the deck opened, none of the three daily papers bothered to report it. Only the *Gateway,* even then the voice of the university, found it newsworthy. That was because some students stormed the barricades the day before the official opening and paraded across the bridge, led by a donkey.

The Great Escape

Grandfather Cashman liked the penitentiary. That's the one that used to be in downtown Edmonton, with a main cell block that later became a warehouse for Big Four Van Lines (and later still was a warehouse for Hill Security). It had a vegetable garden where the Clarke Stadium is now, and it had a coal operation which was called the Penn Mine and which tunnelled under the stadium property.

Gramp was business manager at the penitentiary, and since he was able to come and go as he pleased, he was not subject to the urges which drove Black Jack Johnson and Atchison and Monty the Mexican to plot the Great Escape. Gramp was a gentle, whimsical fellow whose relaxed enjoyment of the contradictions and foibles of human nature made a deep impression on his grandsons. Before coming to Edmonton at fifty he had run a clothing store in Orillia, Ontario, and had sold his famous fellow-townsman, Stephen Leacock, a wedding hat on credit. At the appearance of each Leacock book, he would laugh and say, "Well, he hasn't paid me for my hat yet." He was also amused by the horsehair industry which flourished in the prison. When a tradesman entered the gates to make a delivery, the prisoners would raid his horse's tail for long hairs from which to make the belts and watch chains they traded for tobacco.

He and his pal Matt McCauley, the warden, were curlers of some talent, and Grandmother Cashman would groan when she would see him coming up the walk with one of the monstrous trophies which went to successful curlers. She would also groan when she saw him coming up the walk with a young prisoner who had just been released. He used to operate a sort of one-man John Howard Society on behalf of young prisoners who were in for the first time, and, he figured, also for the last time. They were still shaving the heads of prisoners in those days, and when a man came out he was pretty well branded as an ex-convict until his head reforested. To spare promising young prisoners the shame of appearing hairless in public, Gramp would take them home till their hair regrew.

My grandmother Cashman, kindly and friendly as a person

123

could be, was never very keen about this John Howard service, but at least Gramp never brought home anybody like Black Jack Johnson, or Atchison, or Monty the Mexican. These gentlemen were very much in the news in the summer of 1909, when they elected not to serve their allotted terms but rather to take off instead. Black Jack Johnson was a huge black chap from the southern states, who was supposed to be in three years for stealing a horse. Atchison had broken the law in Moose Jaw. Monty the Mexican was a con man.

The luck of work assignments had already placed Johnson and Atchison outside the prison fence, digging a ditch about where the Highland Court Apartments are now. They decided to take the first opportunity to get even further outside and invited Monty the Mexican to join them. Monty had to get on the ditching crew first and he asked for a transfer, explaining to the warden that he was a bit run-down and needed some exercise to tone up his system.

The warden said NO! — and that removed Monty the Mexican from the plot, but he hatched his own plot and his own break for freedom, and the aftermath made him even more of a celebrity.

Johnson and Atchison chose July 12, 1909, for their departure. Perhaps they had heard that a government dignitary named Hangman Radcliffe was to visit the penitentiary that day. Anyway, when the guards were at the far end of the ditch, Johnson and Atchison laid down their tools and went over the hill, literally over the hill, and down into bush below the Highlands Drive, while the guards cocked the triggers of their rifles in vain. They'd forgotten to load them. This set the tone for future attempts to apprehend the fugitives.

For three weeks they led the hounds a merry chase through the outskirts of Edmonton. And although the Mounted Police on several occasions announced their imminent capture, Johnson and Atchison were never caught. For a few days, Edmonton was deeply perturbed about such characters being on the loose, especially Johnson who was described as "desperate." One farmer in today's Clover Bar refinery area was so concerned about this threat to his person and fortune that he sat on his front step all night, firing off a shotgun at half-hourly intervals.

Unfortunately the penitentiary had neglected to keep a rogues' gallery, so none of the police or civilian posses knew what to look for, except for the "vicious expressions" said to be on their faces. And the fact that one face was darker than the other.

Two nights after the escape, the quarry got across the river, crossing the Clover Bar railroad bridge at night. The authorities had forgotten to put a guard on this tempting bridge before Johnson and Atchison crossed it but afterwards the bridge fairly bristled with guards. After crossing the river the couple broke into the farmhouse of Richard Ottewell, and while the occupants of this well-kept and well-stocked farmhouse slept, they outfitted and provisioned themselves for the journey south. They took two suits of overalls, two union suits, two sides of bacon, and all the pies they could carry.

Two nights after this, they found some expense money for the trip in a pair of trousers hanging outside a surveyor's shack on the Mill Creek rail line. There were eight dollars in the trousers. The fugitives took the trousers too, and when the unfortunate surveyor woke up and discovered his plight and tried to report the theft, he set off one of the many rumours of capture. As he skittered through the woods in his drawers, he was pounced on by a thirty-man posse who hauled him away — protesting vainly and profanely — and presented him to the police as the fugitive Atchinson.

Another three nights and the two men had worked themselves around to the tall timber of Whitemud Creek, where they settled down to a pleasant, contemplative life, loafing in the day and working at night. Mr. Johnson, in his native southland, had presumably acquired a taste for chicken and also the technique for obtaining chickens in the dark. Each night a chicken would disappear from a henhouse — in Belgravia or Grandview Heights or Allendale or Malmo Plains or Aspen Gardens. One night the fugitives got tired of their own cooking and had dinner with a German family, who hadn't learned enough English to know that their guests had cancelled a previous engagement to dine with them.

As these stories circulated, people began to realize that no one was in danger but the chickens. They began to regard Johnson and Atchison with amused tolerance. The police lost interest in chasing will-o'-the-wisps. Johnson and Atchison moved back closer to town, to the bush in present-day Lendrum. And for all we know, they may be there yet, frying chicken.

Meanwhile, Monty the Mexican plotted his own break for freedom, and Monty's departure turned out to be the Greatest Escape — because a few weeks later he was back. He showed up at the prison gates, explaining to the cheers of the Board of Trade and all boosters of the capital city that he'd rather be a prisoner in Edmonton than a free man anywhere else. So eat your heart out, Calgary!

By the way, we did mention that Monty the Mexican was a con man, didn't we?

George Roy, Civil Servant

The Federal Building throws a long shadow. When the sun goes down in the southwest the shadow reaches almost to Victoria Avenue and 105th Street, and that's historically and poetically right, because it was on the northwest corner of that intersection, in 1885, that Edmonton's first civil servant set up the first Dominion government office. George Roy was the gentleman's name. George arrived here from Manitoba in the fall of 1885, with his wife, three daughters, and a magnificent parchment scroll from Queen Victoria.

We have seen this scroll. It says: "From Victoria, by the Grace of God, of the United Kingdom of Great Britain and Ireland, Queen, Defender of the Faith. To George Roy, of Provencher, in the Province of Manitoba in our Dominion of Canada, Esquire: Greetings: Know ye, that reposing trust and confidence in your loyalty, integrity and ability, we, under and by virtue of the powers vested in us by the North-West Territories Act and amendments thereto — and by and with the advice of our privy council for Canada — do hereby constitute and appoint you, the said George Roy, to be registrar for the district of Edmonton in the North-West Territories in our Dominion of Canada; to have, hold, exercise and enjoy the said office of registrar, for the said district of Edmonton, with all and every the powers, rights, authority, privilege, profits, emoluments and advantages unto the said office — of right and by law appertaining to, during our pleasure. In testimony whereof we cause these our letters to be made patent, and the great seal of Canada to be hereunto affixed."

Nowadays, not even an ambassador can aspire to such a list of credentials, but that's the puff that Queen Victoria gave George Roy when she sent him here in 1885 to be Edmonton's first civil servant. George's title was registrar, and that's about all that the federal civil service did in 1885 — register things: timber rights and mineral rights and land titles. Land titles were something new in the Far West when George came. The government had finally got around to surveying the country and marking it up into pieces that people could take title to. Before that, all a settler had was squatter's rights. So it marked considerable progress when legal land titles came into being and George Roy arrived to register them.

As a youth in Lévis, Quebec, George probably gave not a single thought to going west. He started out to study medicine at Laval University, but gave it up as too long and too tiring. He then drifted into journalism and for a time ran a French-language newspaper in Windsor. Then he drifted into Bishop Taché, the pioneering western bishop. Bishop Taché was in Quebec recruiting missionaries; he decided to recruit some lay-men as well, and enlisted George Roy and three of his friends. He told them they were crazy to be doing nothing in eastern Canada when, with all their education, the West held a magnificent future for them. It was 1869; George Roy was twenty-three; in the midsummer they set out.

They reached St. Paul, Minnesota, on the railroad. Then, deciding to save the steamboat fare, they got a raft and floated down the Red River into Winnipeg. They were four young men on a raft, drifting down the river and watching for the spires of St. Boniface Cathedral, the landmark that showed for miles over the flat prairie. There was Marc Girard, who was to form the first government of Manitoba. There was Joseph Royal, who was to become lieutenant-governor of the North-West Territories. There was Joseph Dubuc, who was to become chief justice of Manitoba and the father of Edmon-

127

ton's Judge Dubuc. And there was George Roy, who was to become Edmonton's first civil servant.

George became a millionaire before he became a civil servant. When he first arrived in Winnipeg he roomed for a time with Louis Riel. In 1872 he married Marjorie Langevin, and prospered mightily. By the height of the Winnipeg boom he owned a hotel, eight fur-trading posts, and many square miles of land. In 1883 there came a panic that ended the boom, and George lost everything. He lost it all and had to get a job, but it didn't bother George Roy one bit. For all his early success, he really didn't care much for business and was just as pleased to be out of it. So he got a job with the government and went to St. Norbert, Manitoba, as registrar. In 1885 he came to Edmonton as registrar, our first civil servant.

George's plan was to build a house for himself and family, and fix up one room as an office in which to transact all government business. He looked around and chose three lots on 105 Street at Victoria Avenue, on which to build his house. But there was a drawback to this location — there was no street except on the survey maps — so Edmonton's five hundred citizens pitched in and cleared a street out of the forest primeval.

J.H. Picard, the pioneer jack-of-all-business, built Mr. Roy's house. It had a picket fence, complete with an old-fashioned country stile to keep out the dogs which roamed through Edmonton in yelping, thieving packs. If you wished to transact business with the Dominion government, you had to go three steps up and three steps down on the other side. The Roy children used to shriek with delight whenever a certain lawyer came to transact business. The lawyer was well fortified most of the time, and would perform the most wonderful gymnastics getting over the stile.

In the fall, the children would go away to school in Winnipeg. They went by steamboat — down to the Grand Rapids on the wonderful steamer *Northwest* — then across the lakes to Winnipeg on another boat. It was a fifteen-day trip. While they were away, that entertaining lawyer still performed his balancing act coming over the stile, and more and more people came to claim title to land, and to mineral rights. They paid twenty-five cents extra for mineral rights, and many a comfortable oil income of today is based on the twenty-five cents paid to George Roy.

George didn't make anything for himself, although he was ideally positioned to make it, and a lot of chaps would have done so. George was too honest, and then he was a perfectly rotten businessman anyway. He once traded the northeast corner of Jasper and 104th Street for a coat. George wanted a light smoking jacket, or smock, to wear around the office. He was in Larue and Picard's store one day and saw an alpaca coat that just suited him. So he traded the northeast corner of Jasper and 104th Street for the coat. George was also an easy mark for settlers from his old home town of Lévis, Quebec. They beat a well-rutted path to his door. George seldom got any of these loans back, but that didn't bother him. He was a man of unshakable serenity.

Along in the nineties the Dominion government figured that Edmonton was a big enough operation to warrant separating the office from the registrar's home. They put up a brick building on Victoria at 106th Street, a building which later became an armoury and has since been taken over by the provincial government. George didn't change his routine for the new building. He kept office hours of ten to four, with an hour and a half for lunch — not bad when store clerks were working fourteen hours a day. It gave George lots of time for what he liked to do best, which was nothing. Like the chap in the Gilbert and Sullivan song, George Roy did nothing in particular and did it very well. He did it so surpassing well, with the courtly charm of the French-Canadian gentleman, that he was one of the most highly regarded fellows in early Edmonton.

At one time, George had two of his sons-in-law working in the registration office, Antonio Prince and Jules Royal. Roy, Prince and Royal gave rise to one of the standing jokes of early Edmonton. It was said that the Dominion office had a king, a Prince, and a member of the Royal Family.

The years went by in complete serenity for George Roy. By 1910 he was sixty-six, and although the civil service had no policy on retirement then, it was suggested to George that he might like to take his pension and let a younger man step up. George Roy's serenity was exceeded only by his calm independence. They could keep their miserable pension. If they wanted him out, he would quit, period. So he did, and settled down to enjoy life to the full, which is to say, unhampered by work, unhampered by any activity save good eating and good fellowship.

George was a very stout man and Dr. Blais tried to get him to go for walks; said he'd feel better and live longer. But George said he felt fine, and as for living long — well, he lived to be eighty-eight, passing on in 1932, in the house he built to be Edmonton's first federal building.

Fighting Joe Clarke

Clarke Stadium was the only possible name. That's what Alderman Hugh John Macdonald said when he moved that the stadium be given that name. Fighting Joe Clarke, champion of the underdog, had been mayor of Edmonton five times, an alderman eight times, and a candidate every time since he'd roared in from the Yukon in 1908. Those were valid enough reasons for suggesting the name, and Joe had been an athlete and booster of sport, but there was yet another reason for Alderman Hugh John to call it the only *possible* name.

Fighting Joe Clarke's political style was derived from his approach to athletics, a style that first drew notice in eastern Ontario in the 1880s when he played slambang lacrosse. He played in quick succession for teams representing Prescott, Brockville, Morrisburg and Athens. In his Edmonton years, when people would ask him how he'd happened to play for so many teams, he would explain with a jovial growl, "Well, when I got expelled from one school I'd move on to another."

In 1892 Joe made his first mark on the West. He arrived out in Regina to join the Mounted Police, and his prowess in track-and-field events soon made him the toast of the troop. The lad who had come to ride horses could run like a deer. Joe never claimed he could run 100 yards in 10 seconds. He was always very modest about that. Then he would grin wickedly and growl, "But I've beaten more men who say they can than any other man in western Canada."

130

Joe turned this talent to profit at an open track-and-field competition which the Mounties arranged in Regina. Joe entered all the events and won them all, raking in the total prize money of $108. In the hop, step and jump he travelled 47 feet 11 inches. Then a few weeks later he jumped all the way back to Ontario. Policing the plains had not been the adventure he'd been promised. There was far too much spit and polish and riding practice. As in his later political days, Joe had no inhibiting reverence for red tape when he thought something should be done. The Mounted Police, however, held a higher regard for red tape than young Constable Clarke. They pursued him all the way home and had him in court on a charge of desertion. As Joe explained the outcome, "Fortunately the magistrate before whom I was tried happened to be my uncle. I got off with a hundred-dollar fine. The usual rap was six months."

Having completed a brief career enforcing the law, Joe went to the University of Toronto to study the stuff. His rugged build and rugged individualism made him a star outside-wing on Varsity's rugby football teams. He was a cruncher, especially on defence. His greatest day on the gridiron was one on which he wasn't due to play because of an injured neck. Joe helped the cause by leading the cheering, and those who heard Joe at games in Edmonton years later could testify that no one could produce more decibels.

But hard as Joe cheered, Queen's ran up an overwhelming 19 to 2 lead in the first quarter. Joe Clarke, champion of the underdog, wanted to do more for his down-trodden Toronto Blues. In spite of his injury, he went into the game and set his sights on the nimble Queen's halfback, Chicky McRae. He rocked Chicky back so often and so hard on his nimble heels that Chicky had to withdraw his services. Toronto went on to win 21 to 19. When Joe was asked afterwards how he could play so well when racked with pain he growled, "Hell, I had two hundred bucks bet on this game."

More important to us, however, than Joe's heroics on the thudding turf, was a friendship he was making among the students at the University of Toronto. A most unlikely man for Joe to claim as a lifelong friend was a young student of political economy named William Lyon Mackenzie King. Unlikely, but the roaring extrovert and the devious introvert remained lifelong friends and this friendship was the key to what follows.

In 1898 Mackenzie King was pursuing his careful path to the top, but Fighting Joe Clarke was off for more adventure — to Dawson City on the gold rush trail. There, in the long summer evenings, he added a sport to his repertoire — baseball — but dropped boxing. In renouncing the ring he did pick up a distinction. He became perhaps the only heavyweight in history to get a broken ankle from a sock on the jaw. In the cause of charity Joe agreed to a bout with Kid Owens, pride of the Mounties. Joe stepped out into the ring and struck the approved pose. The Kid came through the pose with a solid right to the jaw. Joe went down in such a way as to crack his ankle.

Joe was a member of every sport commitee in Dawson. When he stormed into Edmonton in 1908 he was only a few weeks becoming secretary-treasurer of the Eskimos' professional baseball team and only a few more weeks getting into politics. Real estate man Stuart Darroch put a city lot in Joe's name so that he could contest an election for the Liberals. From then until he died in 1941, Joe waged noisy campaigns on behalf of the underdog, and as civic elections were annual events he was seldom silent. He was a large man who could enjoy a good weep at a Mary Pickford movie or a sentimental Irish song, and he came by this honestly through his father, a native of County Armagh.

The appearance of Fighting Joe Clarke on a platform was the signal for a noisy demonstration, and it often had the same effect in the city council chamber. On the night of August 6, 1914, Alderman Joe and Mayor Billy McNamara enlivened a meeting with a display of fisticuffs. The row started harmlessly enough with a discussion of economy in civic government, but then by stages the heat of discussion mounted. Joe called Billy a liar and after further talk amended it to perjurer. Then Billy said Joe had no more courage than a rat, and then the fists flew. Billy and Joe crashed through the door to the fire escape, out into the startled night air, then rolled back into the council chamber. Then they surged down the steps and out onto 99th Street, and fought to a draw.

The *Bulletin* reporter wrote that they "intended to resign

because they had so disgraced themselves and the city that they could no longer hold office as elected representatives of the people." But that was silly. Why would Billy or Joe feel guilty about a good scrap in a good cause? After the scrap they were better friends than ever; because that was the way of the stout-hearted men.

In or out of office, Joe was a force. He was out of office when he engineered the coup which made Clarke Stadium "the only possible name" for that place of sweaty endeavour. It was in 1929, when the city was sending a delegation to Ottawa to press the cabinet for cessation of coal mining under the old penitentiary site. The penitentiary had closed in 1920 and the inmates had been moved to Prince Albert, but the pen coal mine had been leased and the operation was threatening the whole east end with collapse. Anyway that's the impression one gets from records of the city council.

The city fathers decided to send a delegation to Ottawa to press for a halt. Joe was not then in office, but because of his friendship with Mackenzie King he was included. Joe was overjoyed. He was indifferent to the coal mine but wished to present a scheme involving the surface of the penitentiary site — in particular the vegetable gardens north of the tracks.

In pursuit of this strategy, Joe, along about North Bay, disappeared. The delegation went on to Toronto, doubled back to Ottawa, and upon entering the dining room of the Chateau Laurier found Mackenzie King having lunch with none other than Joe Clarke. In his back pocket Joe had a lease to the property that now holds Clarke Stadium. The prime minister had given it to him that morning. Edmonton would have the site for ninety-nine years, at an annual rent of one dollar, to be developed as an athletic park.

There was no money to develop the site, with the great depression settling in, but this economic slump revived the political fortunes of Fighting Joe Clarke. Joe was not by any means a man for all seasons but he was certainly the man for that season of blighted achievement and stunted hope. The underdogs became the majority and they returned their champion to the mayor's desk in 1934.

Joe's critics would tell you how he would have his feet on the desk when a distinguished visitor entered the mayor's office and how he would look up and growl, "Well, what the hell do *you* want?" His boosters would tell you how he would order the police to transport a junior baseball team to a game in Wetaskiwin, with the gruff comment that "the cops are better off taking these kids to a ball game than chasing 'em down a back alley." Only once as depression mayor did he withhold compassion from the underdog. A prisoner at the bar was asked by the magistrate how he'd happened to get into such a deplorable state the previous evening. "I was drinking with Mayor Clarke," said the accused. Joe happened to be among the spectators, waiting to represent a client. "You're a liar!" he boomed — for which he was fined ten dollars for contempt of court, and made the Toronto papers.

The year after the depression returned Fighting Joe Clarke to office, it did the same for his old friend William Lyon Mackenzie King. The city formed a Stadium Development Committee, made Mackenzie King an honorary director, and Joe made a trip to Ottawa to get some federal money for the project. As he boarded the train, Joe said, "I'll get the money. I'll get it honestly if I can, but I'll get the money."

Alas, even Mackenzie King had no money in 1935 and Joe came home empty-handed. But in 1938, when he was out of office for the last time, things were beginning to brighten a little and the city found money for a 3,000-seat wooden grandstand. But it didn't have a name. So Alderman Hugh John Macdonald moved that it be given the only possible name: Clarke Stadium.

The Heroes — 1885

On the south wing of the Legislative Building two ancient brass cannons once sat, aiming out at the river valley. They seemed like toys, so small that their noses just poked over the stone balustrade. Behind them, inside the heavy-leaded windows, was the provincial library, a quiet place in the tradition of libraries, and the cannons did not disturb the peace. However, they were once primed for action on those very grounds, when the Edmonton Volunteer Infantry prepared to defend the settlement against the last threat of Indian attack. Sixty-eight strong, the volunteers organized on the night of March 31, 1885.

Far down the Saskatchewan, Louis Riel and the Métis were preparing to fight. The Métis of the Edmonton district hadn't the same provocation as Riel's men and there was nothing to fear from them, but the excitement had spread to the Indians. If the Indians were ever to make a last attempt to take the country by force, this was the time. The Indians knew it. The white men knew it. District Indians were drifting in towards Edmonton and pitching their lodges on the present Victoria Golf Course. Families who had taken refuge in the fort could see the campfires at night. There were more campfires every night, and they believed the Indian chiefs had divided up the white women among themselves and that the women were to be among the spoils when the men had been killed. The soft spring air was heavy and menacing. Government troops had already left eastern Canada, but they couldn't hope to reach Edmonton for a month.

In this atmosphere the Edmonton Volunteer Infantry was born, the gallant company of soldiers who were so completely forgotten by officialdom that they were never even recognized in the first place. Sixty-eight of them crowded into the public school on the night of March 31,1885, most of the able-bodied men in the frontier village. They drew up a telegram, addressed to the Honourable the Minister of Militia and Defence, Ottawa, and went to the telegraph station to send it. Alex Taylor began tapping out the message, informing the minister of the action taken for the defence of Edmonton, asking him for instructions, and asking him to put the Edmonton Volunteer Infantry on the militia list of Canada. Alex Taylor started tapping. Then, halfway through, he stopped. "It's no use, boys, the line has gone off." Riel's men had cut the telegraph line west of Battleford. That was Edmonton's only direct communication with the outside world. Now it was gone and Edmonton was isolated, and the government troops were a month away. The Edmonton Volunteer Infantry had to hold the fort.

There were few among them with any military experience. William Stiff, a cheerful old bachelor who worked for the

Bulletin and liked to play the fiddle at dances, was elected captain. Bill Ibbotson, the hardware man, was elected lieutenant; and John Mitchell, an Indian agent, was elected ensign. There were three sergeants: John Belden, Joe Hayes and T.B. Henderson. And three corporals: Bill Connors of Connors Hill, Charles Strang and Alex Taylor. And there were sixty troopers, whose names, unfortunately, are not recorded. They were organized on Tuesday night, March 31. The next day thirty of them spent the afternoon in the old Masonic Hall, learning to form fours as Captain Stiff barked the commands. Then they paraded through the few streets of Edmonton, led by the village band. The *Bulletin* commented rather cryptically on the music: "Considering the instruments used, the band played quite creditably." But the village knew the volunteer infantry was in business and meant business.

They knew little of orthodox military theory, but they could shoot. They knew their enemy, they were resourceful pioneers ... and they were preparing to fight for their lives. They prepared with cool, realistic determination, making use of everything they had. They hadn't much but they made full and often amazing use of it. They decided the strongest place to defend was old Fort Edmonton and they set about making it stronger still.

They completely rebuilt the south wall of the fort, doing it in two days. They cleared out brush up the hill behind the fort and knocked down some outlying barns which might give cover to Indians moving in to attack. They found a hundred brush-hooks in the fort, which were being stored there by the Hudson's Bay Company for the Dominion government. Brush-hooks were flails for clearing the brush. The volunteers sharpened the flails and practised using them to repel invaders who might try to come in over the walls. There were eighty old muzzle-loading rifles stored in the fort, ancient things which had been used to suppress the Sepoy Rebellion in India back in 1857. There was no ammunition to fit the muzzle-loaders, so the volunteers set to work making their own cartridges. A shipment of powder and shot, consigned to the merchants Norris and Carey, had arrived on the south bank from Calgary. The river ice was about to go out and was too mushy for sleighs. But the volunteers were equal to the problem. They

136

broke a narrow boat-channel through the ice to the south bank and brought the ammunition across on boats.

The ancient brass cannons were also re-activated. As you can still read on them, they were cast in 1807, and they are stamped with the crest of King George III. The volunteers built solid bases for them and got them in working order, while the wife of John A. Mitchell, the ensign, made powder bags for them on her sewing machine.

They were also preparing a defence against fire, the favourite weapon of the attacking Indian. Indian strategy in the American Southwest was to set fire to fortified buildings and force their enemies out into the open. But the Edmonton Volunteer Infantry men were ready for flaming arrows. They moved in a portable steam engine, belonging to Hardisty and Fraser, and set it up on the fort plaza. They hooked up a long hose to it and prepared to fight fire with water, water at high pressure guaranteed by the steam engine. They dug a well inside the walls and found a good underground stream at fifteen feet. Then they built another wall through the middle of the fort, so that if the Indians should overrun one half of the fort, the defenders could retire to a half-sized fort, just as strong.

This, mind you, was all the work of men whom Ottawa later decreed were not soldiers. And all this time they were working with very little definite knowledge of what was happening outside, either in the camp of the enemy, or in the councils of the Canadian army. The telegraph line was still cut. The only information was wild rumours about Indians moving here, there and everywhere.

On Saturday, April 11, a wild story came over the telephone line from St. Albert that fifteen hundred Indians were attacking Fort Saskatchewan. It was a rumour only, but it created genuine panic in Edmonton. The defenders of the fort set out a string of pickets to guard against being taken by surprise. The line ran from the fort, down the hill to the Edmonton Hotel at the foot of McDougall Hill, and around through the woods on the present Jasper Avenue to about 112th Street. That was where the trail from St. Albert cut through the woods on its way to the fort. Near 98th Avenue and 111th Street, where the trail came out of the woods, the volunteers dug solid gun positions, to give a steady cross-fire on the trail. If the Indians came that way they were in for trouble.

Across the river, the homes of John Walter (down on the flat) and James McKernan (by McKernan's Lake) became armed observation posts. It was a great plan. And it was executed with calm but desperate haste, because there were eighty-four women and children taking refuge behind the defences. The fact that the attack never came does not make the achievement of the volunteers one bit less remarkable.

When General Strange and the 65th Mount Royal Rifles reached Edmonton on May 1, the Edmonton Volunteer Infantry fired a fifteen-gun salute with the tiny brass cannons. General Strange was amazed at the salute. He was amazed at the defences. He told the volunteers so when he made a formal inspection of their rough but ready ranks. That was a proud day for the Edmonton Volunteer Infantry. But it was a sad one, too, because the regular troops had taken control and there was nothing more for the volunteers to do.

They were disbanded on May 2, 1885, after thirty-three days in the defence of Edmonton, and they returned to civil life without even an official thank-you from the federal government. For, despite a number of representations later on, Ottawa refused to give the soldiers of the Edmonton Volunteer Infantry the North-West Rebellion medal. Regulations are regulations, and according to regulations they weren't even soldiers. Heroes, perhaps, but not soldiers. And there's nothing left at the site of their stand to show that they ever prepared to fight. Even the tiny cannons stamped with the crest of King George III are gone from the balustrade of the Legislative Building. They've been moved to the Provincial Museum.

Life in the Woods

In the uncertain days of early summer, tents appear in the back yards of Edmonton, and the more adventurous youngsters move outside to sleep under canvas until fall. Summer days are days of real sport all right, and they recall summer days early in the century when Edmontonians of all ages lived under canvas. In July 1907 the *Bulletin* took a census of tent-dwellers and found that one-fifth of the population of Edmonton was living under canvas. The *Bulletin* found 1098 tents in the woods which still grew in their primeval state through most of the city. There were many fine houses in Edmonton (the *Bulletin* wanted no one to be under any misapprehension about that; especially anyone from Calgary), but houses were not mass-produced in those pastoral days, and the people were coming too fast for the builders. Anyway, life in the woods was such sport that some families who did have houses were closing them up for the summer and taking to tents.

For young, adventurous people coming out to distant Edmonton to start life anew, it took only a little extra spirit of adventure to start it in a tent. Life in the woods was invigorating and restful at the same time. And it was cheap. Yes, for fifteen or twenty dollars you could buy the lumber for a floor and sidings; for a couple more dollars you could buy a licence for your tent — and there you were, sheltered from the madding crowd, sheltered from the elements, in the friendly poplar woods. Where there were woods there were tents, and there were woods everywhere.

There was one concentration of tent-dwellers on a cliff behind the Dreamland Theatre, a cliff which has long since tumbled to the river. There was another flock of tents on Fraser Flat; Riverdale they call it now. There was another on Gallagher Flat; Cloverdale. There was another flock beyond the CNR tracks in the west end. And all along the view lots, which stretched out east and west along the cliffs, there were tents. That was the life!

And talk about "do-it-yourself." There's nothing new about that. In 1907 a housewife could build a house on her sewing machine. Many housewives did exactly that. If the lady of the family was particularly clever with her sewing machine, you could buy her the canvas in the morning and she could stitch up the house before sundown. That was the life! That was the life for one Edmontonian in five. In reporting this figure on July 20, 1907, the *Bulletin* conceded that the weather had been a little rainier than most tent-dwellers would like. "But," said the *Bulletin,* uttering those famous last words, "The rainy season is surely over now."

All sorts of people were tenting. You'd often find three or four young bachelors who would go together on a tent and take turns at the cooking. You'd find new Canadians from central Europe, who would pitch a tent in Edmonton until they found a homestead. You'd find a bookish Englishman, sitting outside with his book and puffing his pipe with solid contentment while his wife prepared tea on the outdoor stove.

When winter came the stove was brought inside the tent and a stovepipe pushed through the roof. The tents were kept very warm indeed by the stoves. They could be kept either too hot or too cold, and since the former was the lesser evil, people got used to having them too hot and never noticed it. And then, before you knew it, it was summer again and the tent flap could be left open and the stove moved back outside.

That was life in the woods; Thoreau never had it so good. Thoreau never woke in the morning to breathe the air of early Edmonton, air washed by the rain and made sweet by the leaves of the poplars. As a matter of fact, *we* don't do so any-more, either. We have cut down the poplar trees to make way for houses, and we don't encourage them to grow because their roots break up the concrete and get into the water pipes. And the water pipes point up the flaw in this homey picture of long ago. Life in the woods was fine and healthy when there weren't too many people living that way. But soon there were too many. They crowded in too close to each other, and disease and food poisoning began to take their toll. The victims were almost all small children. It was a blessing when the builders got enough houses built and the tents disappeared. But if you look only at the pleasant side of the picture, it makes a very pleasant picture indeed; a picture of 1907.

140

Matt McCauley

Perhaps the most surprising fact about Matt McCauley was the fact that he was a man. From all that Matt did, you'd suppose that he was five or six men, or at the least a father-and-son combination, because his career was as long as it was wide. But there was only one Matt McCauley; he was part of Edmonton from 1879 until 1912, and if Edmonton ever has a hall of fame there must be a choice niche reserved for Matt. He was one of the great men, one of the restless men, living by choice on the outer fringe of advancing settlement.

Matt was born smack in the middle of the restless nineteenth century, in May 1850, near Owen Sound, Ontario. His father was Irish and his mother was Scottish. Matt looked like an Irishman, walked with the long stride of the stovepipe Irish, talked with the fire and humourous lilt of both races, and thought like a Scot. The restless striving for the beyond that drove his father from Ireland to Ontario, also drove Matt from Ontario to Manitoba when he was twenty-one years old.

It was 1871 when young Matt landed in Fort Garry, by present-day Winnipeg. For three years he worked at any labouring job he could get, and, through the virtues of energy and thrift, he was then able to go into business for himself with his own team of horses. As a sideline to his teamstering he introduced the first hackney carriage, forerunner of the taxicab, to Fort Garry. He married and began raising a family of eight children, enough to make almost any man settle down. But not Matt. He heard the reports of the Fleming expedition and he grew restless again.

Sir Sandford Fleming's expedition had investigated the possibilities of a railroad through the mountains and had recommended the Yellowhead Pass. Matt also met Frank Oliver, and Frank's optimistic reports on the possibilities of Edmonton made him more restless. The shock that finally jarred him loose from Fort Garry was the civic election of 1879. As Matt told it, there was a close two-way race for the mayor's job. Election night wound up with a free-for-all in the main hotel, in which hundreds of dollars' damage was done. All the participants were arrested. The next day the newly-elected mayor held court in his new capacity as chief magistrate. He found his opponents guilty and acquitted his supporters. Matt said he didn't care to live in a town run like that. In May 1879 he and his family set out for Edmonton.

They were twenty-three days on the open prairie, riding the Red River carts behind the oxen. For one stretch of eleven days they didn't see another human being, but the weather was beautiful and the parkland offered a rich menu of game and wildfowl. The McCauleys came to Fort Saskatchewan first, and farmed just south of the town for a couple of years. Then they moved into Edmonton; and that's when Matt started carrying on as though there were six of him.

He built a house on a view lot — on the property now occupied by the Alberta Telephone Tower, and he was quickly into business. From the barn behind the house he operated Edmonton's first cartage company, and in partnership with Bill Howey he ran our first butcher's shop. His cartage business carried him far out of town, on freighting trips to the north and west. Matt explored a great deal of the country. He liked pine trees and brought back pines to plant around his house in Edmonton. Some of the originals of these pines are probably still standing in the Edmonton Cemetery. Matt was a leader in the cemetery project; he was a leader in any civic project.

For sixteen years he was president of the Edmonton District Agricultural Association. That doesn't sound very exciting perhaps, but that association put on the Edmonton Exhibition and got it running on the solid basis which it still enjoys today. Matt was also first chairman of the school committee, which was formed in 1881 to provide a school in Edmonton. For three years the committee financed the school on a subscription basis; then in 1884, it figured the time had come for a plebiscite, in which the property-owners of the settlement could vote to set up a school district with power to run the school on tax money. Matt was returning officer on that controversy-ridden voting day. He was able to report that "yes" beat out "no," and in Edmonton we set up the first school district west of Winnipeg. Matt was chairman of the new board for three years and a member for nineteen.

But that wasn't all he did for education. In 1896 Frank Oliver was elected to the Dominion parliament and Matt took

142

Frank's place in the Legislative Assembly of the North-West Territories. In 1897 Matt introduced the "single tax" bill, the idea being that school boards and town councils would lump their money requirements together in a single tax. Instead of being dunned separately by the town council and the school board, a property owner would get a single tax notice and pay a single tax. The school boards were also spared the expense of a separate tax-collecting system. It was good common sense. The single tax was approved by the Territorial Assembly, and now it's taken for granted, and no one stops to inquire whether it might have been started by Matt McCauley.

Matt was a good man with theories, but in his time the crying need was for men of action, and Matt could provide enough action to meet any situation. In 1882, for example, there was the business of the claim jumpers. Ever since the Edmonton settlement had outgrown the fort, people had held squatter's rights on their land. The government in far-off Ottawa had not got around to making a proper survey, which would have allowed the settlers to get a legal title to their land, but the settlers got along fine with each other by the gentleman's agreement. They got along fine until some chaps who were not gentlemen started coming to town and building on land that was already occupied. These chaps cared nothing for squatter's rights. The boys could see that action, prompt and vigorous, was the only way to impress the claim jumpers. They organized a Vigilantes' Committee, with Matt McCauley as captain, and heaved the shacks of two claim jumpers over the cliff.

In 1892 the settlement was incorporated, with Matt McCauley as first mayor, and he had to supply plenty of action in his first term. He had to act to keep Strathcona from stealing the land office. The files and furniture had already been loaded onto a dray when the foul plot was discovered. Matt called up the Home Guard, organized the first time for the defence of Edmonton in the Riel Rebellion, and told the boys to be ready to defend Edmonton again. The Dominion government sent Major Griesbach and his Mounties from Fort Saskatchewan to enforce the order for the transfer. But McCauley met Griesbach just east of town and he said, "Major, we are both young men and life is sweet; but if you come into Edmonton there will be bloodshed and the first to die will likely be you and I."

When the fuss blew over, the land office was still securely on Jasper Avenue, and Matt was converting his energy to peaceful uses. His administration raised a few hundred dollars here and there to straighten and widen Jasper Avenue, and in 1893 Matt went to Ottawa and got a charter for an electric street railway. It was the first electric railway charter west of the Great Lakes.

From all the foregoing you might assume that Matt McCauley had no time for sport, and while the assumption would appear logical, it would be incorrect. Matt had time for any sport, but his favourite was curling. He was one of the founders of the Royal Curling Club, and was president for many years. In the 1880s and '90s the Royal didn't even have a rink. Matt and the boys would find a patch of smooth ice on the river, sweep off the snow, and curl with iron kettles — weighted with sand.

In 1896, the first Mrs. McCauley died. Matt married again and raised a second family of four children, for a total of a dozen. In 1901 he left Edmonton for a while to try ranching at Beaver Lake, but he was back in 1905 to represent the old Victoria constituency in the first Alberta legislature.

The next year Matt resigned his seat for yet another new experience. The federal penitentiary was opened here that year, and who was the first warden? How did you guess? Such appointments went pretty well by politics in those days. Matt was a Liberal; when the Conservatives turned Wilfrid Laurier out of the prime minister's chair in 1911, they also turned Matt McCauley out of the warden's office in Edmonton.

Matt was sixty-two by this time, and he thought he would try something brand new but not so physically demanding. The pleasant orchards of the Okanagan seemed inviting indeed, so Matt went to Penticton and became a prosperous apple grower and a man of influence in the Okanagan. There was only one drawback to growing apples. As he approached the age of seventy-five, the one drawback finally got too much for Matt. Growing apples was too easy. It made him restless.

So, when he was seventy-five years old, he left the pleasant Okanagan and went to the Peace River Country to be a homesteader. The Peace River was the last frontier; that was where Matt wanted to be. Like Tennyson's Ulysses, he would drink life to the lees. He cleared and broke a farm near Sexsmith and was at work right up to the time of his death, in October 1930. That was Matt McCauley, one of the great men.

John Brown's Store

John Brown began business about 1882 on Jasper Avenue. And when we say John Brown was in business on Jasper, we mean exactly that. His store was smack-dab in the middle of it, between 97th and 98th streets, facing south. In 1882 it was a matter of little consequence that John Brown was in the middle of the street. There really wasn't one there anyway, and there weren't any other streets. But by 1892 Edmonton was a genuine incorporated town. Far-seeing Matt McCauley was mayor. And Matt and the boys could see that if Edmonton was to escape the fate of Boston, stores like that of John Brown would have to get back in line so that the streets could be straightened out.

Street-straightening was perhaps the biggest project of Matt McCauley's first term as town mayor. Edmonton money by-law no. 4, for example, provided $850 to move a number of buildings back off 97th Street. By-law no. 5 provided $750 to move some buildings back off 99th Street. There was also an item of $25 to buy 107 square feet of property and round off the curve of Jasper at 99th Street. It wasn't much work moving a building; there weren't any big buildings and none had basements. Stores and houses used to be towed around Edmonton like flat-bottomed barges. When W. Johnstone Walker towed his first store from 98th Street to Jasper Avenue near Mike's Newsstand, the transfer took an extra week when unexpected rain turned Jasper Avenue into a quagmire.

So the great town of Edmonton — population eight hundred — was not asking John Brown to do much when it asked him to yank in his store about forty feet and let Jasper Avenue run straight. It was a far-seeing plan. Far-seeing indeed. Had it not been for far-sighted Matt McCauley and company, our traffic problem today would be much worse than it is. The only trouble was, John Brown didn't see it that way. This was his store. He had been in business longer than the Municipal Corporation of Edmonton. He, John Brown, was staying put. The town council, said John in effect, could go chase themselves up and down Jasper Avenue until they dropped from exhaustion. And every time they ran past his store they could damn well detour around it. And everybody else from here to eternity could damn well go around it too.

Well, this was a fine kick-in-the-face for a far-seeing bunch of town councillors. They made John a handsome offer — three thousand dollars for the property and the moving job. That was big money in earliest Edmonton, but the answer was the same: No!

Cajolery and bribery having failed to move John Brown, the councillors turned to their solicitors to see if they could get him out of there. They hated to sic the lawyers on John. John Brown was a nice old fellow, nice as he could be, and liked and respected by all. He hadn't a fault except for this pig-headed determination to stand in the path of civic progress. So, on July 18, 1892, town solicitors N. D. Beck and Pete McNamara filed a prayer with the Supreme Court, praying that John Brown's store be proclaimed a nuisance and that he be commanded to remove it. Having filed the prayer, Brown, the town, and the solicitors for both, sat back and prepared to wait, because Mr. Justice Rouleau of the Supreme Court of the North-West Territories was not expected in Edmonton until October.

There was plenty to occupy them while they waited. Other big things were happening. The town of Edmonton was still hopping mad over the attempt of certain patriots of South Edmonton to steal the land office off Jasper Avenue. That was one thing. Then the Jasper House put up an addition, sixteen feet wide by twenty-nine feet long, for the purpose of a bar (K. McLeod, contractor). Then the horses from the Queen's Hotel ran away from the south side station with the hotel bus and racked up the bus beyond repair ... and the town council set the tax rate at eight mills ... and it instructed the town clerk to purchase a brass trumpet for the chief of the fire brigade ...

146

and everyone wished the electric company would generate enough electricity so that the lights could be kept on at night ... and on September 5 it was announced the lights would stay on at night. But the all-night lighting hit a quick snag. Three of the hotels — the Alberta, the Queen's and the Jasper House — had electric light, and if the lights were on in the hotels, none of the other lights in town would go on. So the company shut off the hotels and there were bitter howls from the innkeepers.

Well, with things like this going on, time slipped by and it was soon October; and on October 12, 1892, Judge Rouleau came to town to hear the case of the town versus Brown. Judge Rouleau heard Beck and McNamara state the town's case. He heard the Taylor cousins, S.S. and H.C., state the case for John Brown. Then Judge Rouleau reserved judgement and took off for home, and the town and Brown prepared for another long wait.

And winter came ... and the *Bulletin* reminded drivers that the town by-law required all sleighs to have bells ... and the *Bulletin* commented that there were no skating parties and no dances, and asked what was wrong with everybody ... and Christmas came, and New Year's, and the social pace picked up satisfactorily, and John Brown continued to do business on Jasper Avenue and continued to run his unvarying advertisements in the paper: "Dry goods ... boots and shoes ... clothing ... groceries ... provisions, and etc." (Week in, week out, the ad never changed.) Until February 18, 1893, arrived and the decision came down from Judge Rouleau. The town, said the judge, was right. Brown would have to move.

But John Brown was not to be panicked by the opinion of one judge. He instructed his solicitors to carry the fight to the appeal court. And more weeks dragged by, and spring came, and with it the season for early-closing of the stores. During the summer months the clerks would be off early, at seven o'clock instead of ten. So instead of working fourteen hours a day, they would have to work only eleven hours and would have some leisure to enjoy the summer evenings. The clerks' association took an ad in the paper asking the ladies to co-operate by doing their shopping early. The appeal court met in spring session at Regina, and the Taylor cousins, S.S. and H.C., went down to plead John Brown's appeal. And N. D. Beck and

Pete McNamara went down to argue the town's case; and on the way back, Pete went in the mile bicycle race at the Calgary sports day and won second prize.

It was on June 18, 1893, a year after it all began, that the appeal court announced its decision. John Brown's appeal was dismissed. He and his store would have to move back in line. Not only that, but John Brown would have to pay all the costs of the drawn-out case — the court costs, the town's costs, the town solicitors' costs, and the town solicitors' trips to Regina. All these were assessed against poor old John Brown. He also had to pay his own lawyers and he had to pay to have his store moved off Jasper Avenue. Poor John, he should have taken the town's original offer of three thousand dollars. As it was, he didn't get the three thousand, and by the time he'd paid all the costs of the scrap, he was out eleven thousand dollars.

But John Brown was not out of the running. He pulled in his store but almost immediately replaced it with a new one, and as late as 1976 the new one was still there, just east of the Alberta Hotel, a wooden shed housing the Tokyo Restaurant. And the traffic was hurtling past on Jasper Avenue, right over the spot where John Brown made his last stand.

Those Magnificent Men in Their Flying Machines

Thrift is counted among the virtues. One weekend in 1911, Edmontonians put on a display of thrift even more spectacular than the show they didn't pay to see. It was the first advertised public showing of the airplane — spelled *aeroplane*. The Exhibition Board was the sponsor and the board figured it was only right that the public should have the opportunity to pay, since it cost a few thousand dollars to engage the aeronauts. But the board reckoned without the economical ingenuity of the paying public.

The aeronauts were hired in connection with the spring horse show of 1911. The show was being held at the new

148

Exhibition Grounds, way out in the east end, and a lot of people thought it was a long way to go even to see a prize Percheron. The boys on the board figured an exhibition by a new-fangled flying machine might give the horse show some added zest. So they engaged a couple of heroes from the Glen Curtiss Company to bring their machine here and fly it around the Exhibition Grounds.

They arrived on April 27, a pair of cigar chewers named Hugh Robinson and Bob St. Henri. They arrived riding a Pullman, with their collapsible flying machine riding in the express car. They spent the evening of the twenty-seventh and the morning of the twenty-eighth putting it together — ensuring that it wouldn't collapse in full view of the thousands who would be paying a dollar apiece to witness the display.

The board figured on a big, paying crowd, for this was to be the first advertised flying-machine demonstration in Edmonton. Two years earlier a carpenter named Reg Hunt had built a machine and flown it in the west end, but it had made only one flight, and although he had an agreement with the Exhibition Board to put on a display, he could never get it airborne again. So few people had seen Reg Hunt's demonstration that the Exhibition Board figured they had signed for a bonanza with the Curtiss aviators.

It was a bonanza all right. For the street railway! Every mobile streetcar was put in service to take thrill-hungry citizens to the fairgrounds. The cars took in eighteen hundred extra fares at a nickel apiece. However, less than six hundred people paid their way into the grounds, as their thrifty fellow-citizens, by the thousands, climbed trees, poles and boxcars to get the thrills for nothing.

About eleven o'clock on Friday, April 28, 1911, some of the thrifty thrill-seekers fell out of their trees with awe as Hugh Robinson rose from the race track and went around three times at a height of two hundred feet. A newspaper report says: "The engine began to chug, and before it could scarcely be believed, the airship was off the ground with no apparent effort." Robinson made two more flights around the track that day, the standard way to demonstrate flying in 1911.

That same year Lincoln Beachey, the aviator, and Barney Oldfield, the race-car man, got to arguing about whether a race-car or an airplane was faster. They raced to a draw, round and round a race track in Nebraska. Perhaps if Barney Oldfield had been racing at ground level, the thrifty Edmontonians would have come down out of the trees and paid to see Barney. But the next day, when the suddenly prosperous street railway hauled more thrill-seekers to the very gates of the Exhibition Grounds, aviator Bob St. Henri made it even easier for the freeloaders. He ventured away from the track and flew his Curtiss biplane right around the fence.

He did it three times, and when the crowds got home that night and picked up their papers they read the screaming advertisement: AVIATOR ACCEPTS THE CHALLENGE! The advertisement screamed on: "On Sunday he will fly to Grandview Heights, the beautiful subdivision of the city beautiful, and will attempt to alight on a certain lot. If he succeeds he will get a free lot in Grandview Heights, the beautiful subdivision. Everybody come to beautiful Grandview Heights and see the wonderful human birds. Absolutely free. Lots in the beautiful subdivision selling for $200 and up. L. Pearce Realty Co."

The next day the thrill-seekers scanned the skies. They invested more nickels to pack the streetcars leading towards Grandview Heights, the beautiful subdivision. The cars were packed to suffocation, complained the *Edmonton Bulletin*.

The *Edmonton Capital* reported the events of that Sunday with some bitterness: "Many persons spent a good part of yesterday scanning the heavens for some indication that the Curtiss aviators were making good on their much-announced flight over the river valley to Grandview Heights. Disappointment and stiff necks were all they got for their patient vigil. The brave aviators were all the time comfortably seated in a Pullman car, speeding south."

Yes, Robinson and St. Henri had flown — on the train. Whether it was because they had been threatened with prosecution under the Lord's Day Act, or because the river valley was so deep and awesome, or because they had a premonition that a lot in Grandview Heights wouldn't be worth a damn for fifty years, or because they had already been paid three thousand dollars for their six aerial efforts, or because they wanted the last laugh on the thrifty Edmontonians ... whatever the reason, Robinson and St. Henri had folded their plane like the Arabs and as silently stolen away.

150

Ananias and Sapphira

The Ananias and Sapphira of whom we speak were not the husband-and-wife team of the Bible. They were a team of mules, a team of snow-white mules who plodded the streets of Edmonton in the last years of the nineteenth century. A white mule is a rarity; two white mules are presumably twice as rare; give them names like Ananias and Sapphira and they become unique — not only in Edmonton but in all muledom.

They were owned and named by Donald Ross, the whimsical gentleman who ran Edmonton's first hotel. Donald was a man of many sly little jokes and Ananias and Sapphira were just two. When the mules joined the staff of Donald's Edmonton Hotel, at the foot of McDougall Hill, they joined a team of white horses whom Donald had named Billy and George. They also joined a pair of cats, a red cat and a black-and-white cat who lived around the hotel for seventeen years. The red cat spent many of his seventeen years manoeuvring hotel guests out of their chairs. If all the chairs in the parlour were occupied, the red cat would scratch at the door as though he wanted to go out. And when a kindly guest got up from his chair to open the door for him, the red cat would streak backwards and steal the chair.

Ananias and Sapphira poked their blunt noses into the charmingly informal Edmonton Hotel early in the 1890s. No one can remember for sure how Donald Ross happened to acquire them, or how they happened to be in Edmonton in the first place, but the probability is that they were old railroad mules. The gentlemen who built the railroads of the nineteenth century didn't have the grade-building machinery of today. They tried all kinds of animals in the heavy hauling jobs, and the likelihood is that as the Calgary-Edmonton Railroad approached Edmonton from the south in 1891, Ananias and Sapphira were helping it approach. Completing the cycle of likelihood, Donald Ross probably bought them when the job was done.

Ananias and Sapphira were soon standard scenery around Edmonton. They used to plough the market garden which Donald ran as a hobby. They pulled a wagon through town delivering the produce of this garden, and they also delivered

151

coal, because Donald had a coal mine in the side of McDougall Hill. Most of the time they performed their duties with good grace, but even to the most tractable of mules there come moments when he will not giddap, he will not whoa, he will not gee, neither will he haw. He will do exactly as he damn pleases. Those personality tests which big companies give job-seekers today would sum it up: "A mule does not work best under direction." No big company of today would hire a mule in any capacity, but in the day of Ananias and Sapphira a mule could do a lot of heavy work when he or she felt like it.

Half horse and half donkey, a mule had more power than a horse and more endurance than a donkey; so mules were seldom out of work. Their strong backs were considered fair compensation for their strong heads, their strong hind feet, and their strong bits. Ananias and Sapphira were strong of bit, and because of it their mulelike rebellions against constituted authority were mostly rejections of the command, "Stop!" In moments of rebellion they liked to run away with their driver, and when they took off with a full wagon they left a trail of cabbages or coal. Sapphira, the lady mule, was bigger and stronger than Ananias and was the agitator in most insurrections.

When Ananias lay down and died one day, Sapphira was inconsolable so Donald Ross figured a change of scenery might help her. It was 1898. The gold rush was on. Donald's hotel, and the flats alongside, were full of Klondikers outfitting for the long journey to the Yukon. Donald sold Sapphira to a prospecting party, and when the party left Edmonton on March 8, 1898, there were six men, thirty-five horses and one white mule.

Sapphira was perhaps the only white mule ever to hit the gold rush trail, and perhaps the oldest individual — man or beast. Sapphira was then thirty-five years old, and a mule of thirty-five can be compared to a man of a hundred and fifty. That was the last that Edmonton saw of Sapphira, and Sapphira never saw the Yukon. She died on the way — about one-third of the distance along the way, near Fort St. John. And her passing was half tragic and half comic, a fitting epitaph on the mule itself, one of the most pitiful jokes ever pulled on the animal kingdom. Sapphira's undoing was described by Frank

152

Walker, one of the party and later a member of the first Alberta legislature.

Mr. Walker wrote many years later: "We were moving out from Chimrose Prairie, about 12 or 14 miles above Fort St. John. We just got to the top of a very steep hill, coming up from a creek, when Sapphira's legs gave out. She started down the hill backwards, not like an ordinary animal would do by rolling, but end-over-end like a cartwheel. There was an old rotten tree about halfway down, lying horizontally four or five feet off the ground. This tree was about 15 inches in diameter but Sapphira went through it like a knife, and disappeared among the trees 150 feet below. We hastily went down to investigate and bring up Sapphira's load of flour and beans and riding saddle which was on top. When we got down there we found Sapphira right-side-up-with-care, but wedged in between two trees. The pack saddle was smashed to pieces but the food was first class, not even a tear in it. We had to cut down a tree to get Sapphira out; after which she shook herself, got up and walked to the top of the hill apparently all right. But she died about two weeks later; she had been hurt internally."

So passed Sapphira — builder of railroads, servant of agriculture, pioneer of Edmonton, who in old age set out to find Eldorado. Some might argue that Sapphira was just a mule, and an "ornery" mule at that. And while she may have been an "ornery" mule she was certainly no ordinary mule. We can only hope the singers of Western songs are right: that for Sapphira there was a gold mine in the sky — and that another white mule was waiting there.

The Days of Real Sport

It's possible for a very popular sport to decline. Lacrosse, our one-time national game, has declined so much that now it is played in only a few localities. And two grand sports of Edmonton's early days have disappeared entirely.

One of them is the exciting pastime of Model-T jumping. Model-T jumping was very popular here around 1912. The road to Cooking Lake made the perfect arena for the jumping matches because it ran through the Beaver Hills, straight up the hills and straight down into the dales. There was no trimming of hills and filling of dales, and while you will still find roads of this type in Local Improvement Districts — where there hasn't been much improvement — you won't find enough Model-Ts any more to get up a jumping contest. Never more will a Model-T go rocketing up the back slope of a hill — its four hundred pounds of metal and leather quivering with life — and go sailing over the crest, off into space for an exhilarating flight of six to ten feet. Never more will the officials come out to measure the jump by the tire marks and signal the next contestant to gun his mount and take off into the wild blue yonder. Sad that Model-T jumping should have vanished from the Edmonton scene — as completely as horse racing on the river.

Back in the winters of 1906, '07 and '08, all business would cease on Saturday afternoons so that the crowds could line the riverbank and watch the horses race on the ice — from the site of the Dawson Bridge to the steamer-landing at the Low Level Bridge. A half-mile track on ice. The condition of the track was always "fast." A cutter took the place of the sulky for this winterized sport, the cutter being a fast and fashionable sleigh built light but solid for dashing through the snow (and also being the subject of Currier and Ives prints showing winter in Central Park). The local bloods drove a patent cutter known as the Dan Patch Racer, and they took the sport so seriously that they formed the Edmonton Driving Club, with Bob Tegler, the man who put up the Tegler Building, for their secretary.

The drivers had to bundle themselves in furs for the windy race to the steamer-landing, but to top off their costumes each man wore a silk hat with his colours, so that the crowds could tell at a distance how the race was going. Chaps like Stuart Darroch, Alex Reed, Jim McKinley, Oliver Jackson, Albert Taylor, Bob Manson, and C.J. Robert had their individual colours, and a fine sight they made on a winter's day, rounding the Riverdale bend and thumping up to the landing. When the horses thundered hot and panting past the finish line, they were hustled into a circus tent to cool off. It would have been dangerous to let valuable pacers and trotters cool off in the raw

154

winter wind, so the club had a circus tent at the bridge with a coal stove inside, and each Saturday one of the mines would donate a ton of coal.

Not only did the merchants suspend bargain and sale on Saturday afternoons but they supported the races with handsome prizes, and the horses themselves got most of the prizes — woollen blankets, hobbles, harnesses, horseshoes, oats — everything a horse could hanker for. J.C. Pomerleau (who ran the Richelieu Hotel — now the Grand — and kept a pigeon loft at the back for Continental guests who wanted squab or quail for dinner) donated a gold-and-silver shield for the champion ice-horse of them all. Through the winter the results of all the races would narrow the field to two possible champions, and along in March there would be a match race between the two. One year Stuart Darroch's Bermuda Queen beat out C.J. Robert's Nosy McGregor in an epic race for the Pomerleau Shield, and thereby showed that the ratings of summertime performance, by the Harness Racing Association, didn't mean a thing on ice. According to the association, Bermuda Queen was only a Class-C horse, but she loved a track of ice and crusted snow, a track that made many a Class-A horse too nervous to run.

Winter and summer the harness racers would practise their demanding art on Jasper Avenue. They had permission to race along *West* Jasper — that is, from 104th Street to 116th — every afternoon except Saturday and Sunday. And when West Jasper was in such frightful shape that the boys didn't want to risk their horses on it, the police would let them race up and down First Street. The police felt it was their duty. The boys were preparing for an exciting winter sport, a sport for which Edmonton once suspended all less important activities like bargain and sale, and which, like Model-T jumping, has vanished for ever.

Commissioner Bouillon

Civic government in Edmonton is not what it used to be, nothing at all like what it was in 1911, a year dominated by the feud with Bouillon. A.V. Bouillon was our first utilities commissioner when the great city of Edmonton introduced commission government. The theory was that professional managers should run the city under the direction of an elected council, thus removing personalities and politics from the routine of civic administration. It's ironical that our first attempt to remove personalities generated the hottest exchange of them.

Mr. Bouillon was an able man. He was brought here from Seattle in April 1910 at the astronomical salary of ten thousand dollars a year. He might have been a great success had he not made it plain, with icy hauteur, that the elected representatives of the people were bungling amateurs, and that aldermen should not be voting each other city contracts. While the conflict-of-interest principle is now taken for granted, in 1910 some aldermen thought it bad taste on Bouillon's part to raise the matter at all.

With icy, polished politeness he insisted on running all departments personally and in his way. Before long the fire chief quit. Shortly afterwards the chief of police quit, too. Bouillon had been commissioner only five months when the president of the Municipal Improvement League was moved to describe him from the public platform as a "czar." Now, the czar of Russia was strictly an amateur judged by later Russian improvements in totalitarianism, but back in 1910 about as close as you could come to calling a man a dictator was to call him a czar.

Well, a man who earns such a nickname is not the type to back down. Commissioner Bouillon told the press with steely confidence: "If anyone wants to fight, he will find me ready. Petty politicians are trying to keep the city in a state of perpetual agitation. My ship is in fine condition, the decks cleared for action, and I'm going to sail through the storm in which some of these frail political barks are going to be wrecked."

156

A committee of aldermen, whom Mr. Bouillon presumably included among the petty politicians, had been making a survey of civic departments. And the chairman of the committee was moved to reply to this challenge, also through the press. A bulky statement included these two intriguing viewpoints: "Bouillon has failed to come up to expectations," and "Bouillon has treated the heads of departments like dogs." Commissioner Bouillon then informed the press: "These reports are false, defamatory and libellous. I advise Alderman Mould to retract." Neither Alderman Mould nor Commissioner Bouillon would retract their statements or their horns, and on January 19, 1911, the *Edmonton Journal* carried a headline: WAR BETWEEN BOUILLON AND MOULD IS ON TO A FINISH.

And so it was, and before it was finished the warring factions produced some of the finest comedy ever to lighten the dreary records of civic government. Eight days after the *Edmonton Journal* declared the war, Commissioner Bouillon refused to recommend that the superintendent of the power plant be sent east with a civic party on a buying trip. Two days later Commissioner Bouillon fired the superintendent, and also fired the head of the street railway. Bouillon icily declined to give reasons. When the city councillors protested, he reminded them bluntly that they had nothing to say about it. Hiring and firing was a power they had surrendered to the commissioners. The councillors were annoyed no end by Bouillon's brushoff. They fixed him, though; they refused to let him go on a three-weeks' holiday. And the street railway fixed him too. It sent him a bill for $22.15 for four late streetcars he'd ordered to run after Midnight Mass on Christmas Eve.

Having fixed the annoying Commissioner Bouillon temporarily, the city councillors decided to fix him permanently. On February 21 they fired him by a vote of eight to two. They'd arranged it all beforehand and it was passed through the meeting without any fanfare. Bouillon was fired. That was what the council thought, but Bouillon thought differently, and the city solicitor agreed with him, because you couldn't bring up new business at one meeting unless you'd given notice at the previous meeting. The firing was illegal.

Well, the councillors had missed Bouillon that time but they vowed to get him at a special meeting called just for the

157

purpose. The special meeting was called for February 24. But this meeting, too, turned out to be illegal. One alderman had resigned in protest when Bouillon had been fired illegally the first time, and shortly before the special session he discovered that his resignation was illegal and he was still on the council. So, according to law, he had to receive notice of the meeting twenty-four hours in advance. They hadn't sent him a notice because they thought he was off the council. Therefore the special meeting was illegal. At this second failure, a citizen named John Kelly wrote to the *Bulletin* and said, "As one of the heaviest taxpayers of the city I suggest that the members of the city council all resign, and turn over the affairs of the city to the Edmonton high school boys." The *Bulletin* ran Mr. Kelly's letter up under the front-page headline.

Foiled again, the city council decided to have a big public meeting and let the public demand Mr. Bouillon's scalp. The meeting was called for 8 P.M., February 27, in the old McDougall Church on 101st Street. Meanwhile the Edmonton Board of Trade came out solidly in support of Bouillon. So did the *Journal* and the *Bulletin,* and only the *Edmonton Capital* insisted that Bouillon must go. Two hours before the big public meeting, something strange happened. The building inspector suddenly condemned McDougall Church as a place unfit for public gatherings, and the crowd of citizens milling around the church was informed that the meeting had been moved to the Bijou Theatre. Two of the three papers said that when the mob got to the Bijou, it was well packed with council supporters.

The big meeting appeared to be a victory for the city council, a clarion call for Bouillon to resign. The councillors were all set to bounce Bouillon when they were stopped by a Supreme Court injunction. Yes, Charles Gallagher of our town had gone to Chief Justice Harvey and got an injunction restraining the council from firing Bouillon without "showing cause" in Supreme Court. The Chief Justice opined that Commissioner Bouillon was protected by the city charter. Coises! Foiled again!

For days and weeks legal battling went on in court, while less and less work got done in civic departments. Finally, all the arguments were sent to Mr. Justice Stuart in Calgary for a final decision. Edmonton waited tensely. On Thursday, April 2, Mr.

Justice Stuart advised that he had sent his decision by express and it would be in Edmonton the next day. However, it didn't arrive the next day; it didn't arrive in the Edmonton court house until Saturday. And it did look as if someone had intercepted it en route for a quick peek. The verdict was that Commissioner Bouillon could not be fired without a public trial. The council was stuck with Bouillon. Worse still, the aldermen who'd voted to fire him were also stuck with the bill; all the costs of the drawn-out proceedings were charged to them personally. Coises! Foiled again!

Commissioner Bouillon was riding high. When he asked for money to buy a new power plant generator, he refused sharply to give the council any details or any report on power plant equipment. The councillors tried a new tack. They hired two more commissioners to outvote Bouillon on the commission board. So, instead of one less commissioner, there were now two more. Then they decided to hire a "competent engineer" to advise them on big purchases like power plant equipment. The engineer was an English chap, and he seemed very competent indeed, until it was found that his chief engineering experience had been installing toilets at the Ponoka Mental Hospital.

All this time the investigating committee was rounding up evidence against the immovable object, A.V. Bouillon. The city auditor was fighting with Bouillon over the new centralized accounting system. The waterworks superintendent was blaming the muddy taste of the water on Bouillon. Bouillon was about to walk the plank at last, when the Supreme Court threw everything into a cocked hat once again. At the request of an Edmonton taxpayer, F. Fraser Tims, the Supreme Court issued an injunction restraining four members of the council from voting on any new motion to oust Bouillon. This was because of rude things they'd said about him. Well, there were only ten aldermen on the council. Seven votes were needed to fire a commissioner, and if four aldermen couldn't vote, that left only six. The city council of the great city of Edmonton was foiled again.

But this was the last time. The injunctions were lifted finally. Bouillon was tried. In seeking to divorce themselves from the domineering Mr. Bouillon, the civic department heads pleaded the same reason used by Hollywood stars: they charged him with mental cruelty and incompatibility. In the last act of our comic opera of 1911, A.V. Bouillon was fired, fired at last from his commissioner's job which paid ten thousand dollars a year. And was A.V. Bouillon downhearted? Well, a month later, he was managing a big shipyard in Seattle — at forty thousand a year.

By-law 434

The processes by which people of the democratic persuasion govern themselves are changed from time to time. Edmonton is surely the only city in the democratic world that made a profound change in the process because a Chinese restaurant-man hit a customer over the head with a bottle. The incident spurred a change back to commission government. In 1910 and 1911 the city had given this form of administration a try, but the clashing personalities of the aldermen and Commissioner Bouillon had led to such a commotion that the city council took back control of all civic departments into their own hands.

The bottle that changed the course of history was swung on the night of July 10, 1912, at the conclusion of a day that was supposed to be one of good will and celebration, a day on which Edmonton and Strathcona marked their amalgamation with a giant sports meet at the South Side Athletic Grounds. There were five thousand people at the sports, better than ten percent of the combined cities. There was lots of good will right enough, but the old rivalry was still there. In the evening, as the crowds surged homeward, there was a fight in a Chinese café on Whyte Avenue. The Chinese gentleman who ran the café sought to break up the fight by hitting the aggressor over the head with a bottle. Just at that moment, Detective-Sergeant Ernie Seymour walked into the café. He saw the bottle swing. He pronounced the Chinese gentleman to be under arrest and began hustling him off to the police station. It was the old station on 83rd Avenue, the one with the white globe light.

A crowd of indignant citizens followed Seymour and his

prisoner, demanding that their Chinese friend be released. Fred Richards, citizen of credit and renown and conductor of the old Strathcona Town Band, appointed himself leader of the opposition. At the door of the station, Fred blocked the way and demanded that Ernie Seymour let the man go. Ernie grabbed Fred by the throat and tried to shove him out of the way. Constables Bob Unruh and Bob Scott joined the fray, swept the crowd back, pulled the Chinese chap inside and shut the station door.

The door might be closed, but the issue was not. The crowd vowed that this was not the end of the affair, and how right they were. The south side had its men on the amalgamated city council. Alderman Judge Tipton carried the case to the next meeting. Alderman Tipton introduced a motion that Police Chief Lancey be instructed to fire Seymour, Scott and Unruh. The council agreed, to a man, and it wasn't often that the council agreed on anything to a man. But Chief Lancey disagreed. To heck with the city council, he said in effect. He, Lancey, was chief. Seymour, Scott and Unruh would remain on the force. The chief was then advised that Fred Richards had laid a charge against Ernie Seymour, alleging assault causing bodily harm. Well, all right, Seymour could be suspended until the case came to court, but Scott and Unruh were still on the force.

The stout-hearted men of the city council were singed to the eyebrows by this defiance. Were they mad! Judge Tipton was the maddest. He got up and asked to know who was running the city. Had the council any authority or was it all held by the superintendent of some department?

Then the discussion turned to the personal merits of Ernie Seymour. Alderman MacDonald didn't think the council ought to discuss Ernie when the question was before the courts. Alderman Fighting Joe Clarke said MacDonald had no right to suggest that, because MacDonald's legal firm was representing Seymour. Then Alderman MacDonald said he had no more use for Seymour than a snake in the grass, and if he were chief of police he'd fire Seymour in a minute, but in the meantime he should not be condemned without a fair trial. Joe Clarke tried to say something, and Alderman MacDonald said he didn't care to pay any attention to Alderman Clarke: Joe Clarke didn't know any law, he never had any cases. Then Joe Clarke said, if he took the kind of cases Alderman MacDonald did, his office would be full all the time. That was the way they ran city governments in 1912. (In Prince Albert that same year the boys fell to fisticuffing each other in the council chamber, and a riot was averted only by the city solicitor, who had the presence of mind to shut off the lights.)

A week later Ernie Seymour's case came up in the south side court, and he was found not guilty of assaulting Fred Richards. Ernie then immediately resigned from the police force, announced that he was going to sue certain aldermen, and that he would lay a counter-charge against Fred Richards, of obstructing a police officer in the discharge of his duties. Fred Richards came to trial a few days later and was found not guilty of obstructing. But everyone was still very annoyed at everyone else, and Bob Scott and Bob Unruh were still on the force.

At this point the historic row might have petered out, but in this simmering situation, on the early morning of August 16, 1912, Chief Lancey ordered a raid on the Afro-Canadian Progressive Association. The association had its clubrooms on 96th Street in a building now known as the Moon Rooms, and on that busy morning the police wagon made nine trips — seven trips with fifty-nine club members and two trips with the confiscated furnishings of the place. The furnishings included dozens and dozens of bottles, packs and packs of cards, and stacks and stacks of poker chips. The cops even took the pictures off the walls, and one was a picture of Charlie Cross, Alberta's attorney general. Charlie, of course, was a Liberal, and the stoutly Conservative *Edmonton Journal* made a pious point of the fact that there was a picture of a Liberal in a gambling den. Very sinister.

While the fifty-nine unfortunates were being booked in and bailed out at the police station, along came Alderman Gus May. Gus possessed one of the stoutest of the stout hearts. He was one of the "ginger group" in city politics, a group that included the three Joes — Clarke, Driscoll and Adair. The editorial voice of the ginger group was *Town Topics,* a throwaway sheet written at the compositor's rack by Joe Adair. From this distance, there would appear slight necessity for any more ginger in city politics, but Gus and the three Joes saw their duty and they did it.

Gus saw the poor unfortunates being brought in and demanded, in his best platform manner, to know why the police should raid the Afro-Canadian Progressive Association when fifty-four worse places were allowed to flourish. Chief Lancey demanded to know the addresses of the fifty-four places Gus was referring to. Gus told Lancey in his best platform manner that the St. Regis Hotel was one of them. And then the fat was in the fire. The St. Regis was run by the chief's sister. Chief Lancey called for his lawyer and plastered three slander suits on Gus: ten thousand dollars for himself, ten thousand for his sister, and ten thousand for the hotel, thirty thousand dollars' worth of slander altogether.

Now it happened that the chief's lawyers were partners of Alderman Jim MacDonald. Jim's firm started proceedings against Gus on August 18, and on the night of August 21, sitting beside each other at a meeting of the city council, were Alderman Jim MacDonald and Alderman Gus May. A chap with very limited gifts of prophecy could have predicted that there would be fireworks before the night was out. The commissioners that night recommended that there be an investigation of Edmonton's morality and the efficiency of the police department in uplifting the moral tone of the city. Mayor Armstrong commented that aldermen who went barging into the police station in the middle of the night were certainly not helping the police.

Then Alderman MacDonald, sitting alongside Gus, put in his lawyer's two cents' worth. Jim said it would be improper to proceed with any investigation of the police and civic morality while one of the aldermen was being sued for his remarks about the way the police were enforcing morality. Jim said the investigation was needed and Gus ought to be ashamed of himself for getting sued and delaying the investigation. Gus bellowed in Jim's ear, "Shut up!" Jim turned in surprise and said, "You shut up!" Gus shouted back, "You shut up!" Jim said, "You shut up, or come outside for five minutes and I'll shut you up like a jack-knife." Now, that was the way to run a city in 1912. The boys bellowed back and forth at each other until the mayor stepped in and demanded, in parliamentary language, that they both shut up. Which they did, for the rest of the night anyway.

The next day there were editorials in all three papers, lamenting the constant delays in city business because someone was always being sued in connection with it, and it was not proper to discuss anything when it was before the courts.

That was August 22. On the twenty-third, Chief Lancey announced that he was quitting. He was tired of aldermen like Gus meddling in the conduct of the police department. The same day, Gus had a conference with his lawyers and they advised him he'd better make a public apology to the chief and get the suits dropped. Gus issued a public retraction, but it was more a legal apology than an expression of sorrow; in fact, if you didn't know it was supposed to be an apology, you'd hardly recognize it as one.

The suits against Gus were dropped, and the city commissioners announced that the investigation of the police and public morality could proceed, and would Chief Lancey please come back and continue his fine work as police chief? But Lancey said an investigation would be even worse meddling than having Gus May barging into the station in the middle of the night. No, to heck with it. Lancey didn't have to take it. He was through.

As the chief prepared to leave town, Gus figured the city council could save itself a lot of time and grief by divorcing itself from control of the police force and several other civic departments — by transferring control from the city council to the city commissioners. He hastily brought in a by-law to that effect, stating that control of the police force, the city assessor's department, the treasury department, the city clerk, the medical health officer, the claims adjuster, and the industrial commissioner, be transferred from the city council to the city commissioners. It was By-law no. 434, introduced and passed, all on the night of August 26, 1912; and the principle remains in force to this day.

The McLeod Building

If Edmonton should ever have the misfortune to be hit by a super-bomb, and if only one building should be left standing, it's a good bet that it would be the McLeod Building. This last part, anyway, would please Kenny McLeod but it would not surprise him, because Kenny built it to last and to be a monument to himself and to his faith in Edmonton as a great city. Kenny McLeod came to Edmonton in 1881, when it was a frontier village set in the woods. All his ambitions for himself and Edmonton were summed up in the McLeod Building.

Kenny was a Bruce County Scotsman, Bruce being a county in Ontario which, in Kenny's day, produced Scots indistinguishable from the Old Country variety. He was a big man, a fine sturdy fellow with a florid, handsome face, a bristling moustache, rather penetrating eyes, and a love of work for its own sake.

Kenny began his career as a carpenter. He came out to Winnipeg in 1879, and in 1881 arrived in Edmonton, having walked all the way with a procession of three Red River carts. He wanted a place to build a house and traded a sack of flour to Frank Oliver for a lot where the Edmonton Plaza stands today. He built himself a house there, and he could look across 100th Street at the poplar thicket, where, thirty years later, he would start the McLeod Building. In his later years Kenny built a fine red-brick mansion, with pillars and a sweeping verandah. It was on 103rd Avenue where the east wing of the City Hall stands today. It faced south, and Kenny could sit in his living room and spend contented hours gazing across the intervening blocks at his favourite sight: the McLeod Building.

It was about 1910 that he decided to build it. By that time Kenny had made a fortune at his contracting and real estate. He went up and down the west coast, from Vancouver to San Diego, looking at buildings, looking for one of quiet distinction that he could take as a model for the McLeod Building. He found it in downtown Spokane, the Polson Building. Kenny hired J.K. Dow, the Spokane architect who'd designed the Polson Building, to design him a duplicate. He also hired the Spokane contractors on the Polson job: Olsen and Johnson. They came to Edmonton to put up his building.

But as soon as he got them here, Kenny began improving the original. He wanted his monument to be "built strong." That was one of his favourite words: strong. Kenny had no formal training in the art of construction; he was a self-made man professionally, and he laid great stress on a thing being "built strong." Strong enough to suit Kenny, meant as strong as it could possibly be made. That's why the windows in the transoms of the McLeod Building were made of plate glass, a quarter of an inch thick. And the transoms were just a final finishing touch. Kenny started with the framework. First he had Mr. Dow draw the steel plans. "That's fine," said Kenny. "Now I want fifty percent more steel than that." So the sizes of the beams were increased, and twelve hundred tons of steel were required. He ordered the concrete footings to be eleven feet square, enough for a fifty-storey building.

Each floor was poured as a separate slab of concrete, eight inches thick. Kenny personally inspected each wheelbarrow of concrete that went into the building. There were three mixers at work along the west wall, and Kenny sat in a chair all day, not stirring away even for lunch (his lunch was brought to him) to make sure that every batch was exactly the right blend of water, air, sand, gravel and cement. If it wasn't, well — "Ye're not puttin' that in my building laddie. Run it through again." When the concrete was all in and dry, Kenny used a carpenter's test to check the results. He ordered the architect, Mr. Dow, to make an exact hairline measurement of the distance from floor to ceiling in one room on the ground floor. Mr. Dow did so. Then Kenny piled all the cast-iron radiators for the entire building into that one room. Tons and tons of cast-iron radiators. And Mr. Dow measured again the distance from floor to ceiling. It had not increased by a hair. That's what Kenny McLeod meant by strong.

His building had another distinction: it was the first in Edmonton to be wired with conduit. The marble, which was imported from Italy, was installed by some gentlemen imported from Winnipeg, and by Kenny's orders it was all suspended from the floor above. As Christmas of 1914 approached, the marble-hangers were working late into the night trying to finish in time to be home for Christmas. They were hanging the last few slabs in the ceiling of the main lobby

— stringing yards and yards of copper wire around quarter-inch steel rods — when Kenny suddenly stopped the work. "That's not strong enough," he announced firmly. "I want fifty percent more wire." So all the ceiling slabs had to come down again and the marble-hangers spent Christmas in Edmonton. When the building opened for business in January 1915, it had been completed to Kenny's satisfaction in every detail.

But we've moved a little ahead of our story here. From the end of construction we must double back to the beginning, which was in August 1912. When Kenny bought the corner of 100th Street and 101A Avenue, he acquired a basement from the previous owner. The previous owner was a railroad conductor — name, alas, now forgotten — who had started to build a hotel in the days of optimism. The conductor had actually swung enough money to buy the corner and dig the basement before his money ran out. Someone then put a tent over the pit and made it an ice-cream parlour called The Sugar Bowl. And then Kenny McLeod bought it. The man who installed the machinery for the building job was Ted Voss, an English-trained engineer who stayed on at the block for thirty-five years afterwards as chief engineer. To Mr. Voss we are indebted for this story.

The steel went up with a great rush in 1912. By the end of that year Kenny had spent $400,000, all he had; but he was still $280,000 short. The skeleton stood deserted for a whole year while Kenny raised the rest. The insurance companies were willing to lend it, but they insisted that he take the whole amount at once and start paying interest at once. Kenny was a canny Scot who would not accept less than a dollar-ten in exchange for a dollar of his own. "Not on your life, laddie." He hit up the City Sinking Fund Board for a loan of $280,000. Sam Smith and G.R.F. Kirkpatrick were on the board at the time. They liked Kenny's ideas, gave him the money, and in short order the cement and the yellow terrazzo tiles and cornices were flying. And the McLeod Building was ready for business in January 1915.

Ah yes, January 1915. By the time the McLeod Building was ready for business, there wasn't any. The boom that had made the building possible had gone flat, and half the offices stood empty. For nearly ten years Kenny McLeod was unable to pay off his loan to the Sinking Fund Board. City treasurer, Frank Barnhouse, predicted on several occasions that the city would soon be taking the McLeod Building for a city hall. Kenny's reactions are not recorded; perhaps that's just as well. Anyway, by 1924 the building was bursting with tenants; the rent money was coming in and Kenny had the satisfaction of paying off the loan and getting undisputed control of his own beautiful building.

In so doing, he disproved a local maxim that Edmonton old-timers always lost their investments. His building also disproved another maxim of wider circulation: that lightning never strikes twice. Lightning has struck twice on the northwest corner of the building and each time it has knocked off the cornice. The first time, Kenny had it replaced with a custom-cut cornice, exactly matching the blasted piece. But it's said that when Kenny got the bill he jumped as high as the building — and that would be 109 feet, or 159 feet if you count the flagpole. So the next time it happened, he had Ted Ledyard, the local stone-cutter, carve a replacement out of grey stone.

You can see that grey-stone cornice to this day. And if you walk over by the City Hall — towards the east side — you can see Kenny McLeod's favourite view of his building, as he used to see it, sitting in the front parlour of his home, in his twilight years.

How to Sell Real Estate to Frank Oliver

As you read this, somewhere in Edmonton a real estate deal is being made. Like many things which were *risqué* in 1915, real estate is now respectable. For example, when the Macdonald Hotel opened in 1915 it was *risqué* for a lady to smoke in the lobby, and a lady who did smoke was shown the hotel's handsome oak doors. In that year, real estate had fallen on evil days, and similarly a cigarette was thought to be the badge of a lady who had fallen on evil days. But both are now respectable,

168

so in honour of the real estate deal that's being made as you read this, let's hark back to Edmonton's real estate deal number one.

It bears the date 1880, when Frank Oliver bought a downtown lot from Malcolm McLeod for twenty-five dollars. There was no cash involved in the deal because there was little money here at the time, but Malcolm McLeod got twenty-five dollars' worth of job-printing from Frank's *Bulletin* printing press. Frank printed our first newspaper in the building he put on the lot, the building you can now see down in Walterdale by John Walter's house. The lot, of course, is still in its original location. It's on the south side of Jasper, looking up 99th Street.

Many years after his historic twenty-five-dollar deal, the Honourable Frank was asked just how he had happened to make it. With his deep, slow laugh he explained that he had thought the transcontinental railroad was going to pass through Edmonton and he wanted to be sure to have some property of his own before the railroad came. "In this endeavour," he said, "I was successful beyond the expectation of my wildest dreams. It was twenty-five years before a transcontinental railroad reached Edmonton."

Perhaps this is why Frank exercised so much caution at the turn of the century, when he bought the southeast corner of 100th Avenue and 103rd Street. Frank built a brick house there, which he occupied during his joint career as editor of the *Edmonton Bulletin* and minister of the Interior in the federal government. And when Alberta became a province in 1905, he turned his house over to the lieutenant-governor to be the first Government House. The public works building which now stands on the site is called the Oliver Building, as a memorial to the fact that Frank Oliver once bought real estate there. This memorial, however, cannot inform the passer-by that, in spite of his caution, Frank bought twice as much real estate as he intended. Yes, the real estate man who sold the Honourable Frank the corner property thought he should also buy the adjoining lot. The Honourable Frank didn't think so, and he firmly declined all suggestions to that end. He built his house, rejecting suggestion after suggestion.

Seeing that Oliver could not be taken by frontal assault, the real estate man figured he might be taken by strategy. So he went into conference and discussed the strategy with a Chinese gentleman who happened to be a friend of his. Early the next morning the Chinese gentleman appeared on the vacant lot next to the Olivers' and began going over it very carefully with a measuring tape. All day long he measured and surveyed and plotted. He stood for long periods, immersed in inscrutable oriental thought. He viewed the property from this aspect, now that. The Oliver family were, naturally, more than a little curious about all this. But to all inquiries, the Chinese gentleman smiled broadly and indicated he could not speak English. The next morning he was back, and this time he had brought a friend, another Chinese. They spent the day as before: measuring, surveying, conferring; measuring, surveying, conferring.

Finally, Frank Oliver could contain his curiosity no further. He went out himself to discover what all this was about. The second Chinese, like the first, indicated that he could not understand English. But, smiling broadly, he talked rapidly in his own language, tossing in at intervals the one English word: "laundry." Laundry? Laundry? The sales resistance of the Honourable Frank Oliver, statesman and newspaper publisher, collapsed at the sound of that word.

The real estate man feigned delighted surprise when Frank rushed into his office twenty minutes later and insisted on buying the lot right away.

The Snubbing of Reginald Crowder

The snubbing of Reginald Crowder represented Edmonton society of 1902. And Reggie's reaction to it represented social protest. Reggie was welcomed by Edmonton society when he first appeared on the scene in 1901. Some twenty-two summers had passed over his aristocratic English head, he had easy manners that made him an asset to a garden party, and at the same time he was at ease shooting or playing poker with the boys. A rare bird in the society of 1902, Reggie was doted on by the ladies, and their husbands liked him too.

Apparently the one person who didn't care for Reggie was his pater. The pater had weighed Reggie's virtues against his shortcomings and decided that he was fit only to join that company of exiles known as "remittance men." So Reggie was dispatched to Canada with the assurance of a quarterly remittance as long as he stayed here. And Reggie was a complete remittance man, right down to the last shilling of his quarterly bank draft. Unfortunately, like many in his company, Reggie used to come to the last shilling long before the next remittance was due. And early in the winter of 1902 the action he was forced to take, because of his financial crisis, led to the incident known to turn-of-the-century society as The Snubbing of Reginald Crowder.

With the last shilling gone and no remittance due for six weeks, Reggie accepted a position in a place where much of his last remittance had gone. He accepted a position as bartender. Reggie's pride was hurt but he was not a man to rail at the inevitable, and his gentlemen friends thought even better of him for standing on his own two feet. (Standing on your own two feet was regarded almost as a gymnastic achievement in 1902.) So the men thought more of Reggie than ever, but not so the ladies, who were ever the rulers of society. A number of the elite objected vigorously to men who dispensed liquor, especially to their husbands. Reggie suffered instant social downfall and met the stony stare of rejection from ladies who had only a short time ago pressed on him invitations to tea.

The Snubbing of Reginald Crowder became a matter of some civic importance in the town of four thousand people. It even became the occasion of editorial comment in the *Strathcona Plaindealer,* and although the *Plaindealer* said it was a "tempest in a teapot," teapots were pretty important in 1902 society. The tempest reached its full fury over the invitation list for the Bankers' Ball. The Bankers' Ball was a highlight of the winter season. Bank men were rated socially with military officers and, like military officers, they were expected to maintain a status out of keeping with their pay. However unfair these social demands were, a banker's promotion often depended on how he met them, so it's easy to see why the Bankers' Ball should be a social event of first magnitude.

Early in January the usual invitation committee was set up

to decide who was worthy to come to the Bankers' Ball. The committee was dominated by ladies, and when the name of Reginald Crowder, Esquire, was proposed for the list, it was promptly struck off by a majority vote of the ladies. The men were livid, and the complete staff of one bank threatened to boycott the ball if Reggie was not reinstated.

Reggie's upbringing made the fuss abhorrent to him and he'd as soon have chucked the whole thing, but pride kept driving him in alternate directions. One moment, his English public-school pride would tell him he couldn't possibly go, and then it would tell him that he couldn't possibly stay away. Finally, he decided that he must go, but he must not go meekly. He must show his tormentors the ultimate in contempt — and yet must not offend the many good chaps who were his buddies. He thought of a way.

He appeared at the ball in the finest of Bond Street formal attire. His vest was dazzling white. His tie was white. His gloves were white. But not his partner. Reggie's partner was an Indian girl. The attitude of white society towards the Indian population was then at its least enlightened, and the fact that Reggie's partner was a real smasher and the most vivacious dancer did not make her any more acceptable to Edmonton's establishment.

The opening set of Lancers was called and Reggie's enthusiasm rose to a soaring pitch. He fairly pranced through the set numbers with his Indian lady. They were the centre of attraction in the Lancers and in every dance that followed. The husbands of Edmonton's society leaders fought to dance with Reggie's girl. The Bankers' Ball was a disaster.

The last heard about Reginald Crowder was his departure for Calgary, where he hoped to find a more accommodating climate in which to spend his next remittance.

The Toonerville Trolley

There is a contemporary idea that rock'n'roll is a contemporary idea. But it is not so. We had rock'n'roll in Edmonton as early as 1912, from the very first time the McKernan Lake streetcar rolled away from Whyte Avenue and 104th Street, and rocked out along 76th Avenue to its woodland terminus at 118th Street. In good years this one-track one-car line would lose five thousand dollars. In average years it would lose ten thousand. And after thirty-five years of effort, in August 1947, the Edmonton Transit System succeeded in getting rid of the McKernan Lake streetcar. The transit system has been richer without it, but Edmonton has been poorer.

There was, from the very beginning, no reason for the McKernan Lake line. That was one of the charms of the thing. It just happened that when the boys were drawing up the agreement to amalgamate Edmonton and Strathcona, some of the boys from Strathcona slipped the streetcar into the agreement, and not a single item of the agreement could be changed without a plebiscite. The plebiscite had to be taken separately on each side of the river, and any change would have required a two-thirds approval on each side. With this arrangement, there was obviously no more hope of getting rid of the McKernan Lake streetcar than there was hope of making the thing pay. But the people who ran the street railway found the Toonerville Trolley such a burden that they were driven to take this desperate chance in 1931. They put it to a vote on November 11.

The defenders of the Toonerville Trolley were few, but they rose to defend it with such courage, cunning and orotund prose, that the rascally attempt to "do in" the streetcar met the defeat it deserved. Never in the history of political conflict has so much been owed by so many to so few. But before we examine their campaign to save this curiosity of street railroading, let us examine the proposition: "Was the thing worth saving?"

There was a good deal of grief attached to its operation, especially at night. As you may remember, the line just ended, for no more apparent reason than it started, at 118th Street and

76th Avenue. There was no Y-switch at the end of the line. The motorman would change trolleys, move his crank to the other end of the car and start back towards civilization. At night, the motorman's chief difficulty was seeing the end of the line. The headlight on the car made but little impression on the darkness of the forest. On the last mile there was scarcely a landmark to give the motorman his bearings. Some genius at the car barns figured out a way to hang a light from the end of the trolley wire. But this light was either blowing out from an overcharge of current, or was being shot out by boys playing hooky to shoot rabbits in the woods. So it was a light that failed, often.

As a safety check, Mr. Owen, who had a house a half-block from the end of the line, would leave his porch light burning after dark, and when the car bucketed past the porch light the motorman would shut off the power and glide to a stop. One night, however, Mr. Owen went to bed and turned the light off. The Toonerville raced right off the end of the line at full throttle and crashed to a stop thirty feet beyond in the bush. A crew from the barns was engaged all the next morning, hauling it back to its track with a block and tackle. Another night, when fog hung low over the woods and fields of southwest Edmonton and visibility hung suspended in the ice crystals, Dr. Will Alexander of the University of Alberta brought a barn lantern from his house at the end of the line and stood in the open doorway of the streetcar, holding the lantern forward to give the motorman some view of the track ahead. Was this worth fighting for?

Then there were all the track troubles. In 1912 the tracks had been laid on the prairie, without benefit of gravel ballast, and when the prairie was spongy with spring, the rock'n'roll motion of the car would gradually force the rails apart until the car would drop down between them. At full throttle, this drop of only four inches could be a mighty one indeed, and the boys would ride out with a block and tackle, and boost the car onto the rails again. One time they had to send back to the barns for a railroad tie because they couldn't find a tie in the swampy roadbed on which to anchor the block and tackle. Was this worth fighting for?

Once, in the spring of 1928, the roadbed dissolved so com-

174

pletely that the car could not run beyond 109th Street. In the wetness of that spring, McKernan's old lake emerged from its hollow at 111th Street just south of 76th Avenue, and the tracks were awash. After this, Bill Cunningham, superintendent of the street railway, decided he would have to build a gravel roadbed. And since he could not dispense with the line, he would at least get some use out of it by turning it north at 112th Street and running it to the back door of the university. So gravel was ordered, and Bill went away on a trip, intending to be back in time to tell the boys to turn north at 112th Street. But the weather was good, and the boys laid gravel so quickly that by the time Bill returned they had gravelled the original roadbed right to 118th Street. Ah well, the best laid plans of mice and men gang aft agley. That's what Robbie Burns said, and that's what Bob Chambers used to say, too, because Burns had said it. Bob was the literary Scot among the skippers of our own Toonerville Trolley. He drove the car to its full breath-taking limit to give himself more time for Robbie Burns at the woodland terminal. "A man's a man for a' that," he would say to his passengers. "Isn't that the grand stuff, now?" Then there was Harry Hutton, and poor Alec Wilson. Alec was killed one night when the trolley wire blew down in a storm and crossed a high-tension wire. And then there were the memories: of winter rides to go skating at McKernan's Lake; and summer rides to picnics at Whitemud Creek. Was all this worth fighting for?

There was, though you would scarcely believe it, a man in our town who didn't think so. That was Commissioner C.J. Yorath. Commissioner Yorath could not lose sight of the fact that the Toonerville Trolley was losing ten thousand dollars a year. Every month, along in the early 1920s, he would advise the city council how much the line had lost in the month just concluded. So a small band of gentlemen, who thought the Toonerville Trolley should be preserved, embarked on their campaign to save it. These gentlemen had intense personal interest in the matter. They were the university professors who lived in a pleasant rustic little colony at the far end of the line. If the wonderful Car Number One should cease to run on the outer reaches of 76th Avenue, these gentlemen would be stranded. So they collected a war chest among themselves, bought a great many dollars' worth of streetcar tickets and distributed them among people closer in, who never bothered to ride the car. These people were glad to ride a few blocks for nothing. The next month, an alderman asked Commissioner Yorath how the Toonerville was doing. "Well," said the Commissioner, "I've got to admit it improved in the last month, though I can't for the life of me explain it."

Commissioner Yorath left the service of the city shortly after that to become general manager of the new Gas Company, but others stepped forward to advocate the overthrow of the Toonerville Trolley. In the fall of 1931 they hatched a plot to do away with the streetcar and replace it with a bus, which would follow a more realistic route than the streetcar. They had it put on the ballot for the civic election, and they expected to get away with it using arguments like "the line is losing ten thousand dollars a year," and "nobody lives out there, anyway."

The professors at the end of the line, the "few" to whom we referred earlier, realized there was no point in debating the deficit. So they decided to contest the assertion that they were so few. They bombarded the editor of the *Journal* with letters suggesting that there were all sorts of people at the end of the line. Tom Ferrier, assistant superintendent of the street railway, had made a survey and reported finding only fourteen people out there, either professors or their families. The *Journal,* wishing to be rigidly fair, made an independent survey and discovered twenty-eight. But that was not enough. The professors surveyed the population and reported thirty-four people, in a letter to the editor. The next day two more people were discovered, for a grand total of thirty-six, and that was cause for another letter to the editor. Then someone found a shack along the Whitemud Road in which six people were living, for an even grander total of forty-two. Dr. Alexander made an exhaustive estimate of fifty-nine, and that was cause for another letter to the editor. If the plebiscite hadn't come on so quickly, they might have run the population up into the thousands.

The editor of the *Journal* tried to counter the letters with editorials, but the editorials only helped to publicize the campaign for preservation. The professors were classical scholars, accustomed to making symbols out of things, and

176

they managed to make some surprising things out of the Toonerville Trolley. They wrote some stirring stuff. Dr. Broadus wrote about fundamental human rights. Mrs. Broadus wrote. So did some gentlemen with Latin names. And Dr. Alexander turned his fine classical style to implications of sinister plots at city hall. He wrote about the steam-roller tactics at city hall, the junta at city hall, the dictators at city hall, the cabal at city hall. The people of the district, whose numbers were increasing with every survey, demanded transportation in a streetcar; a streetcar, not "a cold, cramped, rattly, smelly, never-to-be-depended-upon, sardine-can bus." This made the McKernan Lake streetcar sound like the greatest advance in transportation since the invention of the wheel. And even the editor of the *Journal* had to admit that the Toonerville was never cramped.

Planning their campaign, the professors realized that north side voters would probably vote for the extinction of the car. But south side voters would have to vote for extinction too. So they would defeat the northside vote by winning the south side. They picked the six key polls on the south side, worked hard, wrote hard, had leaflets printed, phoned people and buttonholed people, and when the votes were counted on the night of November 11, 1931, old Strathcona had spiked handsomely the efforts to overthrow the Toonerville Trolley. Although 2,188 said, "Away with it," 3,081 said, "Let it run." So it ran happily for another sixteen years, losing ten thousand dollars a year in the jolliest fashion imaginable. When enough people had built homes in southwest Edmonton to make it a paying proposition, it was abolished at last.

Mr. Garside, the legal adviser of the City of Edmonton, told the city council that two bus lines in the area would certainly be construed as the equal of one single-track streetcar line, that this would satisfy the requirement of the amalgamation agreement that there be service maintained in perpetuity, and that since the bus was now universally accepted as a substitute for the streetcar, it would not be necessary to hold another plebiscite. The city council acted on this advice. And while Mr. Garside was held in the highest personal and professional regard, we must disagree with his contention that two bus lines are the equal of the McKernan Lake streetcar. We'll never again see the equal of the Toonerville Trolley.

Raymer the Jeweller

Emmanuel Raymer walked a long way to open Edmonton's first jewellery store, all the way from Winnipeg, over plains which had been rent by the North-West Rebellion only one spring earlier. It was the first jewellery store in Edmonton, and also in Alberta. It was at Jasper and 99th Street, on the northeast corner, in a store that had been built as a trading post by old John Sinclair and ended its career in the 1950s as the Jasper Food Basket. When Raymer set up his stock there in the spring of 1886 he was at the west end of Jasper Avenue, then called Main Street. The trail was not cleared west of Raymer's. It angled off to the top of the cliff and followed the cliff to the fort.

At that time there were perhaps six hundred people in Edmonton, putting the most optimistic face on it, and as winter approached there was often anxiety about whether there would be enough food. But the six hundred were trying to build a civilization in the wilderness — a civilization, not just a town — so it was just as important to them to have a jewellery store as to have a grist mill.

Raymer's was a veritable lighthouse of civilization in the poplar jungle. Women, who wondered how on earth they had ever let their husbands talk them into leaving Toronto, could stroll by Raymer's and find distraction in the windows. When school was out, the kids would stop by Raymer's to see what he'd put in the window that day. When Indians and other citizens of the woods were in town, they also made it a point to view Raymer's window.

Raymer's was a local attraction, and Raymer was a local booster. Although he imported merchandise, he made things with local material. He made wedding rings out of something he called Saskatchewan gold — gold panned from the river down below the town. He also made diamond rings with something called Saskatchewan diamonds. He got these out of the river, too. He used to pick up crystal quartz in the gravel, and if a real diamond was beyond a young man's means, he and his bride could start out quite satisfactorily with one of . Emmanuel Raymer's Saskatchewan diamonds.

Raymer himself did not marry. Not while he was in Edmonton. With a blend of luck and determination he managed to remain a bachelor, and an exuberantly carefree one, the life of many a party. He was also Edmonton's leading tenor. He sang in the Methodist church choir. He was the tenor lead in the cantata, *The Rose Maiden,* the first musical production of any pretence put on here; that was in 1894. He was often to be found across the street from his store, in Scott Robertson's house, gathering with other singers around Edmonton's first piano. And he was forever bursting into song on his bicycle. When bicycles were the newest sensation and the "in" thing was to go on a picnic by bicycle, Raymer could keep the crowd pedalling at a steady pace by singing all the way, and never getting short of wind.

Raymer was popular with the ladies, but he was popular with the menfolk too. He was one of the founders of the Edmonton Club, in 1899, and the club had some of its first meetings in the room above his jewellery, store.

For twenty years Emmanuel Raymer managed to avoid matrimony. Then in 1906 he went on a trip to Toronto and was caught. His best friend in Edmonton had been a chap named Fulton, who worked for the Imperial Bank. Fulton was eventually transferred back east, and when he died a few years later, Raymer called on Fulton's widow to offer his condolences — and that was the beginning of the end of the carefree bachelor. The new Mrs. Raymer wouldn't hear of living in Edmonton. So Raymer sold out his pioneer jewellery business to the Jackson brothers and moved to California, and never came back.

However, he left much of his work here, because he dealt in goods that are as permanent as anything in life, and because he was an excellent salesman. He may well have been the greatest pickle-jar salesman of all time. In the affair of the pickle jars, as in many a story of human achievement, necessity was the mother of invention. In 1904 Raymer was offered a terrific bargain on a vast quantity of jars. They were such handsome things, and the price was so right, that he couldn't afford to pass them up. When he got them here and saw the crates stacked up in the back of the store, he realized with some qualms that he had enough pickle jars to supply the normal demand for at least a generation. But Raymer was never stuck. When a fellow-bachelor, not knowing much about wedding presents, would come into Raymer's seeking a wedding gift for a friend, he would pretty much leave it up to Raymer to decide what he should give.

For many a bride of 1904 or '05 or '06, the happiest day of her life was made happier still by the acquisition of six to eight pickle jars, all silver and cut-glass, and all exactly the same. They were from the shop of Emmanuel Raymer, our first jeweller — a man to remember.

Goofy McMasters

In this age of mass mediocrity it's good to be able to recall Goofy McMasters. Goofy was never mediocre. Goofy was awful. As a boxer, as a soldier, as a bearer of sandwich-boards, Goofy was awful. He was awful at the Empire Theatre that night, when, as "Heartless Harold, the Alberta Assassin," he pranced up to the ring, made a nimble leap over the ring ropes, caught his foot in the tie rope, and plunged headfirst into the water bucket, knocking himself cold. Only Goofy McMasters could be so wonderfully awful. It was one of his ninety-six fights as a heavyweight boxer. He managed to lose, or at least failed to win, the ninety-five others. It was the pattern of his life, of all his endeavours.

In the nineteen-twenties, particularly in the thirties, and on into the forties, Goofy established criteria for ineptitude which will never be challenged. As boxer, soldier and advertising man, he was the worst — and yet he managed to be the worst with such abiding integrity, such earnest dedication, and such overriding dignity of spirit, that he is remembered not only with affection but admiration.

Goofy was a man. At the Salvation Army where he lived, and at the police station where he often recovered from parties, they recognized Goofy as a man. The people at the Salvation Army knew him as a man (even though he once demanded half the money on the drum for coming up to get saved at a sidewalk service). So did the police, who would shoo him out of the cells when he was sober enough to find his way home. He was hardly ever charged and brought before the magistrates for the traditional five dollars or five days.

The police knew better than anybody how hard he worked to earn his money. He came by it slowly and honestly, losing fights, attending parades as a militiaman, skating erratically around the Gardens between periods at hockey games, lugging sandwich-boards, moving furniture, walking up and down Jasper Avenue with a tail and pitchfork to advertise the heat of a certain brand of coal, riding up and down in a bathtub to advertise a certain plumbing company, or dragging a cow up and down Jasper Avenue while dressed as a bullfighter to advertise that Eddie Cantor was appearing at the Capitol Theatre in *The Kid From Spain*. And he put on a funnier show than Eddie Cantor when Bossy got sore feet and lay down and refused to move.

Goofy never made any fast bucks. Except, perhaps, for the five he made for running in his stockinged feet — at ten below zero — from the St. Regis Hotel beer parlour to First and Jasper, and back again. You could always tell when Goofy was in training for one of his ninety-six fights. He'd trot along the street, instead of walking, and would stop for a fast foot shuffle and a couple of shadow punches at each lamppost en route.

In his role as a pugilist, Goofy generally referred to himself as "The Battler." He'd go in the ring with any man, and had the strength of six — or, at any rate, he could lift an army marquee tent, which according to regulations required six men to lift. The Battler was a spectacular puncher, executing monstrous uppercuts from the floor, which were so long in coming that his opponents were rarely in range when they arrived. But the crowd loved to see him throw those punches. Goofy knew they came to see him fight and so he figured he must be a better fighter than his record would indicate. And he was the only Alberta boxer ever to appear in the *Pathe Gazette,* one of the first movie newsreels. For his performance, he received a cheque for twenty-five cents, which he framed and hung in the many shoeshine parlours where he worked.

Goofy's pre-fight warm-ups were spectacular. He would flex his muscles by pulling on the ring ropes and making the gruesome sounds expected of the Alberta Assassin, (or of another of his aliases — the Unknown Undertaker). Once, in Ponoka, when the Alberta Assassin was going through his warm-up, he flexed too hard for the temporary ring. He pulled the corner post right out, and the whole platform came down with a crash. One spectator threw a shoe. The Assassin was a bouncer as well as a boxer. In the confusion he forgot his assignment for the night, picked up a chair, and chased all the fans out of the arena.

At Brooks, the Battler scored the only knockout of his career — but it was on a spectator, a police magistrate. He was boxing a frightening heavyweight named Dan O'Dowd, who had once gone eight rounds with Gene Tunney. At one point, O'Dowd uncorked a ferocious swing that just missed the Battler's chin. It was so close a miss that the Battler decided he had better not be around when O'Dowd uncorked another one, so he dropped to the canvas expecting to be counted out. However, the referee would have none of this and he threatened to hold up the Battler's purse if he didn't get up and fight. So Goofy sprang up and made a gallant bid to K.O. his opponent. He backed up and charged across the ring with his fist coiled. But the blow never landed. Dan O'Dowd stepped aside, and the Battler went on out into the fourth row and K.O.'d the magistrate. Another time, at Stettler, the Battler contributed something new to the manly art of self-defence. A boxer named Billy Bonn was making a target of the McMaster countenance, so the Battler turned his back and waded in, in reverse, with fists flailing. Once again the referee foiled his plans.

Goofy turned promoter once. He promoted a fight at Tom O'Malley's barn near St. Albert, starring himself versus "Thrasher" Sam Logan. This was a draw, and so were two hilarious sequels fought at the Star Dairy on 102nd Avenue and 159th Street. Goofy's duels with the Thrasher got so much publicity that boxing fans in the Peace River country wanted to see the Alberta Assassin in combat with their pride, a very competent heavyweight named Jack Thibault. The Assassin's manager consented very reluctantly, but the Assassin was enthusiastic. Doing some roadwork on the south side, he had noticed a large tree blown part way over by the wind, so he had himself photographed leaning against it. When the picture reached Fairview in the Peace River, it showed the Alberta Assassin toning up his muscles by straightening up a tree. When they got to Fairview for the fight, Goofy's manager persuaded Thibault's manager that the fight would last longer if Thibault's arms were taped so that he couldn't bend his elbows too much. The Battler gave the fans a great fight, throwing punches all over the ring. Finally a long blow hit Thibault. He got mad, burst his bonds, and the battle ended abruptly.

One of Goofy McMasters's greatest fights was with himself. He was hard at work one morning, shining shoes at a stand where the Tip-Top Tailors shop is now. Jack Kelly, the sportswriter, came up behind him as Goofy perspired over a shoe. "Battler," he said, "there's a guy behind you wants to fight!" The Battler swung around, caught a fleeting glimpse of a man with his dukes up and swung from his heels. His fist connected with the mirror, a huge plate-glass mirror, and smashed it. Battling McMasters lost his shoeshine concession over the incident, but he wasn't worried or bitter. He knew there were plenty of other concessions and other jobs.

Goofy's military career was not so well known as his boxing and advertising careers, mainly because it was conducted out of sight — with the 19th Alberta Dragoons at Sarcee in peace time, and overseas with the Loyal Edmonton Regiment in wartime. His military career followed the inevitable pattern, because he didn't get into action. Perhaps the generals had heard that Battling McMasters never won any fight he was in; but he was a useful member of the regiment while it was in training. His superiors put him in charge of the grounds and barracks and as a badge of office found him two armbands of a particularly vile yellow, which pleased him tremendously.

When the regiment was on manoeuvres Goofy entertained each night with a wrestling act, teaming with an Edmonton shoemaker named Steve Jostle. Goofy had wrestled professionally as the Edmonton Bonecrusher. One night when he and Steve were performing on an estate in Hampshire, the rustic farm hands were so dismayed by the savagery that they phoned the lord of the manor to hurry over and avert the slaughter.

Goofy was left in England when the regiment sailed for Italy in 1943, and was back home before them. But on the night the Loyal Edmontons came home, the Battler put on his uniform and joined the parade as a sort of supernumerary, out of step as always, ready and willing, but unable.

In any case his military career did not have any effect on the conduct of the war. But it did have an effect on Goofy's sandwich-board technique, and also on the street-advertising technique of his spiritual descendant, the redoubtable Pete Jamieson. Goofy was already an established Jasper Avenue tradition that day in 1935 when Pete Jamieson was sent out on his first town-crier mission. Pete was an usher at the Dreamland Theatre. Patronage was slow at the third run of the Nelson Eddy and Jeanette Macdonald movie, and the manager sent Pete up the street to holler up some business.

At the sign-painter's shop, where they used to come to pick up jobs, Goofy would discuss with young Pete the application of military marching technique to the carrying of sandwich-boards. It was Goofy's opinion that when you came to a corner and wanted to make a turn, you should give a smart "hipe, one, two, three," then make a sharp turn as though on parade, and then step off — "hipe, one, two, three" — on the left foot. Thirty years later, Pete still marched in military style along Jasper. Although Pete marched like a general advancing at the head of a victorious column, Goofy, by tradition, marched like the sole survivor of some military disaster. But he was giving his best effort. He never gave less.

On his return from the actual war theatre, Goofy was rewarded with the shoeshine concession at the Memorial Hall. His great strength, bearing down on a shoe, could make it glisten, and if he can be said to have had a permanent occupation, this was it. However, he never had a permanent location. He had a knack of making each one temporary. The stand at the Memorial Hall, for example, was next door to the beer parlour, and he lost that location. But Goofy wasn't worried. He knew there were other locations and other jobs.

Harold McMasters, also known as Goofy, also known as Battling McMasters, also known as Heartless Harold the Alberta Assassin, lived as only he could live. And he died as only he could die. It was in 1950. He'd spent the day working at a carnival on 97th Street, and when the day was over he asked if he could have half a bucket of dill pickles which were left over at a hamburger concession. He wanted to take them to a party. No one could refuse Goofy a request like that. He took them to the party and ate them himself, and then fell asleep. The party went on, and the others paid no attention to him. They thought he was just asleep. But he had died, peacefully, as he had lived, no trouble to anybody. It was no mediocre soul which had slipped away.

The Bijou Theatre

Movies are bigger now. They're longer. They're wider. They're louder. They're in colour. But would anyone say they're more fun than they were in 1908 when Pop Lawrence came to Edmonton to open our first movie house?

Mr. Lawrence wasn't too sure about the future of movies or the future of Edmonton when he came here, so he was careful to bring a return ticket, with which he could beat a retreat to Fremont, Ohio, if necessary. The return portion boosted the total price of the ticket to twenty-three dollars. Pop Lawrence had a projector in his luggage, and this historic bit of entertainment hardware slipped into Canada unnoticed. At any rate it was unnoticed by the customs. Pop was afraid the tariff demand of the border guards might doom the project economically, so when an official glared at his trunk and said, "Anything to declare?", Pop decided he should not begin with his brother-in-law's movie projector. He began instead with a pair of shoes he had bought in Detroit. "Have to charge you duty on those," said the customs man. He collected and moved on, and the historic progression moved on towards Edmonton.

Pop had a partner in the venture, a chap named Bill Hamilton. When he and Bill arrived in August 1908, they found Edmonton talking excitedly about the streetcar system (which was about to acquire a streetcar), but there was no excited talk about movie houses. Al Cameron, manager of two legitimate theatres, the Orpheum and the Opera House, said he wouldn't take five thousand dollars to run a movie theatre. Movies could never compete with the living stage. For one thing, movies were so dreadfully lowbrow.

Pop found out about this feeling. He had two backers for his movie house, and the wife of one of them would never come near the place. The place was called The Bijou — a favourite name for such halls of entertainment — and it was on 100th Street, across from the site of the present Centennial Library.

Patrons of the Bijou paid a dime, and got two reels of entertainment. The second reel was the feature film. The first combined a comedy and an educational feature. Now the films which came to the manager of such a place were less than simply "silent." They were totally devoid of subtitles or of any aid to understanding the flealike hoppings of the pale figures on the screen.

Much of the production on a movie was done right in the house. As a first step in production, Mr. Lawrence hired an orchestra to accompany the action on screen and fill in the gaps when reels were being rewound. This was quite a gap, because movie machines had to be cranked by hand, in both directions. It was against the law to use an electric motor; the owners of legitimate theatres had insinuated this law into the statutes.

The feature films were uncomplicated action-packed affairs, full of to-ings and fro-ings in which the good guys were easily distinguished from the bad guys. But when a full house of 205 patrons had paid a dime apiece, Pop figured they were entitled to sound effects. So in addition to the orchestra, Pop would provide a play-by-play commentary, standing beside Joe Elwood, the projectionist. To enhance a drama of the Wild West, Pop and Bill once decided to give the crowd the sound of real shooting. Bill went behind the screen with a pistol and a pack of blank cartridges, intending to synchronize his bangs with the action on the screen. The first bang went off on schedule, but then the pistol jammed. As a chase flickered across the screen, Pop jumped to his feet and shouted, "Believe me, folks, there's a lot more shots than that being fired."

The comedies required little narration from the manager

but the educational shows were a problem. When the distributor sent ten minutes of film on coal mining or lumbering or growing tobacco, Mr. Lawrence had to go to the library and read up on coal mining or lumbering or growing tobacco until he could speak for ten minutes on the subject.

By 1909, Mr. Lawrence was able to bring his family from Ohio. Soon after their arrival, Mrs. Lawrence and the two young daughters went to the Bijou. The daughters watched the show and listened to the voice of the narrator for a while. Then one turned around to see whence the voice was coming. "Oh look! There's papa hollering the show!" To give the audience a chance to holler, the Bijou then added singsongs to the bill of fare. The words of popular songs like "Shine on Harvest Moon" or "Only an Outcast" were flashed on the screen, and the hollering of the tune was led by local singers. Three of them used to alternate, a girl and two men.

He introduced another innovation — the first newsreel. On May 6, 1910, word came over the telegraph that King Edward VII had died. That night Mr. Lawrence went back downtown to the telegraph office and sent a cable to London ordering a film of the king's funeral to be sent "right away, C.O.D." He knew the film would take two weeks to get here and would arrive on a Friday afternoon, along with the Old Country mail for Mike's Newsstand. Just waiting for the fateful day was tense enough, and it became worse when the two rival theatres announced that they would show the king's funeral, starting the following Monday. The theatre that was first with the newsreel would gain unassailable prestige. Tuesday passed ... and Wednesday. And Thursday almost passed. Then at 3:30 P.M. the Bijou was advised by wire that the funeral films had reached Calgary.

Mr. Lawrence had five thousand handbills printed in a hurry, advertising the Bijou's scoop. On Friday morning he rounded up thirty kids, at one dollar each, to be ready to rush the handbills through the town. Then, early Friday afternoon, he went over to the CPR station in Strathcona to get the precious film straight off the train. The train arrived right on time, at 3:30, and the film was on it. Clutching the package under his arm, Mr. Lawrence ran to a butcher's shop and phoned the theatre to send the boys out with the handbills. Well, no, he didn't exactly phone the theatre; the Bijou didn't have a phone. He called Connelly & McKinley's funeral home, which was then next door. When Mr. Lawrence got back to the north side, people were already drifting into the Bijou to see the king's funeral. And it ran over and over again for six days, from one o'clock in the afternoon to eleven at night, while Mrs. Jack Bartley played Chopin's "Funeral March" over and over on the theatre's piano.

But then it was back to business as usual, with the comedy, the feature on industry, the action-packed Western and Pop Lawrence hollering the show. Movies were more fun in those days.

John B. Gardiner

In the 1920s people of the west end would see a man on a market wagon, going around supplying vegetables to the stores. There was something unusual about this vegetable man, something that set him apart from others of the profession. You could tell that, just to see him. But you couldn't tell, just to see him, that only ten years earlier he had been a millionaire. And now, to support himself, he was growing cabbages in what had been the pleasure gardens of his estate. Thereby hangs the tale of a man, which is also the tale of the city — the story of John B. Gardiner, father of Capital Hill.

He was born in Mount Forest, Ontario, a town whose prospects were far exceeded by his own ambitions. He landed out West about 1880, with a job clerking on the CPR and an ambition to make a million dollars. In 1883 he could see that railroading was not the route to a million, so he went homesteading near Brandon. Nine years of that convinced him that prairie farming was not the way either, and he went into insurance. In a few years he became chief agent for Northern Life, from the Lakehead to the Pacific; better than clerking or farming but still a slow way to make a million. So in May 1906 he arrived in Edmonton with an eye out for prize real estate, and in October he bought 214 acres along the first bend of the river and gave it the name Capital Hill. His friends thought the price (and the location) were way out of line, but a string of real estate booms — each greater than the last — brought the City of Edmonton out to Capital Hill and to John B. Gardiner, and by 1913 he had his million.

He wanted the houses of his subdivision to be the finest in the city and he set an example with his own home on Summit Point. (It was Gardiner Point in those days.) From his verandahs and ornamental gardens he could look down to the river 160 feet below, sweeping along at the foot of Capital Hill. And he could show his guests the new city's concrete towers poking their heads above the shoulder of land to the east — the domed Legislative Building, the McLeod Building and the Tegler Building.

When John Gardiner and his wife drove downtown to the centre of booming activity, they didn't ride in one of the roaring open-air Cadillacs favoured by younger real estate barons. They glided along in a silent, glassed-in, electric brougham, which steered with a rudder bar. It went five miles an hour, not fast enough to disturb the fresh flowers in the car, arranged in cut-glass vases. In summer the flowers came from the gardens, in winter from the greenhouses. Dignified and sixtyish, John and his wife seemed the duke and duchess when they went out driving, but they liked to work around their estate in overalls and straw hats. After nine years of the Manitoba homestead, flowers and vegetables were a pleasant diversion, and the Gardiners were often mistaken for the gardeners. Year by year their estate spread — along the brow of the hill and down into MacKinnon Ravine — in a series of walks, rock gardens, fountains and summer houses. It was a place fit for a king, or a pioneer with vision.

John B. Gardiner, unfortunately, had too much vision for his time. Early in 1914 he was thought to be worth $3.5 million because he owned property thought to be worth that much. But when the boom collapsed in the late summer of 1914, seventy percent of Edmonton's real estate was found to have no real value. Seventy-five thousand building lots were suddenly so worthless that men who had deemed themselves wealthy on account of them could not finance the taxes on them, and they reverted to the city. They were all vacant lots.

John Gardiner had sold hundreds of lots in Capital Hill but only three had houses on them, and the area remained in that state for nearly forty years.

When the boom deflated, most of Edmonton's millionaires moved away and many did well in new surroundings, but John Gardiner was past sixty, too old to start out again. He hung on, hoping for a revival and enjoying his own estate. When his mansion burned down, he moved into the coach house. When the last of his money was gone, he started growing cabbages in the gardens and selling them to west end stores. And when he had finished his rounds, he could return to his estate and enjoy the bend of the river and the sight and the lights of the city he had believed in. A man like John B. Gardiner could enjoy them as much as when he had been a millionaire.

When he was gone, the ruins of his estate provided Edmonton's finest rustic picnic ground. The ruins were enough to intrigue the least imaginative — a rustic gateway at the end of Summit Drive, hedges gone wild, grass which must have been planted, stone fountains and pools, intricate stonework along the brow of the hill. And not a building on the place, only an excavation where a large house had obviously been.

There was a mystery about the place, and mystery is a rare commodity in Edmonton. It doesn't keep well in bright sunlight. Yet, there it was, something from an Italian mountainside in the west end woods, a final bequest from John B. Gardiner, the most remarkable vegetable man.

Campaign Charisma

When Edmonton was young, a splendid mini-swamp oozed and gurgled at Jasper and 116th Street. This swamp had a speciality which set it apart from others — plump bulrushes that made bright every election night, soaked in kerosene and carried flaring to herald the advance of the conquering candidate.

Elections were a participating sport and lest someone think

"every man and his dog" is a figurative description of the extent of involvement, let him consider the newspaper account of Edmonton's first election rally, held May 10, 1883. The *Bulletin* breaks its account of the speeches to report: "The proceedings were varied at this point by a first-class dogfight in the schoolroom. So far as is known, no money changed hands on the result. Both dogs were kicked out and quiet reigned once more."

The dogfight came just as Frank Oliver was beginning his appeal to the electorate, and it's a good bet that a good portion of the electorate was in the one room of the one school. It totalled 252 men — of Edmonton, St. Albert and Fort Saskatchewan. In the first election day, that following May 29, Frank received 154 votes, François Lamoureaux received 94, and Stuart D. Mulkins received 4.

We sent Frank to the Legislative Assembly of the North-West Territories. Edmonton couldn't send a man direct to Ottawa then. The limit was Regina, capital of the territories. Anyway, there seems to have been some confusion in Ottawa about where Edmonton was. The Edmonton telegraph station was located at Hay Lakes, thirty miles southeast.

There was no secrecy about voting in 1883. A man stepped up to the returning officer and stated his name, business and choice of candidate, and this was entered in the book while the scrutineers peered over the returning officer's shoulder. If the scrutineers weren't satisfied that the man was entitled to vote, he could be made to swear that he was white, twenty-one, had lived a full year in the electoral district, and hadn't sold his favours to any candidate.

The advantage of this system, as the late lieutenant-governor of Alberta, Dr. J.J. Bowlen, once explained, was that "it showed a man in his true colours." The only colouring books of those ancient voting days were those of the returning officer. In some parts of the country a man would vote "red" for the Liberal, or "blue" for the Conservative, and the book would be marked accordingly. If a voter, or one of the scrutineers, couldn't read, they could still be sure the returning officer wasn't cheating. This open-air system, as Dr. Bowlen explained, also showed the voter in his true colours. In the sneaky anonymity of the secret ballot, a man could promise both candidates he'd vote for them and no one would know what he'd really done behind the curtain.

The hardy pioneer voter didn't care who knew his vote, including the party workers. And that was one of the first flaws of the "fresh air" voting system. The party workers could see how the candidates stood all through the day and would know when it was time to go out and hire some people to swear they hadn't accepted favours from any candidate, and were white, twenty-one, and entitled to vote.

In the next election, of 1885, Frank Oliver claimed he was defeated by a rush of off-duty Mounted Policemen, hired to come in from Fort Saskatchewan by the rascally Conservatives. The Conservatives, on the other hand, blamed the rascally Liberals for cutting the telegraph wires to St. Albert, so that the news of the Conservative swing in Edmonton wouldn't influence the vote in St. Albert.

Even when the secret ballot was introduced, the colour was a long time fading from elections. We were still pretty close to the frontier. Allie Brick, who represented Peace River in the first Alberta legislature, used to drive a team of moose to Edmonton for the sessions and would keep them in a pen in the present Queen Elizabeth Park. Following the federal election of 1907, a gentleman from Vegreville wrote to the editor of the *Journal* to expose the Conservative candidate, who, the writer claimed, had offered him five dollars for his vote. The writer wanted to expose the candidate for not paying off.

There was one group that used to sell its favours openly to both parties in that era. That was the Edmonton Citizens' Band. The band would be hired by both parties, in case of victory, and on every election night would assemble by the Alberta Hotel, ready to parade the victor through the town. Election night 1907 turned out to be a victory parade for Frank Oliver, and at about 10 P.M. the parade moved off up Jasper in a drizzling rain. But the loyal opposition still had a trick left. As the parade approached First and Jasper there was a cordon of inebriates, recruited from the saloons. They had locked hands and were spread across Jasper to break up the parade. This wily knavery might have succeeded if it hadn't been for Ned Marshall. Ned played tuba in the band. He conked one of the

192

Conservative mercenaries with his tuba, the cordon broke, and the victory parade poured through.

There was the aerial campaign of Sherburne Tupper Bigelow, Conservative candidate for Clover Bar in 1926. Mr. Bigelow, the genial young lawyer, had just arrived in Edmonton to practise law and he agreed to "show the flag" by running in Clover Bar. One obstacle to election was M.J. Hennig, who held the seat for the United Farmers. The other was the fact that Bigelow was completely unknown. So he set to work correcting that deficiency by hiring an airplane, and he and his pilot spent an hour or so showering Clover Bar with literature extolling Bigelow.

Up to that point it was a great success, but Bigelow's campaign, alas, "peaked" too early. He and his pilot succumbed to the temptation offered by the well-fed livestock for which Clover Bar is famous. They began diving on pigs, cows and horses to see if an airplane would make them run. It would. In no time, Bigelow had much of the electorate chasing livestock across the lush, rolling hills. The afternoon was no help in his election campaign although it was possibly of great value to his later position as chairman of the Ontario Racing Commission.

Political fervour has certainly produced some remarkable results in Alberta, but no results so remarkable as the ones reported from the Clearwater riding in 1913. That was the year that 150 percent of the voters turned out. There were 80 registered voters and on election night it was found that 120 of them had voted. Clearwater has long disappeared from the electoral map. The Valleyview highway to the Peace River country runs across the northeast corner of it, and it looks almost exactly as it did when 120 of the 80 voters went to the polls. Sixty-seven percent of the candidates found this so remarkable that they wanted everybody to hear all the details. In fact they wanted the courts to hear all the details. But the returning officer was such a modest fellow that he didn't want to talk about the remarkable achievement — especially in court. His modesty prompted him to take off for Ontario.

So we'll never know the full story of how it was done. We can only be sure, because the official records say so, that 150 percent of the voters turned out.

The Barn

Noel Coward wouldn't have been caught dead at the Barn. Lucius Beebe wouldn't have been caught dead a hundred yards from the Barn. Cecil Beaton wouldn't have been caught dead two hundred yards from the Barn. Oscar Wilde wouldn't have been caught dead three hundred yards from the Barn. The Barn was totally devoid of class. It was unshakably, unalterably without class and it was Edmonton's premier gathering place in the years of the Second World War. Around the eleventh day of each November, when young companions long dead are remembered and young days beyond recall are recalled, there are men all over the English-speaking world who still remember the Barn.

It is now almost impossible to describe what Edmonton was like in the years when the Barn was the premier gathering spot and the city of 125,000 was surging with young men in uniform looking for something to do; young men from the United States, the United Kingdom, Australia and New Zealand, touring downtown looking for something to do. There wasn't much. The Macdonald Hotel had a supper dance on Saturday nights, for which there was a three-to-four-week waiting list. On 97th Street there was a joyous centre of romp and riot called the Palace Gardens, a second-storey arena where the patrons drank openly and kicked each other down the stairs, and the police patrol wagon would stop by periodically and remove the wounded from the sidewalk. Then there was the Barn.

The Barn was on 103rd Street. To place it exactly, it was where the Hudson's Bay Company's ticket office is now, plus the sporting goods and men's shoes. The building that was the Barn was torn down when the Bay doubled the size of its store. It was an annex to the Bay's raw-fur department, which was in a building of its own because raw furs don't smell so good and may have bugs. The annex was a garage before it was converted into Edmonton's premier gathering place in 1940, but it was a barn before that, and the dance-hall conversion left no doubt that a bunch of horses had once slept there.

Of course it's possible to transform an old stable into

something elegant, something that Noel Coward and Lucius Beebe and Cecil Beaton and Oscar Wilde would be quite agreeable to being caught dead in. But the old Hudson's Bay stable was not transformed or transmuted. It was simply redecorated. The orchestra stand was fixed to look like a loft, and the booths were built to look like stalls, and the walls were decorated to look like the inside of a barn, though that was completely unnecessary. And young men came from around the earth to dance at the Barn. Americans, Australians, Englishmen, Canadians. Night after night they crowded into the Barn to dance on ten tons of rubber. The dance floor was lying on ten tons of old rubber tires.

The tires, and the idea, were the promotion of Robert A. McInnes, a veteran ballroom manager credited with giving Mart Kenney his start in Vancouver. When his old Tivoli Ballroom burned down around him in 1939, McInnes was a manager without a dance hall. So he got the Barn idea, sold it to Edmonton businessmen Art Carlson, Charlie Dow and Harry Armstrong, and they had it ready to open in the late summer of 1940, featuring the music of a band called the Stableboys.

It was a genuine expression of Edmonton 1940. Churchill and Hitler were then locked in the Battle of Britain, and it's doubtful that they had much time to think about the Stableboys, who were trying gallantly to blow the fifteen-piece Glenn Miller and Artie Shaw arrangements with a nine-piece band. However, thousands of the young men who would dance to the Stableboys, as they passed through Edmonton in the British Commonwealth Air Training Plan, would carry on the air war afterwards.

The young men were bound to feel at ease in the Barn, since they were billeted in the livestock barns on the Edmonton Exhibition grounds, commandeered by the air force for a manning depot. They brought to the downtown Barn a younger, less desperate version of "eat, drink and be merry for tomorrow we die." That would come later. At the Barn it was eat, drink and be merry for tomorrow we get posted to Mossbank or Vulcan or some such ghastly place.

The Australians, the New Zealanders, the English, the Scots and the Welsh came first, and then in 1942, since the Americans were in the war, they came to the Barn, too. And although the conversation at the Barn was not the type that would make Noel Coward or Cecil Beaton reconsider being caught dead there, it was pretty sparkling stuff for the ages of the dancers. In wartime, with men moving in and out, a young person might see another young person once or twice and then he'd be gone, so both could shoot off their best conversational ploys in one or two evenings of top-grade conversation.

Life at the Barn was a party, and it should be explained — for those who came in late to the Edmonton scene — that it was a BYOB party, for the cocktail lounge was nearly twenty years down the road. While beer was sold in hotels, men and women drinkers were rigidly segregated. The law was as oppressive as any devised by a Nazi army of occupation, but the architects of the Barn offered the ultimate in loopholes. They built slots under the tables (slots just the size of the bottles the patrons brought in) and the bar sold ginger ale. It was part of life at the Barn, part of the rhythm of the place. And the subject of rhythm brings us to the drummer.

The drummer was Art Ward. When the war ended and the Edmonton Flyers became the centre of attention with their Allan Cup heroics, Art Ward would achieve his lasting fame as a broadcaster of hockey games. But in the first half of the forties he was the drummer at the Barn, pounding the drums with the same plodding sincerity that marked his play-by-play broadcasting. He also performed another service for the customers.

Art's service grew out of the wartime rationing on whisky. To demonstrate that war can be what General Sherman said it was, even thousands of miles from the fighting fronts, the government rationed whisky at the rate of thirteen ounces per adult per month. In those simple times, few men of twenty-one had a taste for whisky — beer was exciting enough — but they were entitled to a permit to buy thirteen ounces a month anyway. A Canadian serviceman who patronized the Barn and was old enough to have a permit, but not to have acquired a taste for the distilled, could sell the permit through Art Ward.

Art was aware that the government didn't approve of this sort of transaction, but he figured that in his small way he was fighting for justice, the same cause that the young men shuffling past the bandstand were fighting for. As the

196

uniforms shuffled past, Art realized that the boys in American uniforms had more money than the boys in Canadian uniforms, and that they were both fighting the same war. So if he sold a Canadian's permit to an American and got the Canadian boy some of the money he should have been getting anyway, then it was justice.

That was a long time ago now, and Art Ward is gone and the Barn is gone, and so are many of the thousands of young men who shuffled around there. But on the eleventh of November in places all over the English-speaking world, they are remembered.

The Wonderful Steamer Northwest

Towards the close of the nineteenth century the most exciting sound of the Edmonton summer was the great steamer *Northwest* whistling as she passed the Highlands on the approach to Edmonton. If this were a seaport, the last sailing of the *Northwest* would be celebrated in song and ballad. Her whistling past the Highlands gave people time to get down to the landing by the present powerhouse.

The *Northwest* was a powerhouse in her own right. She was a stern-wheeler, 275 feet from bow to stern and 60 feet from the water line to the tops of the twin stacks. If you put the *Northwest* on the field at Clarke Stadium, she would just fit between the 15-yard lines, and the stacks would be as high as the lights. And you could put her on the Clarke Stadium football field because she had a wide flat bottom like all the boats which plied the rivers of North America. She was nearly all above the water line, with only two feet below the surface. She was a three-decker, with the freight deck on the water line, the passenger deck one flight up with thirty cabins and a dance hall, and the hurricane deck with the pilot house, up on top.

The *Northwest* was part of a three-boat relay team that could whisk passengers to Winnipeg in ten days, just one-eighth the time it took to go overland. The *Northwest* ran from Edmonton to Prince Albert, the *Lily* ran from Prince Albert to the Grand

Rapids, and another boat took the freight and passengers from the lower end of the tricky rapids to Winnipeg. The boats were built way up the Red River in Minnesota, then came down the Red past Winnipeg, through Lake Winnipeg and Lake Winnipegosis, and were hauled up over the rapids at high water. Once they were over the rapids, they were in.

The first boat in was the *Northcote,* which reached Edmonton in 1874. The *Northcote* was cheered wildly when she pulled up below the fort, because she ushered in a new era of rapid transit. Until the telegraph line reached Edmonton in 1879, the river boats were Edmonton's quickest link with the outside world. No wonder, even in later years, that the sound of the *Northwest* whistling past the Highlands was the most exciting sound of the summer.

The presiding genius in the pilot house was Captain Josie Smith, part Indian, who could handle the mighty *Northwest* like a canoe. He had known the river in the days of the canoe and the York boat, when a craft like the *Northwest* would have boggled the mind by its magnificence. When the captain was at dinner, which was prepared by a cook known as Old Man Gourd, his son Alec took the wheel. The crew included a mate, an engineer named Jack Shannon (who settled in Edmonton and founded the Reliance Welding Works), a clerk, and fifteen or so deck hands to load the freight and the wood which pioneers on the scattered farms along the river would pile by the landings.

And then there was a cabin boy. The teen-ager who landed this job had an enviable position, something like the kid who gets the job of batboy for the Montreal Expos. All this, and $15 a month too. It was nice work for the summer, and strictly a summer job. Through the winter the river was hard-surfaced, and in the fall the river was too low even for a steamboat that needed only two feet of water. So the navigation season began about May 24 and ran until the end of August.

The *Northwest* tried to beat the sand bars with a flat bottom just two feet below the water line, but this created another problem. The big ship was helpless in a windstorm. Any wind spun her like a leaf. The ship was almost wrecked in Edmonton when a wind caught her on the way from a picnic excursion to Big Island. The picnic crowd had been let off at the present site

198

of the High Level Bridge. As the ship was drifting to its landing by the powerhouse, a sudden wind blew it broadside against the bank under Scona Hill, and for many anxious minutes it appeared that the *Northwest* would topple over onto the land.

Wind was a periodic nuisance, but the sand bars were chronic because they kept changing position as the current rearranged the river mud. When the steamer nosed into a sand bar, log booms would be dropped on either side of the ship. Then a donkey engine would tighten the chains attached to the log booms and lift the nose of the ship over the bar. In addition to her other talents, therefore, the *Northwest* could pick herself up by her bootstraps. There were no docks for the river steamers, but the *Northwest* carried her own. She could ram her flat nose right into shore, making such a good dock that a team of horses could drive right on. The *Northwest* didn't need a dock, but she did have a hitching post at every port of call.

There was music on the *Northwest*, too. At night a fiddler swung out in the dance hall — and one of the best fiddlers on the river was Captain Josie Smith. Smith could handle a fiddle with the same ease as he handled the boat, and he was available for music in the evenings. The *Northwest* travelled by day only — too many snags and sand bars under the muddy surface of the river for night work. As darkness fell, Captain Josie would run the boat into shore and tie up to a tree.

The *Northwest* supplied six Hudson's Bay stores between Edmonton and Prince Albert. The trip took about five days in normal water; but when the river was high, Captain Smith could barrel six hundred miles downstream in only forty-eight hours, almost like flying. But fast as she was, the railways were pushing closer, and the iron horse could run all year round. In 1891 the CPR reached Edmonton from the south, giving faster freight and passenger service to Winnipeg. Even so, the *Northwest* managed to stay in business until the end of navigation in 1897. And even as her own era ended, she ushered in a new one. On her last summer, the *Northwest* hauled the derrick and drilling equipment for a wildcat well that the Dominion government was drilling north of Myrnam. When she returned to Edmonton she was pulled up on the bank where the power plant stands today and was converted into a warehouse.

What finally happened to the *Northwest*? Well, if Edmonton were a seaport, and sea-minded poets were prowling the waterfront looking for material, the final sailing of the *Northwest* would be the subject of many a sea ballad. The end came in 1899. In early August, unseasonal late rains came. And the rains kept coming, day after day. The river rose to its banks. It flowed harder and faster, driven by the press from upstream. It drove up over the banks and covered Rossdale and Walterdale and all the flats.

In her last resting place on Rossdale, with the flood water pushing past, the great old steamer seemed to be afloat. And then she *was* afloat. With a wrenching shudder she broke away from the earth and floated free, out into the main current, bow again pointed downstream. Swinging around the first bend, the timbers under the engines gave way and the engines dropped to the bottom of the river. The flood then carried the great old steamer to the Low Level Bridge, which was under construction, and drove her up against the centre pier. She hung there ten minutes, then slipped around over the flats below Grierson Hill, smashing the surface buildings and machinery of Humberstone's coal mine. Then she swirled away, disintegrating slowly and surely. The *Northwest* had come back to the river.

Inauguration Day

Those were wonderful days, the days surrounding September first, 1905. They were wonderful nights too. In fact the nights were almost more wonderful, blue and sunny and typical of Alberta as the days were. The new capital blazed with lights as it never had before, as the power plant decreed a week of free power — all the electricity the proud citizenry could put to the task of helping Edmonton beat out Paris for the title, "City of Light."

The first place the proud citizens decorated was Alberta College, headquarters for inaugural revels. They hung string upon string of coloured bulbs on the college. Down on 98th

Street the fire hall was ablaze with mottos and designs, executed in coloured lights. Across from the fire hall the Alberta Hotel was transformed into a barber pole by strings of red, white and blue lights. The length of Jasper Avenue — oh, way up to Fourth Street — there were arches proclaiming the greatness of the new province and of its capital city, population eight thousand. The arches were hung with sheaves of grain, boughs of evergreen, and more lights. The Hudson's Bay store and Revillon Frères were spangled with white stars. The residential streets were bright with Japanese lanterns hung in the trees. The very night was dazzled. It made you think of that song "Hail Alberta," suggested for the inauguration by the *Bulletin*. The *Bulletin* published "Hail Alberta" on the front page. To the tune of "Rule Britannia," it went:

Hail Alberta, Alberta fair and grand,
Noblest pra-ha-haha-hah-vince of our land ...

There was music of even better quality at the Thistle Rink on the eve of the inauguration. Vernon Barford conducted a "grand concert," with an orchestra of nineteen and a chorus of forty-one. And the ratio of ladies to gentlemen in that pioneer capital was neatly underscored by the make-up of the chorus: twelve ladies to twenty-nine men. The concert was first rate. Edmonton has heard few sounds so dramatic as the chorus singing the opening hymn: "God prosper him our king."

The days preceding the inauguration were marked by many special events. "C" Squadron of the Mounted Police staged a musical ride. Edmonton's lacrosse team beat Calgary in what the *Bulletin* described as a splendid exhibition of Canada's national game. Alas, the baseball team from Wetaskiwin showed deplorable lack of respect for the team representing the new capital, pounding them 8-0, but Wetaskiwin was part of Alberta so it didn't really matter. The merchants were busy selling Alberta. In all the store windows were the things Alberta could grow and make.

Then came the greatest day, September first, the day to inaugurate the province. It started officially with a parade. The parade came down Jasper Avenue, then looped around and went down McDougall Hill to the fairgrounds. That's where Sir Wilfrid Laurier would formally inaugurate the province. Sir

Wilfrid rode at the head of the parade. There were fifteen hundred school children, twelve hundred walking and three hundred little ones riding on nine wagons. The fire department was in the parade ... and the South African veterans ... and the Strathcona Band ... and a float advertising Ochsner's beer ... and a float advertising Harry Shaw's La Palma Cigars ... and the Farmers' Society of Equity ... and the St. Albert Band ... and the Plumbers' Union. And you've no idea how metropolitan that was. Edmonton had put in running water only the year before, and here the plumbers were unionized already. It was a wonderful parade. It led twelve thousand people, more than there were in all Edmonton, to the fairgrounds by the present Renfrew Ball Park.

There the lieutenant-governor, Mr. Bulyea, was sworn in. And the Mounted Police made a cavalry charge across the racetrack and stopped right at the platform where the high officials were sitting. And then the Mounties dragged their artillery up the hill to fire an official salute. And Sir Wilfrid Laurier made a speech. Sir Wilfrid said he had been in the West eleven years earlier, in 1894. At that time Moose Jaw had still been in the primitive state which its name suggested, and in all Edmonton there weren't more buildings, public and private, than he could count on the fingers of his two hands. If anyone had told him that in eleven years he'd be back in Edmonton for this imposing occasion, and speaking to such a distinguished gathering, well, he'd not have believed it. The progress had been astounding. The next great need of the province, said Sir Wilfrid, was railroads but he would not say any more on that subject lest he get into the realm of politics. However, even in saying that much, the skilful Sir Wilfrid had made it clear to all those smart people that if they wanted railroads, the Liberal party could meet the best offer of any other, in particular the Conservative party.

Then the governor general, Earl Grey, made a speech. That was Lord Grey who gave the Grey Cup for football. He didn't mention the cup, but he did say: "The fertility of your plains, the service of your railroads, your Dominion experimental farms, and your cold storage facilities have done much to make this province what it is."

Then Sir Gilbert Parker, the man who wrote the historical

202

novels, made a little speech. Sir Gilbert was a British M.P. He said Britain depended on Canada for food in peace and war. Well, that made the crowd feel good. All you had to do to make a Canadian crowd feel good in those days was to tell them that Britain was depending on them. It was late afternoon when the inaugural ceremony was over, and the crowd surged back up the hill.

As daylight failed on that first day, the electric lights blazed up again because there was more celebration to come. There was a patriotic rally in McDougall Methodist Church that evening, which the visiting dignitaries attended. The church's minister, the Reverend Dr. John Potts, gave the oration and said Alberta needed a good system of education and a good provincial university, and that it should keep inviolate the Sabbath day.

The finale of the great day was the Grand Ball at the Thistle Rink. The *Bulletin* said the scene was one of bewildering beauty, with the youth and beauty of Alberta making a pleasing spectacle. Though the ball was to be the climax of the great day it came perilously close to anticlimax. Midway through the ball the overworked Edmonton power plant sputtered and staggered. A breakdown was past due. The plant had been straining its meagre resources for too many blazing nights. The brightness in the Thistle Rink dimmed to a foggy yellow twilight and total darkness seemed inevitable. And then ... and then ... the boys at the power plant roused their dynamos to a final effort. The lights showered brightness again and Edmonton's inauguration day closed in a blaze of glory.

The Capital City

Edmonton is the capital of Alberta, but let us not be complacent. A smidgin of wary vigilance will always be in order. Edmonton is still only the provisional capital. A determined government could move it somewhere else. It would take an extremely determined government, of course, but that's how the statute reads.

Alberta was "erected" — that's the word — in 1905 by a parliamentary device called the Alberta Act. Saskatchewan was erected simultaneously by a device called the Saskatchewan Act. Now, since Regina had been capital of the North-West Territories, and since Queen Victoria herself had named it so, there was no argument about Regina's continuing as capital of the province. But there was plenty of argument in Alberta, which had no tradition in the matter. The arguments were so plentiful and so heated that Parliament shied away from making a firm decision. The Alberta Act made Edmonton temporary capital only and said in effect, as they say in Madison Square Gardens, "May the better contestant emerge victorious." In the view of Calgary, Banff, Vegreville, Cochrane, Lacombe, Red Deer, Wetaskiwin and Athabasca Landing, there were better contestants than Edmonton. Claimants to the title of "capital" bombarded members of the federal parliament with letters, delegations and newspaper editorials.

Vegreville, with a population of seventy-eight, was a vigorous contender with several arresting arguments based on the climate. It was very healthy. Vegreville air was the best, having more ozone than air in other towns. There was so much ozone that people suffering from tuberculosis, asthma, rheumatism and malaria had been greatly improved, if not downright cured, by residence there. Vegreville had an open-air rink, and three masquerade balls had been held out in the open there the previous winter. In fact the winter climate was the clincher in Vegreville's claim. The town was farther from the mountains and therefore beyond the range of chinooks. Horse-drawn sleighs would bog down when chinooks turned the snow to slush. Vegreville was not vulnerable to attacks from chinooks and was therefore the logical site for the capital. Attacks were also the basis of Banff's aspirations. Banff could be fortified best in time of war. The capital would necessarily be the centre of university education, and the mountains of Banff would be very educational.

The claim of Athabasca Landing was geographical. It was at the centre of the proposed new province, as it still is. Now in this contest Calgary had a colourful editor, Bob Edwards, to help the cause. But Edmonton had a colourful editor too. Frank Oliver was founder of the *Bulletin;* he also happened to be a member of Parliament and a member of the cabinet — minister of the Interior, no less. In obvious reference to Frank Oliver, the Calgary papers made rude remarks about political favouritism but said that political favouritism would avail Edmonton naught. The *Herald* said: "The people of the extreme north are greatly annoyed, not to say positively alarmed, over the magnitude of the movement (throughout Alberta) to locate the permanent capital at Calgary." To this, Frank Oliver's paper, the *Bulletin,* sniffed: "Few passions are more desperate or vociferous than baffled greed." And in further support of Edmonton's just claim, as if any more were needed, it reprinted an article from the Toronto Methodist magazine, in which the writer stated: "Edmonton is the most romantically-located place I have ever seen."

However, romance was no part of Calgary's claim. It was based on the premise that the city of Business and Bustle by the Bow — that was its commercial slogan — was the population, transportation and financial centre of Alberta. And in support of the contention that it was the Wall Street of Alberta, the *Herald* ran weekly comparisons of money orders sold at the post offices of the two towns, and Calgary was certainly ahead on money orders. On February 2, 1905, a mass meeting was held at the Odd Fellows Hall and it was decided that Calgary must send a delegation to Ottawa to counter the poisonous presence of Frank Oliver. Eight stout citizens were named. Their mission was to stage a sit-in on Parliament Hill. Calgary wanted no favours, only what it was entitled to as the population, transportation and financial centre.

Edmonton also sent a delegation and this brought the *Albertan* out fighting mad. The *Albertan* struck the noisiest note

of the campaign with an editorial headed: EDMONTON'S COWARD-
ICE. "The people of Alberta," roared the paper, "will not soon
forget the cowardice of Edmonton in the contest for capital of
the province. The action of the people of Edmonton is one of
the most despicable in the history of provinces. Edmonton is
asking the government to restrict the power of the new
province, to destroy one of the most sacred rights of a new
province, the right to select the capital."

So that was Edmonton's cowardice. The cowards of the
extreme north were ducking a fair fight with worthier
opponents by asking Ottawa to make Edmonton the capital.
However, Edmonton feared nobody — well, anyway, not
Vegreville.

The *Bulletin* printed a story "from a private source,"
presumably Frank Oliver, saying that Edmonton would be the
winner, and Frank then made a speech about it in the House of
Commons. Frank didn't say anything about Edmonton's
desire, nothing like that. Frank talked only about the
government, why the government was right in thinking
Edmonton ought to be the capital. The government was moved
by noble concern for the Grand Trunk Pacific Railway, which
was building a second transcontinental rail route through
Edmonton. The government was guaranteeing the bonds of
the Grand Trunk, and what a fine thing it would be for the
bondholders to have a provincial capital beside the track.

The crystal logic of Frank's explanation was appreciated
only in Edmonton. When the Alberta Act was finally passed
and given royal assent — on July 20, 1905 — the choice was
left to the people of Alberta. Section Nine of the act read:
"Unless and until the Lieutenant-Governor-in-Council di-
rects, by proclamation and under the Great Seal, the seat of
government shall be Edmonton."

The other contestants still had a chance to persuade the
Lieutenant-Governor-in-Council to "so direct by proclamation
and under the Great Seal," but the shifting fortunes of national
political parties were working to the advantage of Edmonton.
The Liberal party happened to be in power. You'd hardly expect the Liberals to name a Conservative as first lieutenant-
governor. They didn't. They picked a stout Liberal, G.H.V.
Bulyea. And you'd hardly expect a Liberal lieutenant-governor

to ask a Conservative to head the first provisional government. He didn't. He asked A.C. Rutherford, a Liberal and patriot of Strathcona. Mr. Rutherford's right-hand man was Charlie Cross, militant citizen of Edmonton.

Calgary's formidable R.B. Bennett was leader of the Conservatives. Bennett vowed that his government would move the capital where it belonged. A provincial election was called for November 8, 1905. The Liberals won in such a landslide that even Bennett was defeated. But Calgary wasn't out of it yet. W.H. Cushing was as sturdy a Calgarian as anybody, and even though he was a member of Mr. Rutherford's first cabinet he gave the first legislature a motion that the City of Business and Bustle by the Bow be named permanent capital. The vote failed by sixteen to eight, the unkindest cut of all coming from the Honourable Member from Olds, who voted for the north when sectional loyalty was expected to put him in the Calgary camp. When assailed for his perfidy, he explained that he was a curler and whenever he had come to a bonspiel in Edmonton he'd been treated really well.

For this reason, and for other reasons perhaps even better, Edmonton became the capital of Alberta and beneficiary of the big business that government has become. But it's temporary. It could still be moved elsewhere by proclamation and under the Great Seal. So let us be wary and vigilant, and in case of emergency ring the fire bell which warned the citizens the night Strathcona tried to steal the land office. Remember the location of the bell. At last report it was in the city's Cromdale warehouse, the old ETS garage near the Exhibition grounds.